Breaking t

'Children begin by loving their parents;
as they grow older they judge them;
sometimes they forgive them.'

OSCAR WILDE

# Breaking
# the Chain

ABUSE, REVENGE, REDEMPTION:
THE TRUE STORY OF
A DAMAGED CHILDHOOD

## Andy McQuade

MICHAEL O'MARA BOOKS LIMITED

First published in Great Britain in 2008 by
Michael O'Mara Books Limited
9 Lion Yard, Tremadoc Road
London SW4 7NQ

Copyright © Andy McQuade 2008

The right of Andy McQuade to be identified as the author
of this work has been asserted by him in accordance
with the Copyright, Designs and Patents Act 1988.

A CIP catalogue record for this book is available
from the British Library.

Papers used by Michael O'Mara Books Limited are natural,
recyclable products made from wood grown in sustainable forests.
The manufacturing processes conform to the environmental
regulations of the country of origin.

ISBN 978-1-84317-252-9

1 3 5 7 9 10 8 6 4 2

www.mombooks.com

Designed and typeset by Martin Bristow

Printed and bound in Great Britain
by Cox & Wyman, Reading, Berks

# Contents

*For my mother, Veronica,
and my brothers, Iain and Anthony.
And for my father, Eric.*

# *Prologue*

THE BEDROOM starts to shrink as it always does at this small hour of the morning. Shadows on the faded wallpaper are spun like a vast creeping web; deformed twitching fingers of light and darkness exploring the length of the walls and furniture, touching and reshaping my small room into an ever-changing, terrifying and alien world.

The child that is me lies there in my bed – not scared, not calm – and my heart beats dull and heavy, a relentless drum that rocks and rolls in my head. The tinnitus, brother in arms to insomnia, eventually fades out. This is my nightly cue to slip away into that indescribable place between waking and dreaming, but something is different this time. This time I am trapped inside that waking unconsciousness – a twilight world that defies description. It's a child's world; inaccessible to my future self, the memory gradually wiped out by adult logic and reason – but like chalk echoes on a blackboard, the faintest of images will remain for ever. Beckoning and taunting me to try to remember.

Then the figure appears . . .

# 1 | *Beginnings*

I NEVER KNEW my father. You can spend every waking moment with a person, watch them die and realize you never really knew them, and that's how it was with us. It suited us both that way – until we had no choice, either of us. By then it was almost too late for a happy ending because we did not truly understand what happiness meant.

In my quest to discover my father's past and understand what had created him, I had to confront the secrets hidden in 1930s Glasgow, but owing to conflicting reports I found it impossible to work out exactly how and where my paternal grandfather and grandmother had first met. As I can count on two hands the number of occasions my father and I conducted anything close to a conversation – and half of those were stories later revealed to be fantasy or warped parables – I've had to rely on the little information that my mother had learned and then had confirmed by others.

In one of those rare and uncomfortable verbal blips, my father once told me that my grandfather Francis, a foreman in the then bustling port of Glasgow, spotted young Agnes McQuade Buchanan as she walked with friends along the waterfront and fell in love with her at first sight. Another time I heard that Francis had become seriously ill and been nursed back to health by Agnes, whereupon he'd fallen in love with his healer. The real facts are now lost, so it may well be that there is some truth to both accounts.

However, one definite fact underpins this part of the story; my grandmother, whom I'd never meet, possessed a heart larger than the city of Glasgow. By all accounts she was the sort of person who'd give her last penny to someone in need, and thought nothing of sacrificing pieces of herself if it could do others good. It's this part of her that looms largest when I try to imagine what she must have been like, because she instantly reminds me of another amazing woman who would play the most important role in my own life many years later.

The Glasgow of that era was a formidable place. Racked by poverty and deprivation, its reputation as a harsh and forbidding host was well deserved. 'No mean city' was one of its many aliases, but any time my father would slip into drunken and slurred memories of his childhood, he would fix me with those piercingly dangerous eyes and simply mutter, 'Evil place, son . . . evil place.'

Gangs were many and razorblades were routinely carried, and damaging blows were exchanged as casually as punches in a boxing ring, but this was a sports arena of industrial proportions; concrete warrens and teeming tenement blocks loomed like sky-high filing cabinets storing flesh and blood.

The particular area of Glasgow in which my grandparents set up their family life, the Gorbals, had its own near mythic reputation of violence, giving birth to some of the most dangerous men in Britain and swallowing up the lives of many more. Rising above the squalor and inbred violence on those estates was no mean feat. But despite its self-perpetuating legend as a fearsome and deadly place, it also had at its heart a sense of real community among the ordinary people who struggled with everyday life. There, like London's old East End, poverty could not destroy the natural human urge to look after one's own, and people like my grandmother epitomized that quality.

If little is known of my grandmother, then even less can be said of my grandfather. My father never uttered one word to me about him. My only childhood meeting with him provokes memories of a short, slightly overweight and physically unimposing man. But he possessed, just as my father would one day, a cold and domineering personality. He was a man who ruled his world with a rod of iron – literally, as well as metaphorically. When I was six or seven he came to stay with us, said nothing to anyone – including my father – and left after seven days of sitting in the same chair, glaring into the nothingness of the bleating television without ever appearing to see anything or show any interest in the curious grandchildren watching from a safe distance. One thing is certain about him though: beatings to all members of his family were routine and brutal, and he established a climate of fear that would permanently affect my father, uncles and grandmother. In my grandmother's case, fatally. A chronic alcoholic, his violence needed no provocation or justification, and my forebears were conditioned into the art of random cruelty from their earliest days.

It was November 1943 when my father Eric arrived into this unpredictable and ominous setting. The youngest of four brothers and a physically small child, it is likely he bore the brunt of the violence that my uncles passed down from their father to him. When I was about nine years old, two of my uncles once visited us on separate occasions and I remember wondering why my father eyed one of them in particular so nervously with an alien lack of authority and confidence. I loved it, because for a whole week I had no fear of his rages while these strange and sinister relatives took over his house.

Years later I would come to understand that my father, as the youngest son, had somehow escaped the worst of his father's explosions. Perhaps his brothers couldn't forgive him for that. Almost certainly they passed on the lessons being taught to them and, like an abused animal, he never forgot or forgave.

It was under this insidious programming that my father and his brothers learned to fight each other, which they did savagely – broken bones and stitches became part of everyday living, despite my grandmother's presence and the goodness she always showered on her family.

Raising a family on the meagre wages of a docker created additional pressures. A violent household struggling with severe financial hardship is the perfect breeding ground for crime, and my father and uncles appeared to fall into it with consummate ease. My father once told me, almost with a hint of regret, about how he and his brothers extorted money from small shopkeepers to prevent 'accidents' befalling them or their properties. He also spoke of strangers who made the grave error of wandering on to their patch being robbed and slashed with razor blades. But in those times, in that part of Glasgow, such behaviour wasn't particularly exceptional; a stranger walking down a dark street could lose his life if he bumped into the wrong people.

Then, in the early 1950s, when my father was eight years old, my grandmother fell ill with tuberculosis. It was possibly the worst thing that could have happened to the family. For the boys, just escaping the slums of the Gorbals would be a great achievement; but fleeing from the world my grandfather was fashioning for them would be a near miracle, and the only person who could have helped them achieve this lay dying in the upstairs bedroom.

The tragic nature of Agnes's incapacity might have provoked the release of hidden tenderness in my grandfather, but instead it merely unleashed the full fury of his inner demons. Perhaps he blamed her for falling ill and saw it as a weakness and selfishness on her part. More probable is that he was terrified of losing the one good thing in his life – the sole glimmer of light in that deprived family. Whatever his reasons, the self-destruct button was flipped and he couldn't stop himself.

The beatings didn't just continue as they had previously – they got worse. He'd beat her as she lay stricken in bed, often dragging her from her sickbed to perform household chores in the middle of the night and forcing my uncles to watch her struggle with tasks she simply couldn't manage. Then one night, in the middle of an exceptionally biting winter, he came home in his usual state of saturated rage, dragged her out of bed and threw her outside into the freezing night telling her to stay by the front door or else he'd murder her. A few days later, she died.

But she got her revenge. As she lay dying, after the priest had read the last rites, my grandfather threw himself at her mercy and knelt at her feet, sobbing and pleading with her to be pardoned for everything he'd done. With one of her last breaths she replied, 'You're begging for forgiveness now, Frank, but you'll not get it. It's too late for that. It's too late.' Hours later she slipped away for ever.

An unwilling witness to the unbearable final exchange between his tortured parents, my own father would be haunted by these words for the rest of his life.

After their mother's death, the boys' future lay in the hands of someone who cared little for them, and they were left to their own devices. Without a moral compass to guide them on the right path, they were free to wreak havoc under the dubious influence of their father and fellow tenement dwellers. Initially, though, my father had different ideas, perhaps because he had been spared so many violent beatings, and was protected by the memory of his mother's love and kindness. Whatever the reason, he gave serious thought to becoming a priest, and even spent a year in a monastery. Ultimately, though, he decided that religious life was not for him, and he left the priesthood to pursue a more physical career in the boxing ring.

Every boxer likes to believe that they 'could have been a contender', but in my father's case it was probably true: he was so fast with his fists that before you'd realized his shoulders had even twitched, he'd plucked a fly from the air. I'd also heard stories from reliable sources of him being attacked one night by small gangs of men and walking away without even a scratch.

Unfortunately, his dream to embark on a successful boxing career came to a premature end when, at the age of sixteen, he got involved in a pub fight and was head-butted and left with a permanently damaged left eye.

Unwilling to pursue a life in the priesthood, and unable to establish himself in the boxing world, he was left with little choice but to join his brothers in the violent underworld that surrounded him. However, in one of his characteristic moments of doing the unexpected, he opted to take a different path, and instead jumped on a train bound for England, where an unknown future lay ahead.

While my paternal grandmother was helplessly abandoning my father and uncles as she lay dying from TB, at the other end of the country my maternal grandmother was also undergoing a difficult separation from her children. In complete contrast, however, hers was by choice.

My mother Veronica was six years old in 1953 and her two brothers only a few years older when their mother took them to Chelmsford train station for a day out and simply left them there. They were found by a surprised railway employee and were promptly despatched to social services where, in the best traditions of those misguided times, they were split up into three packages for hire or purchase in local children's homes.

The reason why my grandmother deliberately chose to leave behind three small children so casually on a station bench has never been fully understood. Thirty years later, my uncles

Chris and Tony managed to track my mother down, whereupon she learned that a year or so before the final abandonment, my grandmother had done the same thing with her two sons, sparing my mother from the trauma on this occasion. A local newspaper ran a story, featuring a photograph of my two young uncles, under the headline: 'Do you know these children?' Fortunately, someone did recognize the boys, and they were reunited with their mother, albeit temporarily.

A few years before my uncles had found their sister, they had managed to locate their birth mother, but they learned little about why she had left them. Even when my mother made face-to-face contact with her estranged parent, all the questions that had plagued her since childhood were never properly answered. The only explanation offered for my grandmother's behaviour was that she simply didn't want to deal with her children any more and had had enough. She refused to elaborate further, and the topic was closed for ever. Birth mother or not, my own mother left that first meeting with more questions than before and with an overwhelming sense that my grandmother had no interest in the fate of her offspring. After a few more brief visits, it became clear to my mother that she was wasting her time, and that she would gain nothing from any further contact with someone so lacking in basic human compassion.

As a child, my mother was shy and untrusting, scared of everything around her, especially people. It's doubtful she received much affection before her mother's final rejection, and by the age of six she was totally alone, separated from the only people she knew and loved, surrounded by overworked social workers, with a broken doll as her only possession. Years later, when I was old enough to grasp the enormity of what she must have endured, she simply smiled as she recalled her situation. 'I loved that doll so much,' she beamed. But that was, and still is, her way – to see the good in every situation.

The fostering process is not unlike being displayed in a pet shop. The younger and cuter you are, the greater your chances of finding a new owner. My mother, therefore, had a head start on her brothers and it wasn't long before Mr and Mrs Smith, searching for a companion for their own daughter Kaye, became the new custodians of a scared little girl clutching an old doll for all it was worth.

Mr Smith had served in the army and saw the practical applications of military life applied to house and family. He wasn't cruel nor even harsh with his small family platoon, but nonetheless made sure that everyone conformed to his rigid, uncompromising way of running things, and if that meant forfeiting the gentler side to his nature, then it was a necessary sacrifice. His wife, however, fell into the 1950s ideal of what makes a good mother: devoted to her husband's needs and unquestioned authority – albeit with affection for her 'new' daughter very low on her list of priorities.

Perhaps if Mr and Mrs Smith had asked Kaye what she had wanted first, my mother's new life might have been very different. Although the Smiths undoubtedly had their daughter's best interests at heart, they may have been surprised at her answer and acted differently. Although my mother was made to feel quite welcome by her foster parents in that correct and neat middle-class house in a pretty middle England village, it became obvious from the start that Kaye did not welcome the new addition to her family and shunned my mother from the off. The Smiths' plans had been unexpectedly scuppered, but rather than admit defeat, in that good old-fashioned English way they decided to make the best of a bad job and see it through to the end.

It would be wrong to say that my mother's new parents were unkind to her, but any child in her situation, having known no real affection before being discarded like an unwanted pet, would need a great deal of love and care to overcome such a trauma, and through no fault of their own, the Smiths simply couldn't provide that level of support. As she was often reminded by her foster father, little girls should be seen but not heard, and so, in the absence of physical affection or even the odd kind word, she retreated and closed herself off from that well-ordered house, finding solace in other ways.

While her new home may have offered little in the way of embraces or real human warmth, the surrounding countryside and gulleys of Cherry Hinton were a different story entirely. Every opportunity she had, she would steal herself away to the nearby fields and woodland, literally throwing herself headfirst into the landscape and discovering a beauty and peace that gave her much comfort. Her happiest moments would be spent breathing in the pure countryside air and taking delight in the shapes and perfection of the natural world. 'It would fill me with absolute wonder,' she once told me, 'and I couldn't understand why all these fields weren't filled with people marvelling at it too.'

If she'd known what the future had in store for her, she may have remained for ever in those welcoming long grasses and faded away into the blue expanse overhead.

Although the Blytonesque surrounds of Cherry Hinton offered temporary escapes from her stiff and proper home life, my mother took the first available opportunity to pack her bags at fifteen to find something 'different'. It was a natural and instinctive move. She had never been allowed to forget her status with the Smiths, which was clearly reinforced by the fact that she had remained their foster child, and was never legally adopted. Mrs Smith was fond of saying, 'Blood's thicker than water . . .' and although the phrase was never uttered with any malice, she seemed oblivious to the upset it would cause my mother.

So, in 1963, almost ten years after being rejected by her birth mother at Chelmsford station with her two brothers, she sat alone on another railway platform bench with a small suitcase by her side containing her few possessions. This time, however, her destiny was in her own hands. She had no real idea where she was headed and only knew that she had to find a place where she would be accepted and – perhaps – loved. With very little money, no academic qualifications and without a clue about what lay ahead, she ended up in a Berkshire town called Reading, a bustling urban hive that was worlds away from the thickets and thatched roofs of Cherry Hinton.

Reading wasn't without some history and character, as kings and queens had sojourned there while travelling to and from London, and Henry I was buried in the town's twelfth-century abbey. Even Oscar Wilde had spent some time there (albeit at His Majesty's pleasure in the local prison) and immortalized his stay in his poem *The Ballad of Reading Gaol*.

Aside from all its history, the Reading of my mother's day was more famous for its cheap and available workforce, and its land. Huge companies set about exploiting these resources until Reading's red-bricked Victorian buildings became lost in the shadows of industrial parks and tower blocks.

Despite a lack of qualifications, my mother found herself work as a petrol station cashier in the middle of the town. Unfortunately, the job had its drawbacks; if shoplifters walked off with a handful of Mars Bars or packets of biscuits, the money came out of her already meagre pay packet, and if the ultimate crime was committed – a customer driving away without paying for petrol – her wages would shrink to almost nothing. In spite of such stringent rules she stuck at it and didn't mind the work too much. She maintained a hardy old-school attitude and tried to make the best of a bad job. Besides, working late into the night allowed her mind the freedom to roam to the hills and woodland of her youth, which now seemed no more than a distant memory.

She was still only sixteen when she met a smooth-talking young man one evening as she sat working at the till. His good looks and flattering attention swept her off her feet – for a while at least. She had long hours to fantasize about a better life as she worked her lonely ten-hour shifts. He breezed in, spilled out promises of an exciting world that he'd create for her, made her pregnant and breezed out even faster – back to the wife whom he'd kept hidden from my mother. She was understandably devastated. Broken-hearted, alone and carrying a child who would have no father, my mother knew she would find little sympathy returning to her foster parents. Indeed, as an unmarried mother, her return would be nothing less than scandalous.

Some women in her situation, with neither emotional or financial support, would have been forced to take steps to terminate the pregnancy, but this was 1964 and the Abortion Act of 1967 had yet to be passed, which meant the back-street method of dangerous drugs and coat hangers was the only solution for the less affluent. Instead, she resolved to keep the child and decide how she would support them both in the months that followed.

It was at this most vulnerable time in her life that she met the fast-talking, wisecracking man who was to become my father, albeit in name only. In all other things he was to become my terror and the beast under the bed; the monster whom I would one day have to face up to whether I wanted to or not.

# 2 | *A Fateful Meeting*

M Y PARENTS first met in a cafe in the centre of Reading when my mother was on a lunch break. To a teenage girl from the sticks with little life knowledge, my father cut a suave and impressive figure. Well dressed and toned from his short-lived boxing career, he must have looked almost dashing. Every photograph I had of my father is now destroyed – my mother saw to that as soon as she had the chance – but I do remember an old black-and-white photo of him in his late teens, wearing a smart jacket and striking a film-star pose. It wasn't hard to see the attraction; he looked like a cross between James Dean and a young William Holden. His brief time in the ring had been enough to give him the confident swagger of a prizefighter and a tongue every bit as sharp as his suit.

After being forced to abandon his boxing aspirations, he had set himself up as a bricklayer and general labourer, but my mother later noted that he often kept odd working hours at that time – sometimes claiming to be going off to work in the middle of the night dressed in smart clothes. She thought little of it in those early days; young love seemingly sending logic to sleep. The witty Scot effortlessly charmed her, sweeping her off her feet. 'It was the way he could make me laugh,' she later told me. 'At that time there seemed to be nothing to feel remotely happy about and here was someone who could make me belly laugh with his jokes and clowning.'

My mother had revealed her pregnancy to him in the very beginning and he reassured her that it made no difference to him. As far as he was concerned, any child of hers was, in effect, a child of his. Thus, it seemed that she had at last found the happiness she had so often dreamed about. Even when he slapped her across the face one evening, after accusing her of flirting with another man, her spirits remained very much intact. Some might say she should have heeded this behaviour as a sign of things to come, but a young girl in her situation at that time had few options other than to hope for the best. My mother put his frequent rages down to mere immaturity, believing that once the child was born he would calm down. Besides, he would apologize profusely the next morning – and she was deeply in love with him.

My father had always been a drinker, like his own father before him, and my mother was simply too ignorant of the dangers of hard drinking to spot the early symptoms of the disease infiltrating his mind and body, which would one day cause disaster, not only for him but everyone else around him. In fact, it was during one of those early drunken moments that he first revealed one of the most frightening aspects of his personality: destructive unpredictability. One evening, as they sat watching a film, he suddenly announced that she could only keep the baby if it were a girl; if it were a boy, it would have to go.

Understandably, my mother's hopes came crashing down around her. She had swung from the terrifying prospect of bringing a fatherless child into the world alone – still a huge stigma in the 1960s – to the joy of finding someone who seemed strong enough to take on another man's child, and was now being faced with the surreal situation of deciding the baby's fate solely on its gender. At the time of my father's shocking declaration she was six months' pregnant, and had happily nurtured and sung to the child that was moving inside her, convinced that soon she would be holding a new life in her arms. The child's sex meant nothing to her; whether it was a son or daughter, it was hers.

The weeks that lay ahead were agonizing for my mother. She could think of and pray for nothing else other than that the child be born a girl, while my father, like some biblical king issuing judgements for reasons unfathomable to his subjects, seemed completely indifferent. In this respect, at least, he remained consistent throughout his life.

In December 1964, my mother gave birth to a beautiful, healthy female baby. All the pressure of the previous months and the fear of being forced to give up her much wanted child evaporated as soon as the midwife announced, 'It's a girl.' Sadly, her joy and relief were short-lived. When my father turned up at the hospital, drunk, a full day after the birth, he took one look at the beaming mother and her newborn daughter and simply said, 'Get rid of it.'

So 'get rid of it' she did. She had no real choice in the matter. She loved my father in spite of everything, and over the months had become so dependent on him that she felt there was no way she could support a baby by herself. Hence my half-sister Kathleen Marie – though to me she will always be simply my sister – was given away to social services, like my own mother more than a decade before.

After the double trauma of giving birth and being forcibly separated from her child, the depression that descended on my mother was merciless. Her doctor merely prescribed pills and suggested she tried 'cheering up a bit'. If he'd been a fly on the wall during my father's increasingly black and violent moods, perhaps he would have understood his patient's grim smile as he dished out his useless advice.

Having seen one chance for redemption come and go

straight to the care of the local authorities, my mother – true to the nature of the abused woman – clung on to the next carrot that my father dangled: marriage. Again, she truly believed that, like a magic talisman, a ring on her finger would change and mellow my father, and so, in August 1966, my mother gained a husband at Reading register office. But all the ring signified was that she was now my father's property, and to prove this he would beat his wife at night and repent, in tears, in the morning.

It was during these remorseful mornings that my mother learned of his formative years in Glasgow and how his earliest memories consisted of the violence meted out to his mother by his father, and the constant beatings he endured at the hands of his own brothers. My mother, full of the goodness and compassion that characterized my grandmother, forgave him every time. My father learned to use the 'abuse excuse' for his own purposes, but I can't judge him too harshly: years later, I'd find myself doing the same thing.

By the time she became pregnant with me, early in 1967, and shortly after being housed by the council in temporary accommodation, the violence had become a regular feature in her life, and even my father's morning-after tears and confessionals had ceased. Where once he would deliver a swift slap to put her in her place, now she had to fend off thrashings that inevitably ended up requiring medical treatment. She bore it with the resignation of someone with nowhere else to go, who naïvely believed that having a family would 'make things better', and who lived with the terrible fear that if she left him he would come after her and beat the life out of her. He'd certainly made that promise before, and she knew he wasn't lying and was more than capable of carrying out such a threat. Unless a person has experienced this type of climate of fear, it is almost impossible to appreciate the debilitating effect it can have, causing logic and reason to fly straight out the window. My mother was no different.

By now my father had racked up a number of convictions for assault, street fighting, and being drunk and disorderly, but perhaps more worryingly for my mother, he had also become involved with many of the local criminals and organized gangs that operated in Reading. Their reach was far and wide, and though my mother may have been naïve, she wasn't stupid. She'd met some of these men and although they were as disarmingly charming as my father had been, she could see beyond their well-dressed, broken-nosed characters to the dangerous creatures lurking within. Occasionally they'd visit the young couple, and casually talk about going after various individuals with hammers and knives. She would often look at them and wonder what they would do to her and her unborn child if she ran away and they tracked her down. It was a risk my mother was not prepared to take, such was the fear instilled in her by my father.

And still that thing called love kept her believing in the possibility of change. In her isolated state, there was no one to tell her the simple truth: that when a man has struck a woman once, he will do it again and again, and that unless he recognizes he has a serious problem it can only continue and worsen. My father, however, sensed no wrong with his treatment of his wife, because it was what he had witnessed during his childhood. He was just another link in the chain, and even beating my mother when she was pregnant did not seem unreasonable to him.

And so she remained trapped. In the late 1960s there were few domestic violence units (certainly none in Reading at that time), no women's refuges and no laws to protect the wife – except in the event of murder, in which case it was a little too late. The police were impotent and powerless to do anything; even when neighbours called them to report that they could hear a woman screaming, the authorities needed an official complaint from the victim, and for my mother to admit that her own husband had assaulted her was tantamount to signing her own death warrant.

★ ★ ★

After months of my mother's singing to me in the womb and her constant caresses of her swelling belly, I was born a fit and healthy child in most respects, but in another I was quite abnormal: I had an extraordinary memory.

I have vague recollections of a bleached white room smelling of disinfectant, which I am almost sure was the delivery room, though it may be from a later hospital check-up. However, my first clear memories definitely start from a very early age. I can still astound my mother with descriptions of lying in the pram, and the sights and sounds of people or events unfolding around me; a hot-air balloon that floated across a vivid blue sky as I watched, hypnotized, while I lay on my back in a garden, listening to the exclamations of my mother and her friend – I was only two at the time. It's almost as if I came into this world ready for the fight, and having to keep my wits about me from day one.

My first abiding memories are sounds. Sounds became an integral part of my life and still are to this day. Remembrances of birds singing, the wind whistling outside my bedroom window, and a biplane flying high overhead would come much later, being overshadowed as they were by far more disturbing noises. Some of my earliest aural memories are the anguished sounds of my mother's screams as my father beat her. Although I had no idea at the time what was happening, I knew it was bad. In fact, it was the worst noise I ever heard – or ever will. My ears became finely tuned and alert to every creak, every shout and every dreadful cry that echoed round our house.

One incident that I'm thankful I don't remember, because I was safely tucked up in my cot in an upstairs bedroom, took place when my father was out and we were staying with friends in Tilehurst, on the Reading borders. My mother and our hosts were sat down enjoying a drink – and no doubt, too, my father's absence – with another friend who was telling them a joke. My father returned, clearly displeased that a good time was being had without his permission, and told my mother to get her coat because they were going out. The guy telling the joke made the grave mistake of telling him to relax, and to let him finish his joke first. My father calmly walked over to where the man was sitting, bent down as if to whisper something, and bit off half his ear. As the poor chap fell to his knees screaming, my father spat out the lump of flesh, wiped his mouth, silently picked up my mother's coat and dragged her out of the house. My mother was too shocked to do anything other than comply, but she'd have nightmares later that evening.

The fear my father inspired in people certainly wasn't limited to my mother. No one said or did anything after the ear-biting incident. So he got away with the violent act while further enhancing his fearful reputation.

Some time after that horrific episode, my mother overheard two men referring to him several times as 'Mad Eric'. If the knowledge that her husband was becoming well known for his madman antics came as an unpleasant shock to her, it still didn't change the fact that she was by now totally dependent on him, pregnant with another child (my brother Iain) and living in the sure knowledge that she had nowhere to run – or at least nowhere that he wouldn't find her. The old threats of having her found and battered senseless if she dared to run away were now replaced by promises to have her and her baby killed. This raising of the stakes merely tightened the shackles, and trapped my mother in a state of fear that was to define all our lives for the next ten years.

# 3 | *Growing Up in Whitley*

FOULKE STREET in Whitley, on the outskirts of Reading, was a collection of Victorian terraced houses glued together with crumbling cement and council indifference. Although the whole area was being torn down – house by house and brick by brick – Foulke Street had somehow evaded demolition and so it stood, defiantly and alone, like the solitary survivor of a massive explosion. Some bright spark at the council obviously realized that although the street's days were numbered, it could still take the temporary burden of being 'home' to some of Berkshire's most desperate citizens. Unfortunately, that's what my family was, and so we ended up moving there.

A film director shooting a movie set in a Victorian slum could have saved a fortune on set design had he or she stumbled across Foulke Street or, as my mother preferred to call it, the street that time forgot. The toilets were outside in a stinking shed that was freezing cold all year round, while the claustrophobic rooms inside the house had a damp, forbidding odour which fell off decaying walls that audibly heaved with the effort of trying to support the leaking roof. The whole house, it appeared, had been designed with the sole purpose of keeping light out and locking in the gloom; shadows in the rooms and hallway having more permanency than the ancient fixtures and fittings that regularly crumbled or fell off their mountings.

The whole house creaked and groaned with every step, and even when we were all asleep it continued to make the strangest noises. I would lie awake in my cot and listen with a mixture of fascination and fear to these structural riffs as they complained and moaned into the night.

My racing imagination bestowed life on shadows, speech to the whining bedsprings and moaning floorboards, and fantastical worlds to all the spaces in between. The realms I visited then and for years afterwards are way out of bounds even to my extensive and elastic memory; whole worlds are locked in my mind, somewhere just out of reach, and they evaporate every time I start to catch the scent.

We had an attic, which for some reason was a place that filled me with horror. As we never used that part of the house, the room was left to disintegrate faster than the rest of the house. Yellowing strips of paint hung slackly off the walls and doors giving it a classic horror film look. One small window let in a mocking strip of light that only served to splash shadows across the room and send motes of swirling dust into a frenzy. I went up there once and had nightmares for months after. The dream was always the same: I would be chained up to a soaking wet bed and slowly, inch by inch, a foul, salivating, insane monster with fangs so long they scraped against the floor would come for me, slow step by slow step, creak by creak to eat me alive. Invariably I'd wake up bathed in my own urine, crying out for my mother, and I'd hear my father shout at her that 'the boy's not right in the head.' For a while I thought it was his special name for me as he said it so often.

The meaning of the nightmare didn't require analysis even back then. I had already learned to fear my father, and although he occasionally tried to make me laugh by pulling stupid faces,

I'd stare dumbly back at him knowing that the person standing before me was the reason for my mother's frequent tears and the strange marks on her beautiful face that I knew should not be there. He was so blind to everything that he put my lack of response down to being backward, and he would often slap me out of the blue – usually when I was staring out into the nothingness, lost in my own little world – demanding, 'What's wrong with you, son? Are you stupid?' After a while, I began to believe that perhaps I was.

Beyond the old house, though, lay great adventures and escapes. Although my mother told me to play directly outside the front door, it was almost as if the waste grounds and demolition sites that encircled our house were calling me to them, and so I would wander there gleefully. Her main fear, as she dragged me back home from the various new continents I'd discovered, was that one day I'd have an accident out of her earshot and lie undiscovered in one of the many tangles of scrap metal or abandoned fridges that littered the wasteland like rusted and charred weeds.

It didn't take me too long to add to her worries. One day I toddled off to the rubble at the top of our street and found a brown bottle filled with some curiously aromatic liquid. My mother had warned me over and over about two things: the first was never to climb into anything with a door that closed – especially fridges – and the second was never to drink or eat anything that I found on the floor. So, naturally I opened the bottle, sniffed it and drank it. Luckily for me it was an innocuous, but foul-tasting, cough mixture or something similar, but it still took a trip to the hospital and reassurances from doctors that all was well before my terrified mother could be calmed down. I was three at the time and can still remember her exasperated disbelief that I had done something so stupid. In my eyes she was being boring, because I genuinely believed that by drinking any strange mixture I'd travel to a magical land.

By this time I had a new companion, Iain. Born in April 1969, my baby brother was a strange one. He never cried or smiled and would watch me with deep curious eyes that seemed impervious to everything. I tried playing with him, tickling him and even pinching him, but he seemed unimpressed by all my efforts. Perhaps he'd understood that my extrovert and ridiculous antics would do no good and he decided on the path of least resistance. Certainly he seemed to be on to something, as my father would often not even notice him; I'd be slapped or pushed over frequently but Iain, like a knowing little owl, rarely triggered my father's anger.

This unique ability of his really bugged me at the time and I'd study him as he studied me, trying to work him out and gain access to his secrets, but he was as inscrutable as a closed flower. I loved him all the same, however, and sometimes I'd even manage to make him laugh – usually when I wasn't trying – and it was a rare and wonderful sight to see that pale, solemn face break out in a grin that almost seemed to belong to someone else.

As a toddler I'd developed a pathological fear of the dark and always had to have a light on in the hallway with the bedroom door ajar. There were two reasons for this: on one occasion, when I was about three, I had woken up in the middle of the night to find a huge spider sitting on my chest. Having witnessed my mother's reactions to these strange creatures – which always involved her jumping on a chair and shrieking – I tried to follow suit, but couldn't. I was frozen, in some kind of narcoleptic state, unable to move no matter how hard I tried. After what seemed like an eternity, my father must have heard my strangled yelps and crashed into the room, whereupon he brushed the spider off me, whacked me round the face and staggered back to bed, cursing me as he went.

The other more serious reason for my dread of darkness was that I would always hear my mother's screams at night, so I came to fear that time of the day; that, and the smell of whisky.

I had no word for whisky then, but I could differentiate between the stench of beer and that other evil-smelling and dangerous poison. To my young and finely tuned sense of smell it seemed more like he'd been bathing in the stuff than drinking it; its odour filled the whole house and my half-opened bedroom door allowed me to gauge the danger levels.

The scent of beer meant shouting and possibly the sound of a brief slap to my mother's face before he collapsed, too plastered and drugged to manage much more than a minor fight. The smell of whisky, however, would put me on high alert. I'd curl up in the centre of my bed with the pillow stuffed tightly against my ears because that unique stench meant only one thing – a prolonged beating that would always have the same outcome the next day. I'd wake up, see my mother and hardly recognize her. I'd scream and cry at the horrible beaten creature standing in front of me whom I knew was my mother, but who didn't resemble her in the slightest. Only her voice reassured me of her true identity. Her face would be puffed up, purple swellings obscuring black eyes and there would always be that terrifying protruding, boxer-punched, upper lip that hung over her lower lip. To my child's eye she looked like a deformed monster. Always it would be the same: she'd put her arms around me, softly weep, and tell me over and over again, 'This is not normal. This is not what happens in other families.' Then we'd both cry and I'd try my best to look after her, which usually involved me trailing her around the house until she told me to stop tripping her up and go play.

One night, when I was three and my mother was pregnant with my youngest brother, the front door burst open and he barged in, reeking of the danger smell. All hell followed him in. Things were being broken, screams and curses were raining down on my mother, and her anguished cries told me that this was worse than anything before. When he came into my room, I was in my usual hiding place in the centre of my bed, praying he couldn't find me. He dragged me out and threw me into the living room. My mother was on the sofa sobbing, holding her face in both hands, a thin trickle of blood running down her neck. I stood there paralysed with terror and something else; something that I'd never felt before, something . . . wrong. It felt wrong and not mine to own, this strange gnawing and ripping feeling that started in my stomach and flooded out in every direction. Like every mother who can recall the moment her child came into the world, so I remember the moment I gave birth to mine. I didn't know what anger was back then, and of course had no way of knowing that one day we'd become inseparable.

My father screamed at me, 'Look at the useless bitch, son.'

The theme tune to *The Persuaders* rang out of the old TV. I felt like I was in a dream and everything seemed to slow down. His voice growled and roared, my body started to shake, and still the theme music went on . . . 'ding ding de de ding ding ding' . . . such beautiful music, full of magic and mystery, and still my mother sat there, that little line of blood drying on her neck. After throwing something at her he told her to get out and sleep in my room. I went to follow her, but he kept me back. He sat me down and embarked on a slurred, rage-filled rant about his father and priests. The only phrase I clearly remember was, 'Fucking priests, fucking priests.'

Then he put something in my hand. It was a hammer. He ordered me to go into my room and hit my mother round the head with it. I was too scared of him and the whole nightmare situation to say 'No'. So I took it, thinking I could use it as a way to escape from him, but before I could run away he told me I had to come back when I'd done it.

My mother was in my bed with the light out, crying as I told her what he'd asked me to do. She put her arms around me and explained to me that my father was sick and that this wasn't what happened in other families. Over and over she repeated this to me until she fell asleep. I returned to the demon in the next room who was sat gazing at the carpet as if he were about to throw up or collapse at any moment. He looked up at me, squinting with those narrow eyes, hinting at such danger that I nearly wet myself there and then.

'Did you do it, son?' he slurred.

I stared at the sick man before me, convinced this had to be a bad dream, and quietly said, 'No.'

He didn't explode as I thought he would, but he just looked back at me, his dragon eyes boring into me until they saw something they certainly didn't expect or like one little bit. The slap from him sent me sprawling across the floor and as he towered over me I saw in his face a mixture of anger and, strangely, fear. He could hardly speak, but spat out, 'Don't you ever fucking look at me like that again.'

Looking back now, I realize that although I didn't understand what hate was at that time, my father had seen it in my eyes as clear as day, and it shook him so much that he hadn't known how to react. Exhausted from the evening's events, I crawled off to my room and curled up next to the gentle creature in my bed and swore that I would always look after her, no matter what.

The next morning, when my mother was in the kitchen making breakfast, she wouldn't look at me. I knew the reason why, but when I finally saw her face, and after my tears had subsided, I came to a clear conclusion based on the young logic of a natural problem solver: when my father *wasn't* with us, my mother didn't cry and was always happy, showering me and Iain with unconditional love and making me giggle for hours; when he *was* around, he hurt her and caused her pain. So, I came to the obvious conclusion that it would be better for everyone if he was no longer around.

At that young age I couldn't work out what this meant in practical terms, except that it was a simple answer to a huge problem, but it was a black irony that he'd given me the answer without either of us being aware of it. Or perhaps he had read it in my eyes as I stood staring at him with all the open honesty that only children have the guts to display.

That dreadful night had one major outcome that would set the stage permanently for our relationship: mutual antipathy. He could beat me all he wanted, which he now started to do regularly, but I had an inner defence he couldn't destroy. I would learn to glare back at him with insolent eyes, which sent him into apoplectic fits of rage. When I didn't want to be beaten too badly, I'd look down at the floor and avert my gaze, letting him think he'd won, but always knowing that tomorrow I wouldn't care about anything he dished out, and would lash him again with that defiant look as surely as a swift slap to his pockmarked face.

Establishing our enemy status became the sole focus of my world. The more he beat my mother, the more I hated him and the greater my inner anger became. It offered solace, strength and a much-needed defence mechanism. More importantly it was something he couldn't touch, no matter what. Or so I thought at the time.

A brief respite to the unfolding horrors that took place in that house came in the shape of my youngest brother, Anthony. While my mother went through all the joys and agonies of bringing a third son into the world in December 1970, Iain and I were packed off to friends to be looked after, as my father wasn't capable. I remember that the people were friendly enough, albeit oblivious to my precocious ways. One night they didn't follow my mother's instructions to leave a light on for me, so I screamed the house down until they obliged.

The next day, the lady of the house was chatting to her neighbour across the garden fence and telling her about the odd child standing before them who had a dread fear of the dark. 'It's not right,' she tutted to her gossipy friend. 'There must be something really wrong with the boy. What does his mother think she's doing?'

Clearly unaware that a three-year-old was capable of

following their conversation, they were both astonished when I piped up helpfully: 'Your house has a monster – I saw it and it told me it's coming to get you.' That soon shut them up.

My father seemed delighted at the impossibly cute little bundle that was my youngest brother, and for a brief period I remember a lull in the nightly screams and smashes. It must have seemed, for a while at least, as if his arrival might actually change things for the better. I can imagine my mother's thoughts at the apparent cessation of the nightly beatings, and how she must have grasped at that straw with such pathetic desperation.

Displaying behaviour that I had never before seen, my father would attempt to make baby noises at Anthony and even smile at him – if one could call that horrible grimace a smile. It was an alien sight to the rest of us, but it still didn't make him any more human as far as I was concerned. In fact, there was always something slightly frightening about watching that grin form on his features; it seemed to me as if his whole face could shatter and split apart at any moment with the strain. Every time he went near Anthony I'd go cold; the thought of him putting his hands on my brother, even benevolently, made me feel ill, and I'd rush to the baby when my father had lost interest, holding him tightly in the hope that I'd wipe away all traces of his having been touched by that vile creature.

Where Iain was impervious and floating on his own little cloud of indifference to anything I could do or say, Anthony was the opposite. If I cuddled him he'd gurgle with delight and if I tickled him he'd almost burst with joy. I was most satisfied with this new addition to our crazy house and hoped with all my heart that he'd never get so much as a slap from my father. I needn't have worried because Anthony soon became my father's beloved; where Iain and I disappointed and disgusted my father with our aloofness and outright dislike, Anthony seemed to hold a magic key that almost, at times, brought out a hitherto unknown paternal side.

From the age of one Anthony would gurgle away in his

seemingly unfathomable baby language, but somehow I could understand what he was saying. He would gargle out an Alphabetti Spaghetti of vowels and consonants that my mother would then ask me to translate, which I always managed to do. The particular toy he'd demand would placate and delight him, the potty would be used and it would quieten him, and the cuddle he'd request from my mother would send him off to a land of sweet dreams. As far as my translation skills were concerned, it had probably less to do with linguistics than with the psychic bond that most siblings possess. Iain and I would later develop an extraordinary link that meant we'd often start saying precisely the same thing at the same time, and if he were having a rough time at school or anywhere out of my sight, I'd suddenly feel down and stressed, and know he wasn't happy for whatever reason.

At this stage of our lives in the early years on Foulke Street I'd given up on Iain being any fun at all. Anthony had progressed to crawling on all fours and despite all my pleading with Mum she quite wisely refused to let me take him outside, otherwise God only knows what trouble I'd have got us into. So it was all down to Iain. Unfortunately, he had nothing but disdain for my childish ways. One day I took him outside to find snails and worms, and to make little paper boats with the names of imaginary countries crayoned on them, in which the poor creatures would sail down the drain, but he was never the slightest bit impressed.

'What did you do that for?' he would ask me, totally perplexed.

So I explained to him my relocation programme for all things wiggly and slimy: 'They're going to live in another country that's much better than here – it's sunny all the time and they have parties.'

He looked at me like I was a total fool. 'No, they won't,' he sniffed. 'They're going to drown.' And off he strutted to find someone with a better grip on reality.

Fortunately I wasn't alone for long, as I discovered my first best friend, Marlene, who lived at the bottom of the road. Marlene was beautiful and I couldn't work out why there was an angel living in our crumbling street; I soon realized that she'd been sent to Earth to play with me. My main memory of her will always be her wonderful smile – it was like nothing I'd ever seen. Whenever we met she would always beam out that blinding greeting and I'd be like a hungry seed under the ground being hit by the full force of a life-giving light. My father referred to her as 'the wee darkie' – not unkindly, surprisingly enough – but I instinctively didn't like that word, no matter how it was said. I once asked Marlene whether she was a darkie, and after giving me one of her little chiming laughs she said, with absolute conviction, 'I am a princess,' which of course she was.

Marlene had no problems suspending disbelief when we launched hapless snails into Reading's sewers with only notepaper to keep them afloat. She was a bit older than me and advised that if we covered the boats in purple crayon they'd go to a place called Africa, where her parents came from, and that they'd probably stay on the beach all day and would be much happier there than here. She did put me right about worms, though, telling me that they'd have to stay behind or else they'd frazzle up in the sun. This new emigration rule was unfortunate because there seemed to be many more worms than snails in the waste grounds, which meant that the search for legal émigrés was a lot harder. After we'd return from a successful hunt, she would coo and ahh to the kidnapped snails, whispering strange words to them, and then, as we dropped them down into the ocean currents below, she would beam ecstatically, singing out, 'One more for Africa!'

'Afreeecaahh!' I'd yell out in reply and then we'd tear down the street trying to follow the magic river underneath our feet until we ran out of breath.

I've no idea how many unfortunate members of the snail

kingdom we consigned to a watery and pungent grave, but it possibly explains my present-day, firmly-held belief that all life is sacred. Guilt is the root of many a religion, after all.

Then, all of a sudden, Marlene was gone. Her parents, the loveliest and warmest of people, would continue to open the door to me, but their answer was always the same. 'Marlene isn't here,' they'd tell me kindly. For some reason I didn't believe them, but instead assumed that Marlene had been really naughty and wasn't allowed outside, or that perhaps they'd discovered our snail games and were cross because there wasn't really anything for those creatures to do in Africa. All I knew for sure was that I'd lost my only real play friend.

Sending snails off to a new life by myself was no fun without Marlene. I missed her joyful company and strange little songs too much. I would still colour the paper purple, and whisper magic words to the snails, but when I'd drop them into the black water below, something didn't feel right. So I decided to amuse myself in other ways until Marlene was allowed back out to play, which I hoped wouldn't be too long.

There was an abandoned old factory not far from our street and I'd discovered a way in. While my mother was preoccupied with baby Anthony, I'd sneak into the dingy, dark building and run amok. Smashing things up was my favourite game and inside that place there were so many things to kick to pieces. Filing cabinets received the greatest beating, as they wouldn't break no matter what I did to them, but empty bottles left by visiting tramps made such a beautiful sound if I clambered up to the first-floor scaffolding and dropped them on to the ground below.

Eventually, though, my mother discovered my new playground, and my destructive fun had to end. In her strictest voice she told me never to go back there in case I was kidnapped by a bad man. For once, I heeded her wisdom; the thought of running into someone like my own father was enough to keep me away.

As the months passed by, it was becoming increasingly obvious that Foulke Street was no longer fit for human habitation and on the verge of collapse. I remember my own frightening experience when, one day, while using the outside toilet, two bricks fell from the high crumbling wall and missed my head by inches. Clearly, it was time for us to be rehoused. My mother was duly taken to view a new home by a sympathetic council employee, but when she saw the hovel being presented to her, she took one look at it and burst into tears. She didn't want much for her family, but to go from a condemned ruin on Foulke Street to somewhere equally as bad was more than she could bear. I'd dearly love to find that kindly council worker so I could thank him for what he did next. He drove her to a relatively new estate on the Reading borders, in a little town called Woodley, and showed her an empty house there. My mother wept again, only this time with tears of gratitude.

Shortly before the move, when it had dawned on me I'd never see Marlene again, I rushed to tell her I was leaving and that she should come too. I knocked at her door all day and the day after and the next, but there was no reply. So I collected a few snails from the usual harvesting ground of the wasteland and stood over the magic vent that once led to Africa. One by one I dropped them all in, with no paper hull or purple decks to protect them, knowing they'd all drown, while I sadly mourned my lost friendship.

# 4 | *Onwards, Upwards and Downwards*

ALTHOUGH the small Berkshire town of Woodley was a relatively new urban creation, it had a past and history of its own, even boasting a manor house. Within reach were some beautiful and picturesque villages such as Sonning-on-Thames, which would later become one of my favourite bike-ride destinations, and which had its own huge lake and woodland areas.

The contrast between the dilapidated Whitley and aspiring Woodley could not have been more dramatic; where the former was stuck in the past, the latter was busy with the job of creating the future. There was a shopping precinct ten minutes' walk from our house and it was large enough to ensure that the only time it was necessary to travel into Reading was to go to the cinema, or in my mother's case to pay the rent at the council offices every month.

Looking back, our council estate was quite extraordinary. It was clean and full of well-kept houses – if you exempted our next-door neighbours, who, rather wonderfully I thought, had amassed a small collection of Ford Capris and Escorts, almost as if they were creating their very own museum of engine parts in their front garden. We lived on Manners Road, which was deliciously apt when I consider how the local residents reacted to us as time passed by.

At the top of our street was, to my amazement, a small park hemmed in by the back gardens of other estate houses that surrounded it. There were swings, a roundabout, a slide and more than enough room to play football. It may have seemed like an afterthought when the town planners decided to drop a few pieces of brightly painted metal into an otherwise redundant bit of ground, but whether intentional or not, it was inspired. Although the estate was quite a good one, most people still had their share of difficulties to deal with, be it financial or otherwise. It was, after all, a council estate; there were few privileges and certainly no privileged there. But that little park, tucked away though it may have been, offered somewhere for kids to escape to and let off steam instead of hanging around the town centre, bored, and finding less innocent outlets for all that energy. Ask any youth living on one of today's many vast concrete estates what their biggest problem is and the answer won't be that they have no money or that things at home are shit: it will invariably be that there's nothing to do and nowhere to go. We never had that excuse in Woodley and so life on the estate was both easy-going and, in general, peaceful. In fact, the only sore point on the whole estate were the inhabitants at Number Two: our family.

The house on Manners Road was unbelievable – beyond my wildest dreams. The front garden was nothing special, comprising two empty concrete gateposts that led to a tiny square of grass dominated by a huge manhole cover laid in its centre. But ignoring all that and opening the front door revealed just how far we'd come from the old wreck we'd left behind in Foulke Street.

A small hallway led into the front room, but I was more interested in the next floor up. I shot upstairs, reaching a landing with doors leading off to the left and right. Two of them looked out on to a small but promising garden, which had as its crowning glory – and I nearly fainted with delight when I saw it – a huge and highly climbable tree.

Having spent my early years in the confined, dusty and light-starved rooms of Foulke Street, the new house felt almost like a palace. The small front room, which my mother insisted we called 'the lounge', featured some tall, white French windows that pulled you out into the little garden, overgrown with weeds, which lacked the myriad of colourful flowers that my mother would spend the next seven years lovingly cultivating. Light in the lounge was in abundance and the only drawback was trying to blot it out when we were watching TV.

My first priority was to get into the garden and try the tree out for size. While I pulled at the French doors to open them, so I could run wild in that little jungle, Iain simply asked my mother if he could be the first to use the toilet, as if it were the most important thing in the world to him. It only seems funny when I remember it now, but at the time it was just Iain; as weird as me, but in different ways. He locked himself in for over an hour and only emerged when my mother shouted out that she'd lock him in for ever if he didn't come out.

Anthony was at that irresistibly cute toddling age of three and just sucked his thumb and followed our mother around, oblivious to the significance of our explorations, but infected by our excitement. My father hadn't bothered to help out with the move and so it was up to us to carry the few possessions we owned into our new and stately council house. Even though the walls were half stripped and completely bare in some rooms, we knew that our mother's energetic approach to everything would result in some colourful changes to the house's decor.

Our two beautiful cats had also joined us on our exodus from Whitley. Dino, a jet-black half-Siamese, and Fluffy, an incredible silver-grey, long-haired ball of fluff. They loved the new place – especially the garden tree. They'd stick their claws into its trunk and howl at each other in feline raptures, and then launch themselves into the overgrown weeds as if they were in the deepest jungle. Both cats seemed to be in heaven in their outdoor sanctuary, which wasn't surprising when I consider how my father thought nothing of kicking or throwing them as hard as he could w hen the mood took him. They feared him as much as I had begun to hate him and so the garden offered them a useful means of escape whenever he was around.

We had three upstairs bedrooms. At the top of the stairs from the ground-floor hallway there was a small room that overlooked the little garden. Ignoring my loud protests, my mother decided this would be a store room until I was 'old enough' to have a room of my own. Next door to that was a much larger room, also with a garden view, which I was to share with my brothers, and our parents' room was next-door to ours.

The indoor toilet was a godsend – no more freezing trips to a spider-infested shed with a door that wouldn't close. I wasn't able see it properly for ages thanks to Iain's lengthy private viewing. The little room next to the toilet contained a small bath, where, once every few days, madness would erupt as three boys were squashed into it for bath night – the hot-water boiler dictated this rather undignified way of cleaning us, as it had to be turned on an hour before bathing and still only managed to fill three quarters of the tub before running cold. For this reason, my mother had to make the water as hot as possible, otherwise it would be cold within five minutes – especially in the winter and with no central heating. And so each time we all felt like reluctant lobsters being lowered into the cooking pot. Iain's position was in the middle of the deep, enamelled bath and little Anthony would be at the tap end, always taking rapturous pleasure in farting in Iain's direction, much to his disgust. Although my mother would pretend not to find it as funny as Anthony and I did, she could never suppress her giggles, which wound Iain up even more.

On the whole our neighbours were pretty fantastic and very welcoming. Of course they had no idea what they were letting themselves in for at that time, but Mrs Jarman from next door introduced herself with a pot of hot tea to welcome us to our new abode. Curious kids loitered outside, sizing us up, and it seemed we'd got the seal of approval because by the end of the day Iain and I were out playing with them. First of all we wrestled a bit, which made them happy as despite my unusual height for a five-year-old – I'd shot up to almost five feet – I was really quite puny and unable to hold my own. Joey Longworth, who was one of the coolest and nicest kids out of all of us, wrestled me to the floor with one arm and then we all went to play marbles.

My father's relative calmness during that brief period between Anthony's birth and the move to Woodley couldn't and didn't last. He had found work as a bricklayer in Reading, but had also discovered the local pub, The Chequers, which was an unremarkable one-level building that from the outside almost seemed like a oddly situated bungalow. To my father, though, it would most certainly become a home from home.

A week or so after moving in I heard some familiar sounds coming from downstairs, and my heart sank. I had honestly hoped and almost, but not quite, believed that the bad times were coming to an end. So much had changed recently that I thought it was impossible for things to go back to the way they were. But his crazed screams and her painful cries welded together like barbed-wire whips that lashed at my ears. There was no escape from it. I tried stuffing tissue in my ears, crawling under the bed, squeezing under the mattress and hoping to suffocate, but my mother's screams played in my head long after the violence had abated.

As my father was fond of punching me around the side of the head – because it tended to leave no trace – I'd become used to hearing high-pitched whines in my ears as the inner organs attempted to recover from the shock. But a few months after moving to Woodley, I was still hearing noises like those made by a giant, high-pitched tuning fork, even when my father hadn't laid a finger on me.

At first it was like an echo of the dreadful sounds I was trying to blot from my memory, but as time went on newer and more unusual – and often quite terrifying – noises assailed me.

I clearly remember the first time it happened, because I'd jumped out of bed to see what was happening with the front door, which sounded as though it was being slammed with incredible force, over and over again. I went out on to the landing to investigate, but no one was downstairs and all were in bed. Putting it down to a bad dream, I tried to go back to sleep. Off it started again. In total confusion and absolute dread, I realized that the sounds were coming from inside my head. Crash, crash, crash – that huge castle door slammed in perfect time to my wildly beating heart and I thought that I must be dying or going mad. As time progressed, other more frightening noises tormented me. Sometimes I'd hear a word shouted deep inside my ears just as I was about to fall asleep and I would sit up bolt upright, shaking with fear, and stay awake until the morning.

Eventually I had no choice but to tell my mother. I'd kept it from her because I really thought I was a loony, and was afraid I'd be taken away and kept with all the other children who were so bad that they weren't able to sleep at night either. It was the sleep issue, or lack of it, that forced me to tell her; even when the noises were at a minimum and only a high-pitched wail kept me unwelcome company at night, I found it impossible even to consider having dreams and would only ever find myself being woken up after passing out in bed in a state of sheer exhaustion. It wasn't uncommon for me to fall asleep suddenly during the daytime, which was a complete waste as far as I was concerned, given that I could have been out playing instead. The doctor who examined me declared I had tinnitus, and gave my mother some eardrops that had no effect whatsoever.

While I was getting to grips with adapting to the nightly raves in my head and the encroaching insomnia that was part and parcel of tinnitus, my mother was trying to cope with bringing up three kids without any sort of support, financial or otherwise, from my father. He preferred to drink his wages away, beat her to a pulp, and constantly tell Iain and I that we were 'not right in the head,' before delivering a full stop in the shape of a punch, kick or slap.

By the time I was six years old the beatings were just an everyday part of life, but I didn't mind them so much compared to the other punishments he dished out. I reasoned that if he hit me it would be one less for my mother and although he was starting to punch me more frequently, he still couldn't touch me inwardly. Inside I had built a little box into which I poured my hatred of him. I'd crawl to my room after a beating, invariably crying, but never from the physical pain. The tears were a reflex response to the accompanying words that spewed out of him: 'You're a fucking idiot . . . You're not right in the head . . . You're a cunt . . . You're a queer . . .' I didn't even know what a 'cunt' or a 'queer' were, but I knew they had to be bad, and any time he brought my mother into his poisonous party of words, he'd always hit the mark as easily as if he'd given me a kidney punch. When he'd finished and told me to 'fuck off', I'd escape to my room and curl up into a ball, breathing fire and rage into my little inner treasure chest. Then I could close it back up inside me and get on with the task of trying to be a 'normal' child, though I had no clue what that involved.

Other children seemed so naturally happy and free to be themselves; it was as if everything that came easily to them posed an unsolvable puzzle to me. I couldn't work out why I didn't fit into their world, which was what I wished for more than anything. They seemed to sense my failure to 'get it' and kept me at arm's length. I was tolerated for the most part because I could go crazy and do stupid things to make them laugh, but all children have a sixth sense and they realized that if they got too close to me, I might pass on whatever affliction that burdened me.

My father was many things, but unfortunately for all of us he wasn't stupid. He may have been sick with a psychotic disorder, but he also had the eye of a hawk and a true predator's heart. He could read me like a book and when he understood that I had started to create a second skin to shield myself from his daily assaults, he simply responded like a natural aggressor does when his victim's binds appear to loosen – he turned the rack even tighter. Those years were easy compared to what was to come, and eventually he'd manage to wipe all traces of defiance from me.

Although my mother managed to get a job at the local sports centre, it wasn't enough to feed three rapidly growing boys, and so she found extra income from working as a housekeeper for a well-to-do family who lived near Sonning in a house so large I thought I'd get lost in it. My mother thought nothing of hard work and would break her back for us kids, but even she had to take a deep breath every morning to face that job. As she couldn't afford a babysitter, our mornings would begin at six and we'd embark on a long three-mile walk to the nouveau riche semi, situated on an upmarket estate with houses that didn't have numbers, only names. While she cleaned and scrubbed we were meant to sit tight in the front room, but it was terminally boring and impossible to do. Instead, Iain and I would escape outside into the back garden – a sprawling and beautiful landscaped area that backed off on to wild woodland. It was here, to my amazement, that Iain came into his own. He really loved the woods and trees, and we'd play great games of cowboys and Indians, which usually ended in one of us falling over and traipsing bleeding knees into the immaculate house.

Our poor mother. I can't begin to imagine the stress and pressure she had to face at that time: two mundane yet demanding jobs, three kids who were rapidly turning into the Dennis the Menace triplets, an abusive husband who was slowly but surely becoming more dangerous and violent, yet still she managed to smile for us and fill every second of her precious spare time with love and hugs.

On the way back home from her cleaning job, we'd always wait for the trains at the railway bridge and wave madly to the drivers – usually to be rewarded by loud horns blasting their reply. The walks to Sonning were tough at that early hour of the morning, but the return journey was always a lot of fun. She would tell us stories from her youth and dirty jokes that I didn't understand, but she'd still fall about laughing until her eyes were moist with tears. When we'd complain that we didn't get it and ask her what was so funny, she'd collapse again. It was from her that I learned the importance of the power of laughter, an understated healing tonic that can sometimes work miracles.

Once we were walking home from that posh house after the owner had snootily told my mother to keep her children under control and that she really had to try harder. 'Why do you work there when they talk to you so nastily?' I asked her. The look she gave me in reply is burned into my memory; a mixture of wounded pride and resignation.

'I have no choice, darling,' she replied. Her words echoed in my head for a long time afterwards: 'I have no choice.' In other words, she was not free. That scared me to the core. Surely life meant more than that? At that moment I vowed to myself that

I would never be without a choice in life, nor find myself shackled and chained and at the mercy of others.

The effects of my deteriorating home life, tinnitus and sleeping problems were starting to manifest themselves negatively in my personality. I could pour as much hate as I wanted into my inner box, but its lid had a habit of bursting open, usually when I didn't expect it and in ways I was unable to comprehend.

Since starting William Grey infant school I'd begun stealing, and when I got home I'd empty my pockets and stare dumbly at the random crap I'd swiped. I had no idea I was even doing it half the time, and would wonder where this and that had come from. I'd walk to the little park and bury the hot crayons, stickle bricks and once even a small blue-strapped Timex watch that I knew didn't even work.

I was aware it was wrong as my mother had impressed on us over and over the value and importance of honesty, and I trusted and believed she was right. In all other ways I was extremely upright and truthful, but I couldn't stop myself committing these pointless thefts. I started to think that I must be truly wicked and that feeling grew like a dark cancer inside me.

These were very curious days that came to define me for a long time after. On the one hand, my nights would be a potent brew of my father's rages and beatings, tinnitus and sleeplessness, and in contrast my days were filled with my mother's seemingly inexhaustible love. Mixed into this was my time at infant school, which was simply one long girl-chasing, war-playing, milk-drinking dream. I was stuck right in the middle of a series of contradictions that made no sense at all.

My mother, it seemed, had set out to instil in me a passion for words and literature. Despite her long and backbreaking days, she would read to me every bedtime, losing herself in the plots of *Brer Rabbit*, *The Famous Five* and *Winnie-the-Pooh*, becoming the characters, adopting their voices, and enchanting me night after night. She'd read for an hour or so and I'd always beg her for just one more chapter. Invariably she couldn't refuse. Whenever she wasn't able to read to me due to tiredness or, as I'd later discover, injury, I'd pick up the books and read them to myself. Half the words meant nothing to me on paper, but my memory was razor sharp and I simply heard my mother reading aloud the trickier sentences.

I was reading *Alice in Wonderland* before the age of seven, with the help of a small dictionary, and I started to live for words, devouring and savouring every syllable. Although new words would stop me in my tracks, it was like finding gold. My dictionary was useless for pronunciation and if my mother were around I'd rush to her with a new discovery and ask her to tell me how to pronounce it. She never did though. Patiently she'd guide me towards the correct utterance of the taunting jumble of letters until I got it right by myself.

Having raced ahead with reading, I found myself growing increasingly bored at infant school, which invariably got me into trouble. It always ended the same way. My sweet teacher, Miss Fitzpatrick, would bear my antics with saintly patience until she'd suddenly snap and scream out, 'Headmistress!' And that meant the feared Miss Curwen. Looking back now I can see how much kindness lay beneath her wizened and gruff exterior, but back then all I saw was a walking vulture. To me she looked at least a hundred years old and walked with a slight hunch, her ancient face seeming to consist of one huge beak and two little black beady eyes; as she prowled the playground she looked as if she were scouting for small mice or voles. I'd stand there mute as she croaked out rules and necessary punishments, waiting for her to pounce and swallow me up, which disappointingly she never did. I was curious to find out how many other children lived in her stomach and how they all fitted inside her skinny frame.

My punishment always ended the same way: she'd caw and creak out a lecture in her bird-like voice, while I wondered how she'd manage to swallow my shoes, and then the ritual was sealed by a swift whack to the palm of my hands with a ruler. I'd always cry, but only because it was expected of me. Compared to what I was getting at home the headmistress was a novice.

During the last few months of infant school, I received a letter to take home to my parents from Miss Curwen. I was petrified. I spent the whole journey home going through a list of my many misdemeanours, wondering which one of them had been so bad as to warrant a handwritten note. By the time I'd got home I was in such a state that I confessed all my wrongdoings before handing my shocked mother the letter. After she'd opened, read and folded it without saying a word, she left me alone to stew for the next night and day. I dared not broach the subject and it wasn't until my mother turned up at school the next day, and I was summoned to the office to join her, that I discovered what the child-munching Miss Curwen wanted: she had heard me singing in assembly and thought I should audition for a church choir in nearby Earley. I was astonished. Until that moment I had assumed she saw me only as a useful surface on which to practice her backhand ruler technique while telling me what a 'terrible child' I was, yet here she was, still capable of spotting hidden potential in the most troublesome child at school. I remember the way her eyes twinkled when she spoke about my singing and how her face softened and all the wrinkle lines fell away, which made me realize just how much of a mask she enjoyed wearing.

I passed the audition and remember the look of unabashed pride on my mother's face as the choirmaster, the slightly tubby Mr Turner who had the kindest eyes, announced to her that her son had a voice like a church bell. I thought it an odd comparison, but my mother convinced me it was a compliment.

My father was less impressed with the news, remarking that I'd turn out to be a poof and that I should be singing with a

Catholic choir if any at all. When my mother insisted that I was going and that was an end to the matter, I steadied myself for a violent scene. To my utter astonishment he simply shrugged, muttered something about 'the wee bastard being a fairy' and carried on reading one of his magazines.

This was one of only two occasions that my mother seemed to score a victory over him, but at the time it didn't make sense that he'd dropped his opposition so quickly. It was a riddle that lasted for years; a link in the chain that only revealed itself when it was all far too late for him, but still in time for me.

# 5 | *Night Terrors*

MY MOTHER had become an expert in the peculiar English art of 'putting a brave face on things', so it was not unusual to see her throwing her arms round all three of us and giggling with delight despite having black eyes or a busted lip. For the most part she pulled it off, but even she had her limits, and the pressure on her was beginning to show.

Her doctor, worried by her physical and mental state, had prescribed sleeping pills in the hope that she could find a little peace and quiet in a period of deep uninterrupted sleep. I'd spent most of my life believing I was the only one with sleeping problems, and it had never occurred to me that while I was lying awake at night, so was she. Where my night thoughts were unformed and confusion-racked, hers were scalpels of self-loathing and helplessness, expertly cutting deep into her psyche.

One warm summer's evening, when I was six, another small nail would be tapped into me a few inches – perfect for another hang-up. While my brothers lay sleeping in their bedroom, I was downstairs listening to the radio when a short burst of crazy smashing and screaming came from my parents' bedroom. Things went quiet for a long time and I assumed that, as usual, he'd let the demon out for a walk, it had done its business and returned to its keeper quite content, which resulted in a relative, temporary peace. I was too afraid to go to my own bed until I was sure the coast was clear, and was glad I held out for that little while longer because minutes later my father pounded down the stairs and headed straight out of the front door, slamming it ferociously as he left. I waited fifteen minutes or so before I switched off the downstairs lights and headed up to bed. However, a bad feeling made me stop before entering my room; something wasn't quite right. I opened my mother's bedroom door to check that she was okay. I touched her arm and asked her if she was all right, but she didn't so much as stir.

The rest is a complete blank. At the time I didn't realize that my mother lay in a critical state following a drug overdose. I was later told that our next-door neighbour, the kindly Mrs Jarman, had seen me playing in front of her house at the unusually late hour of ten o'clock and come out to ask me what I was doing. I explained that I couldn't wake up my mother and didn't know what to do. She immediately ran to her phone, called an ambulance and then shot into our house to try to stir my mother into some kind of consciousness before she slipped away for ever.

The ambulance came, my mother was taken to hospital, social services followed and three dazed children were piled into a car at midnight and taken to a children's home in the leafy suburbs of Sunningdale, which was far enough away from Woodley to leave us thinking our mother had gone for good.

Again, all memory of this time has vanished. I have a vague recollection of a car journey and cuddling Anthony; a strange house with a large woman called Pat; a visit to the hospital to see my mother, and the memory of being petrified that I'd never see her again. All I have left from that experience is a sense of bitter disappointment that I hadn't hammered on any front doors, screaming that my mother wasn't well. True, I was only six and perhaps I was overwhelmed with confusion, but nothing will ever erase the guilt I feel at the fact that were it not for Mrs Jarman's neighbourly concern, my mother would not be alive today.

It was only many years later that I got the full facts from my mother. While I was listening to the radio, the vicious argument in the room above me had ended with repeated punches to my mother's stomach, and something inside her snapped. She had reached a point where she couldn't take any more and wanted out. At that moment, her need to escape was so overpowering that she was unable to see beyond her actions. She shouted out to my father that she couldn't take any more and if the violence continued she'd kill herself. He picked up her sleeping pills, threw them at her and told her to do it – she'd be saving him the job and doing us all a favour. Without really being aware of what she was doing, or stopping to think of the consequences, she swallowed all the pills. My father watched and waited until she'd taken the whole bottle.

It was then, minutes later, I heard the front door slam shut as he holed himself up in the local pub, no doubt watching the clock tick away the last remaining minutes of her life.

When my mother revealed what had happened that night, I was left with a mixture of guilt at my ignorance, sorrow for the dreadful mental state in which she had found herself, but above all, anger; anger at my father for setting up her death so cleverly, but also at her for almost abandoning us that night. It was only when I was seventeen and my own journey led me to a similar course of action that I learned to forgive my mother unconditionally and fully understood what must have going through her mind.

When we were allowed to go home to our recovering mother, my powers of recall returned, the previous week's fear now dissipated. My mother was back on her feet but she needed to rest frequently, and so we gladly helped with the housework and treated her like a queen. Not a word was spoken about where she had been and why – life simply carried on exactly as before. God knows what was running through my father's sick mind after this incident, but we saw little of him for a good while. Ironically, those were very happy times. I stayed at home to help her, he was absent for long periods and all four of us got a taste of how good life could be when he stayed away for more than a couple of days.

Whether my father felt any guilt about the almost fatal steps he had pushed my mother to take seemed unlikely. He acted as though nothing had happened. For a short time, at least, things were quiet and relatively peaceful in the house, but all he was doing was biding his time, waiting for the moment normal transmission would be resumed. It came about two weeks later and I knew, as I lay listening upstairs, that if my mother's near death didn't cause him to rethink his actions then we would be permanently stuck in this situation.

By the age of eight I had become something of a philosopher. Nights turned into mornings as I spent long and futile hours in bed, resigned to having to endure both the tinnitus and the sound of my father's rage. A simple question kept running through my head: why? Yet all the hours spent turning the question over and over were no help at all – my mind was adept enough at dropping me into a sea of question marks and even better at leaving me drowning in them.

Talking to outsiders wasn't an option; I'd been warned about 'being taken away' if I did, and although on one hand I thought that that would be the best thing ever, I also believed it would also mean being locked up away from my mother and brothers. Besides, I still had those odd memories of a matronly lady called Pam, living with strange children, and being told that she didn't know when we'd see our mother again.

The logical step was to turn to God. I'd been singing in the church choir for over a year and the novelty of wearing a dress, singing impossibly high notes and boasting about it to unimpressed classmates was starting to wear off. So I began to pay a little more attention to the sermons.

Our vicar Mr Lark was mild, inoffensive, accommodating and very English indeed. His hands were forever clasped in front of him as if they were super-glued together; his sermons weren't so much fire and brimstone as more a gentle paddle through the meaning of life. He'd softly chime about lambs, shepherds and God's infinite love with true conviction, but it bore no relation whatsoever to my life. There was definitely something missing on that score.

I swiped a Bible and painstakingly read the whole thing. It took me weeks to get through it, as my dictionary didn't list even half the words I was trying to decipher, but by the end I was more puzzled and disturbed than before I had started. Puzzled, because there seemed to be no mention of abusive fathers, and disturbed by the bizarre horror story about a nutty old man called Abraham who almost stabbed his only son simply because God had asked him to. It made out it had a happy ending, though, because God was only testing him apparently, but the moral disturbed me rather than drawing me closer to that God.

Something else that disturbed me about the Bible was that it seemed to contain page after page of punishment, jealousy and anger on God's part. In fact, stories about retribution seemed to loom larger than all the other passages that briefly touched on His love, peace and forgiveness. The writers of the Bible were much more concerned, it seemed, with the punishment and deaths of the sinners and unbelievers; wash them all away and drown them; strike them down with fire or turn them all to salt.

At least the Bible covered the issue of violence – and on a massive scale. The vicar seemed to keep missing out all the best bits from his Sunday sermons about this insane and wrathful creator, destroying and laying waste to whole peoples if they so much as looked at another god. The kindly old man with a long white beard we were taught about at school was, in fact, easily angered, insanely jealous, screwed with people's heads and capable of mass murder on a whim. I started to wonder if he had a Glaswegian accent too.

Still, I stuck with it as best as I could and resolved to give religion my best shot in the hope that I'd get some answers. I started to pray regularly, and talked to God like a fervent devotee for hours into the morning, firstly asking for the nightmare downstairs to stop, and then, when my father was too exhausted or felt satisfied my mother had had enough, I'd pray for his death; not just any death either. I prayed for the worst possible end to this screaming, bellowing madman; I wanted him to feel all the pain he'd inflicted on us in one godly, terrible and devastating mortal strike. It didn't seem like too much to ask from this seemingly vengeful God whose track record made the worst tyrant seem benign.

I prayed and I prayed. I offered my life, my eternal devotion, a lifetime in a monastery, my soul – anything He wanted, anything to remove that cancer from our lives. But my prayers remained unanswered.

Not long after joining the church choir I moved up to junior school, which heralded a new phase in my life. The great thing about the promotion to 'bigger school' was being allowed to shed the embarrassing shorts that advertised my eczema. It had erupted when I was about three years old and had developed into a patchwork of flaking and blistered skin that no amount of lotions or creams could alleviate. Long trousers became my new best friend and the only time I had to fend off the gasps of disgust from my classmates was during PE. For my first lesson I thought I'd get round that one by 'forgetting' my kit, but I wasn't smart enough for our games teacher who reached into a carrier bag, pulled out some navy-blue girls' shorts and a white top, and told me to get changed. It was a lesson well learned as I never forgot my kit again.

On my first day, my form tutor Miss H read out the register and asked each one of us to stand up. She was a plump woman, perhaps no more than twenty-five, with huge brown glasses that covered half her face. As she announced my name to the class, her magnified, bulbous eyes swept over me from head to foot and I could see she didn't like what she saw. I was a 'catalogue kid', standing there resplendent in cheap trousers and shirt, my tie askew, wearing a battered old duffel coat and clutching a second-hand satchel. For my mother to stand a chance of making ends meet, she was at the mercy of various catalogues offering instant and low-quality goods that seemed to take the next ten years to pay back. It was obvious I would never be good enough for my new teacher.

When she discovered I couldn't tell the time, I was told to stand on my chair and tell everyone that I was so stupid I couldn't read a clock. It was true, I did have an almost dyslexic eye for figures back then because they made no sense to me. I tried as hard as I could to understand numbers, mainly to avoid the daily humiliation of being made to stand in the corner, but Miss H and I were on a collision course. She never took a moment to explain patiently to me why x plus y equals z, and so whenever I saw numbers in front of me I'd draw pictures of Spitfires and Messerschmitts, knowing that it would wind her up. Like the petty thefts in infant school, I couldn't help myself. Bit by bit we locked horns. Every day she'd tell the class that we had the most stupid boy in school in our midst, and took any chance she could to make me believe it.

As a result of her unpleasant behaviour, I began to weigh up and judge every teacher by my own set of rules and if I found they were lacking, I'd go out of my way to let them know. If I had the slightest sense that they looked down at me, or showed impatience or hostility toward me, they'd be marked out. I would deliberately let myself fall asleep in their classes, shout

out, doodle, ignore them, tease the girls, pass notes to other kids – I would try to get away with anything I could, and my reputation as the school joker became firmly cemented. My junior school years were an early training ground of perfecting the art of making certain teachers' lives as difficult as possible.

My mother was clearly mystified at parents' evenings. Perplexed teachers would tell her about the disruptive, aggressive and hopeless pupil in Class A, and then the conscientious, hard-working and gifted pupil in Class B. Even my mother didn't think to ask me why this was and merely told me to stop misbehaving. But if anyone had asked me straight out why my behaviour was so unpredictable, they'd have got a clear and concise answer: kindness. I responded to it instinctively. One of our teachers, Mr Stringfellow, was a tall skinny man with a long ponytail like a girl, which someone told me meant he was a hippy, though at the time I didn't know what that was. He was remarkable for his patience with all of us. He never shouted, never gave anyone the impression they were less than brilliant and he had the coolest John Lennon glasses. I simply loved him. There were a few other teachers who also saw my respectful side and with them I'd get my head down and try my best to work, even though most of the time all I wanted to do was sleep. But during Mr Stringfellow's lessons I sweated blood to get his approval and to see him smile – which wasn't hard, as he seemed to see positives even when we made mistakes.

Remedy number one for maladjusted children: try educating with love and enthusiasm. Nothing is more effective or as memorable thirty years down the line than the few teachers who inspired respect and lust for learning in me.

To help mask the gnawing anger that was building, bit by bit, to bonfire proportions inside me, I had successfully fashioned the external characteristics of a happy-go-lucky, though very mischievous and often obnoxious, child. I'd take the lead at playtimes and organize games of Star Wars with the other kids. I became director and lead actor, always playing Han Solo, of course. Luke was too wet, Chewie never got to do much more than grunt, and playing a robot wasn't even worth considering. Besides, Han Solo got to lay a juicy kiss on Princess Leia and so my casting for the main female role had less to do with acting talent and more to do with which girl I fancied the most.

These games were incredibly exciting and allowed pure escape into other worlds and characters, while also building a kind of bridge between myself and the other kids in my year; connections, however flimsy, that had they not existed would have made me one of the solitary children left sitting by themselves at break-times, or worse still, like one kid I knew who would run alongside every football match at lunchtime commentating into an invisible microphone. Other kids would make fun of him, but in a way he made me feel sad, and not a little nervous – I knew that we weren't so different and that if I hadn't created this mask for myself, I might have had my own imaginary microphone.

However, every now and again that mask would slip, and without ever knowing why I'd retreat to the side of the bike sheds and sit down with a book, unable to bear the thought of being in anyone else's company. If a mate came over to ask me what I was doing I'd tell him to clear off and I'd fall back into my world of words where there was always a happy ending and everything seemed so certain.

At home my insomnia had become so routine that it became as normal as the state of sleep that constantly evaded me. It didn't help that my father had devised a new method of tormenting me by dragging me out of bed at any point in between closing time and the wee small hours, after getting wrecked at some unknown location. I'd always feign sleep, but it made no difference. 'Make me a tea, son' meant getting up and pouring him a hot cup of tea – that I'd always spit in – before being forced to sit at his feet and endure a slurring and snarling rant about our 'whore mother' and how we were all little bastards whom he'd get rid of one day. Mostly it was an incomprehensible drunkard's sloshing diatribe, but sometimes he'd be more lucid and scare me half to death by saying we were lucky to be alive. His snake-like eyes were blurred and yellow with the poisons he was destroying himself with, but his mind always seemed to sharpen when he made his awful threats, and his eyes could bore deep into me. I couldn't win: if I avoided his gaze he'd punch me for looking away, and if I did manage to hold my nerve he'd slam me, shouting, 'Don't look at me like that, you wee cunt.'

When these nocturnal intrusions first started they were merely something to be endured – even the threats against our lives were so veiled that at the time I didn't register the latent and real danger. I was more wary of the immediate threat to my person, because there were a whole set of rules known only to him that had to be followed. If I failed to answer a question, it could mean a beating and if I blurted out a reply, it could mean the same. From night to night the rules changed; his rhetorical questions were like the little silver ball on a roulette wheel – red or black? Punch or slap? Some nights I'd get away with it and go upstairs, waiting for him to crawl off to bed, praying that he wouldn't come into my room. There had been one or two occasions when, for no reason, the door opened, he slapped me as hard as he could, and then closed the door again. And with every beating or slap he dished out, a tear or noise meant you got it again.

I felt he deliberately set out to create a world where he was a god that could destroy or create on a whim. We had to be prepared for anything he might throw in our direction and in that respect he was most effective. Our lives revolved around him, and our every word or gesture in his presence relied upon his acceptance or blessing, which were few and far between.

Soon after they were married my mother was introduced to this wholly irrational side of his personality. They had been walking home one night when he asked her to take a different route back on her own, which was a much longer journey. When my mother pointed this out to him, he told her to shut up and do it. She'd already learned not to argue with him, and so she did as he said. By the time she eventually got home he had been waiting on his own for quite a while, and to her astonishment he asked her where the fuck she'd been. When she reminded him that he'd told her to go the long way, he beat her black and blue screaming that she was a liar. What my mother learned was never to question his mysterious ways or else she'd have to face the painful consequences.

That unfathomable quality gave him a frighteningly effective hold over us. Often, he'd give me amateur psychology lessons during those unbearable nights and they'd all involve tutorials about fear and how to dominate people. 'Scare them till they shake,' was an oft-repeated phrase. Alternatively, he'd tell me how he knew exactly what we were thinking about him, and he'd tap the side of his head and sneer, 'Psychology, son. Psychology.' I had little idea what he meant most of the time, as during all those screwed-up sermons he inflicted on me I'd shut his voice out of my head and concentrate on the steady whirr and whine of my tinnitus, but one thing I knew for sure was that when it came to matters of the mind, *he* was the one who needed psychiatric help.

I think it must have been these nights that laid the foundations for the very real fear of him that started to align with the crystallizing anger inside me. Although his rants and rages were initially quite abstract to me on a conscious level, the knowledge that he intended to do us serious harm was there underneath the surface. As time rolled on and my vocabulary and understanding grew, with his behaviour and actions becoming even more frightening, those threats began to shed their cryptic veil and make my blood run cold.

Meanwhile, our neighbours' patience with us was wearing thin and the police had been called to the house a few times. Unfortunately the 'authorities' were both useless and powerless. In the 1970s, a full and signed statement was needed from the battered wife, and then she had to testify in court, which was a bit like asking a woman to walk across broken glass in order to lie down on a bed of nails, or it was in my mother's case. The never-ending fear of my father's retribution would have made her life a living hell, especially as he still maintained close connections with dangerous gangs in Reading, whose members, he'd boasted, could find her anywhere she ran to. On several occasions he had beaten my mother so badly that he wouldn't let her leave the house until her injuries had begun to heal, to try to conceal the full extent of his abuses.

In fact, it was around this time that something odd had been happening to those noises from downstairs. Where once those nightly episodes would climax with my mother's screams, now I heard different sounds, which somehow disturbed me even more. As usual, my father would spill out his profanities and accusations, and I'd brace myself for her answering cries of pain, but instead I would hear only low muffled grunts. I was convinced he was punching her in the stomach. For whatever reason, these sounds marked a change in his routine that I couldn't understand, which made them even more frightening.

I'd leave my room in the mornings expecting to find my mother with her head caved in or bedridden, but she would emerge, face and head intact with no obvious signs of the previous night's beating. However, when she tried to walk I could see she was in immense pain. I couldn't work it out at all and at first I was too scared to ask what he'd done to her, afraid of her response. Eventually, I couldn't stand the frantic workings of my imagination as these nights rolled on, so one morning I asked her what he was doing to her. 'Nothing,' she replied without looking at me, in a way that told me the conversation was closed.

Her answer caused me great unease, because usually she'd share everything and anything with me. Our evening chats, our story nights and shared traumas had created an unbreakable bond that went far beyond the normal mother-son dynamic, yet now she wouldn't tell me what he was doing to her. I knew it must be terrible, whatever it was, and a new level of fear entered my psyche.

It would take her thirty years before she spoke about how, in addition to the normal punches to her head and body, to avoid advertising his violence on her face he'd pin her down, force his fists into a kung-fu attack, and bury them hard and deep, over and over, into her knee caps, causing her unimaginable pain.

As if my sleep time wasn't screwed up enough, a new set of nocturnal visitors had started to make their presence known, adding an even more ethereal slant to my nights. It started about a year after we'd moved into the house and at first I thought the visions were nothing more than bad dreams. I had been getting more than my fair share of those, naturally, and assumed that the nightmares were able to take many forms. I'd wake up in the middle of the night to find my room full of people; not threatening or moving, just watching me. When it first happened I froze in fear – I prayed as hard as I could for them to go away, but still they remained, staring at me, almost as if they were waiting for something. When I'd recovered enough to dive beneath the covers, I waited a full ten minutes before peering back out. To my relief, they were gone. I soon discovered that that was the only way I could get them to leave. I had to physically shut them out before they got the message.

More than anything, I wanted to believe that the visions were merely bad dreams, but I was something of an expert on nightmares by that time. I'd been having them for so long that even the occasional narcoleptic episode (waking from a dream or nightmare and being paralysed for a time) didn't affect me too much – I knew they were a part of my odd world and I dealt with it. But I knew for certain that these night-time visitors didn't feel like any dream I'd ever had. I would wake up, for no reason, and with eyes wide open I would see them, as clear as day, standing there, full-bodied and motionless, as if they were waiting for me to wake up and take notice of them.

When I explained what I'd seen to my mother, she told me what I thought she would tell me: they were simply bad dreams. The odd thing is that I knew, deep down, she believed me. She'd mentioned a few times that she'd seen and felt strange things in the old house in Foulke Street, and so I knew she was open to certain inexplicable possibilities. Looking back, we already had quite enough to cope with dealing with one dark mystery, my father – so working out how to handle some ghostly visitors would have complicated matters even further.

Thus, I simply accepted that these apparitions were part of the house and immersed myself in every book I could lay my hands on about ghosts. After some extensive research and reading case after case of documented hauntings, it felt somehow less petrifying to know that I wasn't the only one who saw them, and when they'd appear to me I'd even manage to look at them for a moment longer than I really wanted to, before covering my face with the pillow or duvet. Most of the people I saw were in their late middle age, with a few perhaps as young as twenty. I don't recall seeing any children, but there was definitely one old man who was always positioned further back than the rest and one older woman who always stood closest to my bed. I couldn't stare long enough to observe their clothing properly and so was unable to identify exactly which era they were from, but one thing was definite – apart from the older lady, who wore a very drab-looking outfit that no one would wear in modern times, there was no one dressed in any sort of period costume; no swirling ball gowns, old-fashioned hats, Victorian coat and tails or distinctive garb of any description. Most of them seemed contemporary, which both worried and confused me. If they weren't ghosts, then what were they?

I'd been reading about hallucinations in my researches and found that it was a concept mainly used by sceptics to explain away what they were unable to understand. In my case, though, I had to give it serious consideration – the combination of a sleep disorder, bad dreams, almost unbearable nights, tinnitus and an overactive imagination made me a prime candidate for seeing what wasn't there. Later reading on the effects of childhood trauma covered the ground of psychosis – how hallucinations were a common feature of this condition – and as an adult I'd do my best to sweep them away with this explanation, but there were major problems with this technical dismissal; I wasn't suffering from any actual psychosis and in any case I still believe the people in my room were *there*. They were fully formed, flesh and blood, real people; it was always the same crowd of unfamiliar faces watching with that strange mixture of neutrality and expectation.

In the end, I blurted out my fears over my possible insanity to the only person I trusted – Iain. He was unfazed as I told him about my nightly visitors and how I knew they weren't dreams but were real, and how they would always vanish the moment I stuck my head under the covers. His matter-of-fact response put my mind at rest and diminished the stress I was suffering. He simply replied, 'Don't worry, I see them all the time.'

In my world where everything seemed fantastic and made of magic, Iain's was one of logic and the simple practicalities of getting through the day unscathed. Consequently, even ghosts at his own bedside didn't cause him concern. His influence grounded me in ways I was unaware of at the time, but it was always there in his calm, unemotional and detached manner.

Growing up, we both shared one very particular interest that became something of a competition: girls. When Iain came home from junior school one afternoon and casually announce that he'd French-kissed three girls in the playground, I realized that I had some serious catching up to do. I didn't tell him that I had no idea what a French kiss was, but instead resolved to find out as soon as possible. The chance eventually came at a schoolfriend's birthday party. Amidst the jelly and ice cream, musical chairs and the soundtrack to *Grease*, sat the pale and enigmatic Paula Jefcut. She never really said much and appeared distant from everyone and everything around her – especially me, it seemed. Her huge watery blue eyes and long fair hair gave her the appearance of one of the princesses I'd read so much about in my beloved *Grimms' Fairy Tales*, and I wondered if Olivia Newton John singing about being 'hopelessly devoted' could tempt her to dance with me. To my amazement she agreed, and soon we were glued to each other in the middle of the living room. I was quite surprised that this beautiful shy princess was clutching me so tightly, but was deliriously happy at the same time, and even though I kept treading on her feet and apologizing, she simply rested her face on my shoulder and said, 'That's all right.'

After the party I walked her home in relative silence. I didn't know what to say to someone like her and had the feeling that my usual crowd pleaser – a Frank Spencer impersonation – wouldn't cut much ice as she was far too refined. When we reached her house and I went to leave, she grabbed hold of my arm, and asked, 'Don't you want a kiss?'

I didn't have time to reply because before I knew it she'd yanked me towards her with strength I didn't know she possessed and our mouths stuck to each other like two inseparable limpets. Then the oddest thing happened. As we were kissing, with me lost in the fairy-tale scenario of a prince and his rescued love, a long, wet object pushed past my lips and my mouth was filled with what felt like a giant slug. I pulled back in horror and demanded, 'What the bloody hell was that?'

Paula looked back at me with those pale eyes, and, wiping off the dribble running down her chin, replied, 'A French kiss. Haven't you ever done it before?' She looked as if she might burst out laughing at any moment, and suddenly the princess I'd been kissing seemed very far away.

'Well, yeah . . .' I stammered, amazed that Iain had done this three times in one playtime. 'I've just never done it like that before.'

After returning home, my lips numb and with a taste of trifle in my mouth, courtesy of Paula, I proudly announced to Iain that I'd French-kissed Paula Jefcut for over an hour. He looked at me nonchalantly, and with a little smile remarked, 'Yeah, she's really good at it, isn't she?'

I was gutted. The fact that Iain's tongue had been in her mouth before mine was, quite simply, wrong. I spent the next ten minutes brushing my teeth vigorously and vowed to check, before kissing future girlfriends, that they had never come within six feet of my younger Casanova brother in case he'd already had his wicked way with them.

## 6 | *Brothers in Arms*

WHERE ONCE my two brothers had been a weird duo of indifference in Iain's case and cute but useless gurgles in Anthony's, they had now reached the perfect age as partners in play. With Iain one year younger than me, and three years between Anthony and myself, by the time I was nine we had started to have a lot more fun together.

When I was younger I'd amuse myself in solitary playtimes with Action Men or by climbing the tree in the garden and fighting off invisible marauding Red Indians or German Panzer Divisions that had flattened our house and were advancing upon my treetop position. It was great fun, but only for so long. I did have the occasional 'out front' games with the kids on our street, but my enjoyment was limited to short bursts here and there, as I never felt completely relaxed with outsiders. To my delight my brothers proved to be more than willing and able to step in and fight for the Wild West – what was more, Iain even preferred being a Red Indian to a cowboy.

'Cowboys are bent,' he sniffed, covered in make-up my mother had used as war paint, which, looking back, made him appear more like a forerunner to Boy George than Running

Bull. I didn't care if cowboys were bent because I was no ordinary cowboy.

Perhaps Iain had a point – all the cowboys I'd seen on various westerns were pretty dull and even outright stupid – except one: Clint Eastwood. My favourite cowboy persona was the man with no name, no home and not much to say apart from letting my trigger finger do the talking. The bent stick with a strand of cotton that Iain used as a bow, with a few twigs for arrows, was simply pathetic when faced with my fully-loaded Colt .45 capgun. The drawback was that Iain would always bring logic and reason into the fray, and so if, as often happened, my cheap toy gun failed to explode its paper caps, he'd start launching his dry twigs from his bow stick, shouting that my bullets hadn't fired, so how could he possibly be dead? I'd try to explain that that wasn't the bloody point, but he was the most stubborn eight-year-old alive and we'd squabble until either my mother intervened or we ended up rolling around on the floor. It was usually while we were arguing that Anthony would ruin things further by diving on top of us, hollering in delight, or shooting both of us and then running away laughing that we were both dead. Neither of them, it seemed, were quite getting this.

While our various war games would sometimes end up in arguments or occasionally tears, we could spend long hours playing hide and seek with no such problems; you hid, were found, were out and then you joined the hunt for the remaining hider. As this pastime was less likely to result in confrontation, we'd often play it until we were called in or it was time for bed. Those were the best of times, and many long summer nights were spent playing this wonderful game.

The summer of '76 came and never quite left. Those burning hot days stole all my energy, brought on hay fever and left me on my own for much of the time, hating the sun. The other kids on the estate raced off to swimming pools and parks, but I preferred to stay indoors, cursing the heat and playing with my Action

Man or reading in the cool of the front room. Then when the late afternoon brought a little relief from the energy-sapping heatwave, I'd go into the back garden to play in the shade with Anthony – Iain had no such reservations about being baked half alive and was away like an Apache with all the other kids.

The evenings were a different affair. The hot nights made most parents relax their normal curfew and allow their kids to stay out later, so all of the estate kids would converge outside our house on the little green opposite, arguing over what game should be played next. I'd usually join in the summer evening fun as the night always increased my desire to be outside. Marbles would give way to rounders or football in the little park, and when the dreaded moment came when the sun was about to abandon us, we'd get in a few games of hide and seek.

We three brothers would take part enthusiastically, and although I always felt separate from the other kids my own age, I was grateful that they encouraged us to join in. The cracks in our fraternal relationship were growing more apparent, though, and had begun to spill out beyond our often fractious role-playing games. It started to become a daily feature of our bickering to insult each other in any way we could, and between myself and Iain the verbal warfare escalated over the next few years to reach cruel and vicious heights.

To my shame I know that I was the one who instigated this negative banter. One of the many insidious inheritances of having an abusive parent is that, no matter what you are told to the contrary, you cannot be protected completely from repeating the cycle of abuse in your own behaviour. It's impossible to avoid. The distress and anger that manifests itself is simply too powerful to resist – I would have needed professional counselling at the time to have had any chance of putting a stop to the conditioning that was slowly taking effect. I would feel sick listening to my father's insults against my mother, and then I'd find myself hurling my own, less profane but no less vicious, insults against my brothers – especially Iain.

He'd stand impassive and unflinching as I launched a tirade of frustrated abuse against him, but the hurt showed, nonetheless, in his eyes and its sting would reach deep inside me. If someone had pointed out the similarities between my treatment of Iain and the verbal abuse I received from my father, it would probably have horrified me into stopping immediately, but as with so many other features of my childhood dysfunctions, I was completely ignorant and couldn't help myself.

After our verbal battles, I'd often sit alone in my room hating myself and sometimes breaking down in tears without knowing quite why. Iain would always forgive me the next day and we'd be friends again. In fact, despite all our brief moments of mutual antipathy, the bond between us was extraordinary. We'd lie in bed at night gripping each other's wrists, and fall asleep still holding each other. Ostensibly we were trying to strengthen the psychic link that obviously existed between us, but it also marked a deep sense of brotherhood and solidarity.

What I was unable to take into account then, and for many years later, was how much of an effect my father's destructive nature was having on my two brothers. Anthony, his apparent favourite, seemed well protected from most of it. On those few occasions when my father was at home in the evening, he would lavish the kind of attention on him that would make my blood curdle. It seemed genuine father-son affection, and acted as a cruel demonstration of how life could be for me, Iain and our mother if we'd only start proving ourselves more worthy.

As far as night-time showdowns were concerned, Anthony slept so soundly that only a bomb could wake him, so he appeared not to hear what was going on. It was a useful defence mechanism. On a conscious level he had dodged the bullet, but subconsciously he was as riddled with holes as we were. External noises have been shown to influence a sleeper's brain functions and dreams, so although Anthony wasn't lying there awake with me and Iain, and dying that slow death every night, he was absorbing it all on a deeper and perhaps even more complex level. He would wake up in the morning oblivious to what had kept Iain and me awake, and was so young and unaware of all the chaos around him that he never even noticed when our mother's face was black and blue. And when my father switched to punching her around her body and knees, Anthony assumed she was poorly, just like we did.

The overriding feeling I had as a child, especially on entering our house from the normal world outside, was that something terrible was going to happen. It gnawed at me constantly. If ever that fear needed confirmation I only had to look deeply at my mother to find agreement. No matter how hard she tried, and regardless of how many songs she sang, jokes she told or stories she'd read us, she could never disguise the expression in her eyes. It was a trapped and hunted look that revealed how, frighteningly, she was powerless to do anything about it. Sometimes, in the evenings when she sat and talked to us about her childhood or life in general, I'd gaze into those deep brown eyes that still knew how to sparkle, but what I saw beyond them was the world she kept hidden from all of us – empty fields of despair, regret and guilt. Then the clock would tick-tock towards our bedtime, meaning *he* would be home before long, and subtly she'd start to change. The happy young woman who told us about the woodland and pastures of her youth would disappear, and she would stiffen up, her eyes darting about nervously as if he was already home. Then she would hurriedly pack us off to bed as if she were hiding us from the Gestapo. Anthony, intelligent and sensitive, picked up all this and more.

Iain, although fully aware of everything that was going on, had learned to hide himself away in the aloofness he wore like a permanent mantle against the weather. He retreated further and further into himself to the extent that he wouldn't say a word to anyone for days at a time, but in the outside world he'd become a different person, giving nothing away about the turmoil going on inside him. I related to that, of course, as playtime offered a perfect escape from the pressures of home.

When my father was still at the face-punching stage of his reign of terror, my brothers and I would come down to breakfast and react in different ways to the state in which we found our mother: I'd start crying, Anthony would ask me what was wrong, and Iain simply got on with eating his cornflakes. What could have been interpreted at the time as an uncaring nature on Iain's part simply hid the deep hurt and trauma that he was going through himself. He never had the beatings I took because most of the time my father didn't even bother to acknowledge his presence. But Iain wanted it that way – he'd developed the art of invisibility to perfection and if that meant complete isolation from everything that was going on around him, then that was the way it would be. No amount of coaxing from my mother to say more, do more or 'try cheering up' made any impression on him. He had his recipe for sanity and no one was going to ruin the mix. We shared wordless understanding for our respective coping methods, knowing that each had our own shields and the material from which they were made was a minor detail.

My father threw one particular insult at me more frequently the older I got and the more my artistic inclinations became apparent. When I first asked my mother what a 'poof' was, she looked rather uncomfortable. 'Like Quentin Crisp, dear,' she replied, before busying herself with the cooking as if to say 'conversation closed'.

All this did was confuse me further. By now I was more used to my father calling me 'wee bastard' or 'cunt' than my given name, and so I knew that it must be a bad thing to be a 'poof'. Of course, the various associated slang words such as 'bender' and 'homo' were in frequent use by all the kids on the estate, but as green as I was then, I still had no idea what any of it meant. The words simply made me laugh. By the end of a play session we were all apparently benders and as everyone else seemed to know exactly what was meant by the terms, I wasn't going to admit to being ignorant.

Fortunately, not long after my mother's cryptic evasion, I got the answer. One night, as I was about to go up to my room for bed, my mother leaned over to me and told me to stay where I was. For me this was a major event. Bedtimes were a no-argument situation – we'd learned that no matter what was on television or however much we whined and begged to stay up later, it was eight o'clock for Anthony, nine o'clock for Iain and ten o'clock for me. I thought at first she wanted to speak to me about something, but instead she turned on the television and tuned the dial to BBC One. Eventually, the opening credits rolled for a drama called *The Naked Civil Servant*. At first my heart leapt – she's letting me watch lots of naked people, I thought. But as the wholly clothed proceedings went on, my disappointment turned to transfixed fascination, and then to jubilation; I finally knew what a Quentin Crisp was! Not only that, but I now understood all those other words that had secretly perplexed me. It was one of the most educational nights of my young life. Men did it with other men. That was all! Big deal, I thought. This in turn led to more pondering as to why that sort of thing should be seen as either disgusting or wrong, but at least I finally had some answers.

It was John Hurt's dazzling performance in the lead role that had the most profound effect on me. I'd seen lots of films and dramas before, but it was as if he'd stepped right out of that creaky Bush television and was there in the room with me. To this day John Hurt never fails to take my breath away. At the end of the programme, I resolved two things there and then: the first was that I would become an actor like John Hurt and the second was that I would try being homosexual the first chance I got. After all, if my father hated them so much then it was the natural lifestyle choice for me.

Bless my mother. I suppose she was so aware of my sensitive, artistic nature that she had started to wonder whether my father was in fact right about my sexuality. She never said as much at the time, but the lesson she clearly wanted to teach me, using the life story of that fearless queen of camp, was another priceless gem that I've carried around inside me ever since: be who you want to be, no matter who or what you are – and never care what other people think or say, and never be afraid to let the world know exactly who you are.

For the most part I took the lesson on board, but it would take many years for it to be fully realized and honoured.

By the time I was nearly eleven, my mother had got a new, better-paid job in a factory in Maidenhead. No longer did she have to hold down two part-time jobs involving scrubbing and cleaning, as well as the more demanding career of bringing up three boys. Unfortunately, though, there was a catch – she had to work shifts. This meant that one week she'd have to get up even earlier, at 4 a.m., and be ferried to the factory by coach, but be home in the evening. The following week she would start work at 6 p.m. and get home in the small hours, see us off to school and then try to sleep a little. It was still no life – she'd merely traded one yoke for another, albeit one that paid slightly more money. As far as I was concerned it was bad news. It meant that I would become 'the man of the house', and though my mother made it sound like an incredible honour, I simply didn't want such a role – in fact at that time I didn't want to be a man at all. As far as I was concerned men had nothing going for them, and the world would be a far happier and more peaceful place without them in it. If the thought of trying to shepherd Iain and Anthony to bed at the allotted hour made me groan, the reality would see my patience fail over and over again.

However, news of my unwanted promotion was made a little more bearable when my mother proudly informed me that the spare room was to be cleared out and I'd be given my own room. The bribe almost worked – I was in heaven at the thought of having my own space, but no amount of her trying to convince me that things would be easier for us financially could ease my sense of impending doom about the thought of spending more time alone with our father. When I told her of my dread at having to be 'mother' when doing the washing up and cooking, and 'father' when getting my brothers off to bed, she laughed and told me I was old enough to manage these trivial tasks. But when I countered with the real reason for my unhappiness, how I was terrified of being left alone with my father for two weeks every month, she threw her arms around me and said, 'Sorry.'

The biggest and best thing about moving into my own space was that the torment of insomnia lessened. Though it still persisted, there were rewards all around me. Before when I couldn't sleep I'd have to console myself with a torch under the covers, reading a book, trying not to wake my brothers. When I ran out of batteries it was absolute torture to have to lie there and count the seconds, minutes and hours to the dawn when sleep usually came. On my own I had a freedom I'd only dreamed about. During sleepless nights I would be released into the world of the night quite literally. After reading for a few hours, I would stand at my small window and gaze at the stars, convincing myself that any moment the UFO that had dropped me into this crazy world would come for me if I willed it hard enough. The stars became my friends, a sight I would always look forward to seeing when I went to bed. They were magical, consistent, like silent and twinkling witnesses to all the dramas of the world – especially mine, I told myself. Once, my father opened my bedroom door to find me so rapt in those flickering lights that I never even noticed he was there. When he asked what I was doing, I dreamily told him – with no fear at all for the consequences – that I was looking at the stars. I waited for the inevitable scathing reply, but to my surprise he never said a word and closed the bedroom door on his way out.

Before my mother started to work night shifts, her presence at home, even if she was asleep, somehow dampened the danger and made me feel that my father was in some way partially restrained. With her absence, though, this invisible safety net was gone, and gave him a green light for the worst nights yet. Gone was the gambler's wheel, which had offered bad odds but the remote chance of escaping his wrath, and in its place was the certainty of a good thrashing and unequivocal threats against our lives if we ever tried to run away.

However, what no one knew was that I'd already found some escape routes out of his reach. One of them was a nearby stretch of heathered woodland, not too far from my school. I'd dug a deep hole, almost covered the opening with planks of wood I'd found, and dressed them with bracken and grasses. Squeezing into the narrow entrance I'd left myself, I'd hole up for hours on end, munching on sweets while travelling through time and space to exotic worlds where dinosaurs roamed and people didn't exist. An added bonus of this secret world was that young lovers sometimes used the heather as a short cut to the woods. They had no way of seeing me and even if they walked right above me, the planks were strong enough to take their weight. If I heard anyone coming I'd angle my lips towards the entrance and shout out to them in disguised voices, or scream out 'Ya bastards!', then revel in their confusion as they looked around in vain for the source of the strange cries.

Most of my time there was spent doing nothing; during my self-imposed seclusion, secreted in my own little foxhole, I mastered the art of doing nothing, just being. Minutes in that wonderful world translated into hours in the real one, and as I lay curled up in the sweet-smelling earth, I'd make plans for a huge underground cavern, fully kitted out with furniture and music, and inaccessible to all but me.

On one occasion I made the mistake of holing up when my father was at home during the day, and I lost all track of time. Normally, if I was late home for tea it was no big deal; my mother would tut, serve me reheated food and tell me to be on time in future, but my father suddenly decided that he was a stickler for timekeeping. He screamed at me, demanding to know where I'd been. I said nothing. There was no way I was going to tell him about the sanctuary I'd created and so I kept my mouth shut, waiting to accept the few hard slaps that were coming to me. As he hadn't been out drinking and was stone-cold sober, I thought there was little reason to be scared. I couldn't have been more wrong.

The slaps came all right, but they weren't the two or three for which I'd readied myself. He beat me around the front room before I committed the cardinal sin – I dared to look at him as he laid into me. The bare hatred he saw written across my face sent him into a blind fury. Screaming at the top of his lungs, 'No cunt ever looks at me like that,' he dragged me by the hair all the way upstairs to my bedroom, took off his belt and went to work on me with the metal buckle.

Although by now I'd developed quite a high pain threshold, the punishment he dealt out on this occasion was like nothing I'd ever experienced before. Blow after blow rained down on me. He didn't seem to care where he was aiming. Hard corners of the buckle smashed into my head like an ice pick and I instinctively curled up into a ball, deciding that my back could take the worst of it, and worrying that if my head got hit too much I'd be in real trouble.

As the attack went on, the blows to my back seemed to stop hurting, even though they were still raining down heavily on me; they started to feel more like the soft taps of a forefinger until I could sense nothing at all. Just as everything started to fade out as my consciousness began to wane, a figure burst into the bedroom and started screaming at him to stop. I looked up and, despite my blurred vision, I could see it was my mother. At first I thought I was dreaming, but there she was, all dark fury, and yelling that if he hit me one more time she'd kill him. It seemed unbelievable that my mother – whom someone described years later as a 'frightened mouse' in those days – could raise herself to such magnificent heights, but this time she genuinely feared for my life and a mother, when dealing with such extreme circumstances, is capable of extraordinary things to protect her children. Normally when I was being beaten she was powerless, because to do anything more would have resulted in a battering for her and an even worse thrashing for me. The rules were quite clear on that score.

So, although I was inwardly cheering my mother's amazing courage, I feared that her selfless actions signalled the end for her and probably the rest of us. All the night-time death threats that fell from my father's whisky-sodden lips suddenly seemed likely to be realized. I felt my bladder relax as warm piss ran down my leg and I prepared to watch my mother being murdered. But then the second miraculous event occurred.

My father ran. He rushed out of the room. He didn't just leave; he fled.

My mother gently cradled me in her arms, caressed me and helped to remove my T-shirt to see how bad the damage was. Whatever she saw nearly made her faint and I had to catch hold of her as she fell backwards.

Even now, recalling that terrible day, I find it difficult to believe it really happened, but it did. At that tender age of eleven, I saw the pure, unstoppable energy that had been locked deep inside my mother – and it was breathtakingly beautiful to watch. Whereas before she'd been the woman whom I loved with every fibre of my being, and whom I looked to for wisdom, solace and love, she had now become my heroine.

After the event, I was kept home from school to recover. My father vanished for a few days and for a brief moment it seemed as if the world had been turned upside down, that after this humiliating defeat my father would have to play by a different set of rules, which involved being wary of my mother's new-found strength. But as with all hopes concerning that unpredictable creature, they were quickly dashed. He came back like a wounded wild beast, more savage than ever and in search of revenge against the woman who had more or less emasculated him in front of his hated son.

★ ★ ★

When I finally returned to school, the first thing I did was to steal a load of random items from an empty classroom one break-time. I hid the stash of stolen goodies in a carrier bag, and then went to the boys' toilet to flush them away, one by one. The things that were too big to flush, I dropped into the cistern. Only then did a certain calm descend on me, but it was a gnawing, uneasy and dangerous peace – a fire blanket that only partially and temporarily contained the raging inferno within.

One of the lessons that day was PE. I'd been warned by my father that if anyone saw my bruised body, my two brothers and I would be separated, taken into care and we'd never see our mother again. I had no reason to doubt him. So I slipped out into the locker room where no prying eyes would see my new tattoos. I was just about to put on my white, cotton sports top, when my teacher Miss W came in, obviously wondering why I was getting changed away from everyone else. Despite my efforts to conceal my injuries, I had been found out.

I froze and so did she, and for a moment she couldn't speak. Her jaw stayed wide open and, probably out of nerves, I started to giggle. Miss W didn't see the funny side though and quietly asked what had happened to me.

I liked Miss W. In fact, I had a bit of a crush on her. She wore rather daft, over-large glasses that were fashionable then, and had gorgeous fair hair that always bounced when she walked. Whenever I was cheeky or precocious in class, she'd meet me head on with the kind of Northern humour that was as dry as it was cutting. I loved her. So, I reasoned that if there was any teacher in the whole school who was likely to call the police, it was her. Torn between two outcomes, I felt the blood rush to my heart so hard that I thought I might pass out at any moment.

She asked me to turn round. Reluctantly I did as I was told, and the voice from behind me became even smaller as she repeated her question. I found myself suddenly frightened by her reaction. For some reason I imagined that it was me who was going to get into trouble – possibly even arrested. I felt consumed with guilt and didn't know why.

When I told her I'd fallen down the stairs, as I'd been instructed to do, she stared at me as if she hadn't heard a word I'd said. 'Put your top on and go back into the classroom,' she said softly, and I knew it was all over. I'd lied, but I wasn't good enough or perhaps I'd been deliberately unconvincing. I assumed she'd seen right through me and that I'd set off a chain of events culminating in a permanent move to a children's home, never to see our mother again.

The whole day I waited for a police car to appear; for a knock at the classroom door as a man in a uniform or a white coat called out my name; for the end of my life as I knew it. And part of me even prayed for it. I was locked in a strange limbo. A chair scraping, a book dropped on to a table or even a small cough would turn into a sharp rap on the classroom door, and I sat and squirmed as I waited to meet my fate. But the knock never came. The days went by, each one filled with a mixture of excitement and dread, but the family wreckers never showed up because Miss W didn't tell anyone.

I've never blamed her, even when I blamed the whole world for all my problems. She was young and inexperienced, and in those days the way people dealt with suspected child abuse was so different to the system in place now. In many ways it seems that today's society has gone to the other extreme. A mere bruise on a child's arm can be enough to arouse suspicions that set in motion a terrifying machine which already assumes the parents' guilt. In the late 1970s, though, abuse – sexual, physical or both – could be suspected or even known to be happening, but without the support services or any effective legal powers to tackle it, little would be done. The consensus back then and in times gone by was not to get involved – as if by pretending it wasn't going on, it would stop. Perhaps, too, such abuse was so prevalent that no one wanted to face the reality of it.

The privacy that was guaranteed when given my own room came at a price that went way beyond putting complaining and belligerent younger brothers to bed each night. The ghostly visits I received weren't, as I'd hoped, confined to the other bedroom, and now that I was alone, it seemed that they were becoming more frequent. To my horror, the ghosts themselves were also getting bolder; each time they would stand even nearer to my bed, and the old woman now came so close to my headboard that I could see her wrinkles. My situation was made all the more terrifying when Iain revealed that he didn't see them any more. I reasoned that they must be following me. They wanted me and I had no idea why. The little sleep I did manage was affected even more. I could no longer comfort myself with the thought that I had my two brothers on either side of me, and the little room I now occupied assumed new proportions, vast and echoing, with walls that seemed to move further and further away as the night passed by.

Sometimes I'd pretend to be asleep and try to catch them out by opening my eyes suddenly to surprise them in the act of whatever it was they were doing, but they were clever ghosts – they knew to emerge only when I was asleep. Always I'd sense their presence, wake up and there they'd be, blank and unthreatening, inactive yet no less scary to my young mind. It struck me that they could have given me a heart attack just by making a single moan, but they seemed content just to be near me and made no noise at all.

Once again I tried to work out where they'd come from. They couldn't have been from heaven because they didn't have wings and they weren't devils either, appearing too normal to have emerged from the depths of hell. I was clueless about their origins, and helpless to do anything about their unwanted presence.

The general strangeness of those days showed no sign of

abating. While the Seymours next door threw wild parties that instilled in me an utter contempt for the Bay City Rollers, I'd also feel things in my bedroom that I couldn't actually see. I'd tell myself that it was all in my head, but I knew I was only kidding myself – I sensed things all around me in that room and although I was never menaced or felt the remotest danger, my eyes would still be big as saucers and my body almost paralysed by the sensation that someone or something was sharing the air that I breathed.

The night would creep on into the early hours of the morning, and weird shadows and odd soft lights would slowly move around my room, at which point I knew that sleep was about to descend on me finally. Often I'd wake up in the morning with the overwhelming feeling that there was something I had to remember, something that had happened, and I'd rack my brains in vain trying to recall what it was – a bit like trying to recollect an amazing dream from the night before that you knew was of great importance.

Thankfully, my freaky nights were offset by the staggering normality of my time at choir. I rehearsed twice a week at church, and attended two services, Communion and Evensong, on Sundays. As our choir had a good reputation, we often sang at large cathedrals and I loved every minute of it. I took delight in the fact that up to five times a week I'd have a legitimate excuse to get away from the house and into the genteel world of the Church of England. However, my fellow choristers were far from saintly. Most of them attended private school and a few of the older ones took an initial dislike to the common-speaking urchin from a council estate. For a short time they tried to put me in my place, but as time went on I could stand up to them and verbally gave almost as good as I got.

The head of the choir, Mr Turner, was a great man. I think he sensed that things at home weren't quite as they should be and seemed to go out of his way to push me to work harder with my voice, and offering me stern instruction on why I shouldn't lock up younger choirboys in the bell tower. He always seemed to have a twinkle in his eye even when issuing a telling-off. Most of all I loved his perfectionism. His standards were so great that we busted vocal chords trying to achieve his high bar; nothing but the best would satisfy him. When he was pleased with a rehearsal, service or concert performance, he made you feel on top of the world. It was purely down to him that our choir was asked to record an album of choral pieces, which gave me my first experience of a recording studio.

Anyone who thought that little choirboys were no less than cherubs in fancy dress would have had a shock if they'd taken a seat on one of the coaches that ferried us to various cathedrals. We sang songs there and back that wouldn't have been out of place on a rugby stag night. When I first heard the older boys singing a beautiful rendition of 'Nobby All' – apparently he only had one ball – I looked nervously at Mr Turner whom I felt was sure to explode, but he didn't. In fact, on every coach trip we went on, he would always be covering his mouth and trying his best not to laugh. As the songs got more profane, the more he buried his face into his chest, pretending to be blissfully unaware of the fully harmonized set of sixteen voices belting out, 'I'm a wanker, I'm a wanker and it does me good like it bloody well should!' The same could not be said for our poor vicar, the gentle Mr Lark. He sat rigid and pale staring ahead in shock, no doubt thinking that Satan had taken possession of his angelic choristers.

As well as the church choir, I also got involved with the church football team. When I played football on my local estate, I would always be the one whom the team captains chose last. By the age of eight I'd shot up like a beanpole and towered above all the other kids my age, which made me feel both self-conscious and unsure how to handle this sudden elevation in height. So, with the church soccer side, coached by Mr D, at least I had a chance to prove myself to someone who had no prior prejudices against my lack of football skills. After a five-aside training session, in which I thought I'd performed reasonably well – apart from fluffing a clear chance of goal and running into one of my teammates – the coach took me to one side, and putting a paternal arm around my shoulder, said, 'Mate, let's face it, you're crap.' My heart sank. 'So how do you fancy going in goal?'

Our first proper team training day was decidedly unchristian. As far as Mr D was concerned, the whole point of the game was to play to win, and this meant using elbows, shoulders and upturned studs on the opposing teams. When our coach sent his Christian soldiers out to war, he certainly wasn't taking any prisoners. When our benevolent choirmaster got to hear about these lessons in professional fouling, he gave us a lecture on the values of decency and fair play, and suggested that Mr D needed to spend more time in church services.

Our first match against another parish choir ended up resembling a war zone. Stunned little choirboys from the opposing team were battered, kicked and sent flying into the mud. One small boy was in tears, but our coach simply stood on the sidelines, arms folded, looking as pleased as punch as we went one-nil up. 'Go on – get into 'em lads,' he encouraged us, as if his team hadn't done enough damage for one day.

The referee must have been a friend of Mr D because no one was carded or even told off, which inspired the more aggressive members of our team to even greater atrocities and whipped Mr D into a winning frenzy.

What he hadn't banked on, though, was that he'd put someone with no hand-to-eye coordination in goal. Despite the injuries the opposition were rapidly picking up, it wasn't too long before they sniffed out our fatal flaw – me. Wild shots came in from twenty or thirty yards out, with each one standing a great chance of going in as I'd either fall over or run into my own goalposts.

After we conceded the sixth goal, I risked a nervous look in the coach's direction, but he was staring down at the floor with his hands behind his head, shouting profanities into the grass while parents gave him filthy looks.

When the final whistle blew I was relieved that I'd only let in seven goals – I thought it would have been much worse. The captain of the other team limped up to me and shook my hand, 'Cheers, mate!'

Mr D, as I expected, didn't shake my hand and instead spat out through gritted teeth, 'Try rugby instead.'

So that was that. I wasn't too disheartened because I knew I was crap at football. I was eternally grateful to him for at least giving me the chance to run out on a pitch and prove it to the rest of the world as well.

Those early days in the choir were fantastic and I'm fairly certain that they kept me sane when my home life was so unbearable. Just as enjoyable as the rehearsals was the journey there. My mother would give me the bus fare, which I'd pocket for crisps and sweeties, and I'd walk as far as the school playing fields before sticking a thumb out and hitching a lift.

I didn't need anyone to tell me it was dangerous – I knew that well enough. In fact, if I hadn't been aware of that cold fact I probably wouldn't have done it. I loved the danger and the rush of adrenalin as I got into the car of a passing stranger, knowing that there was a one in a million chance that I could get picked up by a lunatic and murdered. It wasn't a death wish on my part – it was purely and simply the thrill of the stupid risk I was taking.

I would one day realize the hazards involved when I accepted a lift from a man who told me he'd drop me off even though he was heading in the opposite direction. After a few minutes in the car he started talking about dangerous it was to accept lifts from strangers, and that you could never tell who was going to pick you up because there were all sorts of people out there.

His manner made me feel uncomfortable. I'd had the same

lecture a couple of times before and the drivers would always be exasperated at my idiocy, but this guy – middle-aged and with a thin, gaunt face – spoke slowly and calmly, as if he was talking from experience. To say I was scared is an understatement. He never looked at me once and always seemed to be checking his driver's mirror, as if to make certain we weren't being followed, all the while repeating his creepy mantra, 'Some nasty, nasty people out there.'

Eventually I cracked and told him I wanted to get out and walk the rest of the way. He didn't pull over immediately, though, and carried on driving until, after a long pause, he said, 'Oh. You sure?'

I reached for the door handle and prepared to leap from the moving vehicle, but the car slowed to a halt. Before stopping at the top of the junction that led to the church, the driver gave me a weird grin and said, 'Be careful now, you hear?' I didn't wait to hear anything else and ran all the way to church, soaked in sweat.

That driver was very smart indeed. I suppose he guessed I'd been warned many times about getting into cars with unknown men, and he used applied, intensive psychology to get the message through to me once and for all. In retrospect he had the air of a natural child psychologist and I'm eternally grateful to him for that effective wake-up call. No doubt he would have been delighted to learn that from that day forward I always walked to choir, and once even refused a ride from a kindly old dear who'd pulled over to offer me a lift during a downpour.

I grew to love those walks and would always pause at Earley Bridge, just before the church, haul myself up and wonder whether it would hurt if I jumped and killed myself – or would I die before I hit the ground? I thought about death a lot – too much, in fact. If it wasn't my father's death I was fantasizing about, then it was my own. His would be horrific and as painful as possible, while mine would be glorious and tragic.

At least I was distracted from such dark thoughts by the genuine warmth and friendship offered to me at that mild-mannered house of God, even though His contradictions still confused me. Although I didn't know how to reciprocate it properly, I still loved being in an environment where people were decent and not in the least aggressive. I had developed a deep-seated mistrust of males and yet here I was in a purely male group in which I felt completely at home. I returned their kindnesses in the only way I knew how – I rebelled.

As time went on and things at home and elsewhere got worse, I started to turn up late for rehearsals, swore at the other choirboys and even hit them if they irritated me. I'd goad the older boys into fights that I knew would leave me the worst off, and soon I started to hate being there. Yet I still turned up, pulled by that inexorable force of a steady ship that could offer me some comfort in my deeply disturbed world.

Attending choir had also given me the opportunity to put my light-fingered skills to the test. I'd started committing the ultimate sin by taking money from the Sunday service collections. In the vestry I'd dip my hands into the satin bags containing the cash and I'd steal some of it to feed my growing hatred for the whole idea of church. On my way home I'd throw it over the side of Earley Bridge and it seemed that God's only miracle at that time was that I avoided hitting any of the passing vehicles on the dual carriageway beneath.

I'd always keep a few coins back for sweets and crisps, but usually I had so much that I didn't know how to spend it and throwing it over the bridge seemed the best way to get rid of it, to keep it from the church for which is was meant. I took great pleasure in that, and I'd sing hymns and descants as those pieces of paper and coins dropped down on to the road surface, before heading off home and preparing myself for my own descent into the unknown.

# 7 | *Hide and Seek*

DEATH was definitely becoming the silent sixth member of our household. If it wasn't my father's demise that preoccupied my mind, it was the thought of my family's future massacre. By the time I was eleven, my father's threats concerning our impending appointment with the Grim Reaper were reaching new and worrying heights. Teachers would look at my exercise books littered with bloody scenes of carnage and severed heads, and they'd rail at me for being so morbid – even my mother would wince at my artwork and ask me why I had to draw such gruesome sights.

My father never read books and the only time I saw him look at the tabloids was to check betting fixtures and football results. The only reading matter he seemed to love were American crime magazines. Instead of keeping them hidden under his bed, like a responsible parent, he left them lying around the front room in full view. Indeed it was almost as if these trashy pieces of pulp non fiction were deliberately left out for our reading and edification. There were many different titles on offer, but they all dealt with one subject: murder. Mass murder, gang murders, gruesome slayings, serial killers, unsolved murders – the gorier the better, it appeared. Most disturbing for us were the endless sections on family murders. It seemed as though he'd handpicked every magazine to include tales of the well-respected, loving family man who'd got up one morning and butchered his family. More often than not, the murders had taken everyone by surprise and the articles would feature telling quotes from dumbfounded neighbours, along the lines of 'They seemed like such a loving family.'

Sometimes there would be badly printed black-and-white photographs of the gruesome scenes, showing shroud-covered bodies or invisible murder victims outlined in chalk. I read them wide-eyed with my pulse racing as story after story told me about a world that was light years away from *The Brady Bunch*, but ominously close to ours.

As if I couldn't get enough of real-life horror, I was also devouring Edgar Allen Poe, Bram Stoker and H. P. Lovecraft, but my father's magazines gripped me more than any work of fiction. I could easily differentiate between the fevered imaginings of a horror author – no matter how plausible they might have seemed – and the real-life horror stories reported in those cheap, well-thumbed pages, especially the ones about families who met a grisly end at the hands of the apparently normal husband and father.

I'd draw obvious comparisons and always arrive at the same inevitable conclusion: our father wasn't anywhere near 'normal', so where did that leave us? Or rather, what was he trying to tell us? I was aware and intelligent enough to put two and two together as I perused these ghoulish stories, but if I needed a final kick, it wasn't long in coming.

One evening, when my mother was on the evening shift and my father happened to be at home instead of pickling himself in various sauces at the local, Iain, Anthony and I found ourselves alone in his company. It was a rare event and not one to be savoured. We all felt as uncomfortable as each other; he sat there in his usual chair, silent and brooding, biting his inside lip as he stared at the television, seemingly unaware of what was on the monochrome screen. After a while we'd gone upstairs to make ourselves scarce, but a short time later he told us to come back down, and I braced myself for the usual fun and games involving his attempts to humiliate me in front of my brothers.

We sat on the sofa, three different sized peas in a pod, waiting for something to happen, but nothing did and he sat there if he was all alone in the room and enjoying a private joke at our expense. A gardening programme came on the TV, and as the presenter waffled on about the beautiful array of begonias or whatever, I strained my imagination to convert the various shades of grey and black into psychedelic colours of which nature would have approved. In the back of my mind, though, I was keeping that cat firmly on the tin roof, knowing that my father had never set foot in the garden and thus had no real interest in any programme about gardening. Something was coming: I could smell it as clearly as the stench of Park Drive cigarettes that he chain-smoked. Then, without looking at any of us, he told us to go to bed. Iain, logical and implacable as ever, pointed out that it was only eight o'clock and he still had an hour to go before his bedtime. A swift slap promptly corrected him on that matter. We all got up to leave. I for one was grateful for the early night, but he reached for my arm and told me to stay put.

That familiar sinking feeling grabbed me by the balls and suddenly I felt as if all my energy had been sapped. I sat back down and tried to concentrate on the black-and-white garden flickering in front of me, but the certainty that he was up to something seemed to reduce me to a tiny, screwed-up ball of fear and apprehension. After about ten minutes of silence and me waiting nervously for what was coming, he looked at me and said, 'Come here, son!'

His intonation suggested he was surprised that I wasn't already nestled in his loving paternal arms and perhaps even a little hurt that there was so much physical distance between us.

I almost fell for it, as my mother had done many times previously, and it crossed my mind that maybe all I'd face was a harmless rant, as had happened once or twice before. Besides, I told myself, he was definitely sober and somehow we'd managed not to incur his wrath when we were all sitting together earlier – perhaps the rest of the evening would just involve one of his surreal conversations.

I sat down at his feet and to my amazement he put his hand on my head and gave it a friendly rub. Above all I felt confused, though I couldn't help but relax a little as he started to tell me about his childhood. It was soaked in a nostalgic tone that suggested I had nothing to worry about: the streets of his youth, a friend who'd got crushed by a steamroller, and then a tale of a lost sister whom he'd never mentioned before.

Speaking in a soft, tragic voice that barely sounded like that of my father, he explained that she was beautiful and he loved her, but that one day he'd come home to find her dead in bed, with her wrists slashed. 'She was dead, son . . . slashed her wrists,' his sad voice repeated over and over again. 'Slashed her wrists, son – blood everywhere.' It made his next sentence break me completely. Hand still on my head, his once harsh Glaswegian growl now a soft Scottish brogue, he told me that one day we wouldn't wake up either, because we'd be with his sister after he'd cut all our throats.

I cracked. The room started to spin around and I burst into tears. They weren't the usual tears he'd sometimes extract from me, which were produced to convince him that he'd got through to me and to save myself more bruises – these were genuine, and the strangest feeling lay underneath them, fuelling and spitting them out of me. Nothing seemed real any more and I couldn't get a grip on what I'd heard. He'd threatened all our lives before, but always chewing on red-hot irons and alcohol. Tonight he was sober, calm and exuding a hint of unfamiliar warmth. It made his words all the more terrifying.

He'd got me and he knew it. For the first time ever I didn't get the obligatory slap for 'greetin'. Instead he calmly told me to go to bed. Still close to hysterical, I got up and left him savouring his victory.

Most of the times when I'd been left downstairs with our father, Iain would stay awake and wait until it was over, then whisper goodnight or check I was okay. So as soon as I got to the top of the stairs and reached the landing, I could see Iain and Anthony's door half open, whereupon a small, concerned voice asked me, 'Are you all right, Andrew?'

It was Iain. Just the sound of his voice pulled me together as surely as if he'd put his arms around me and given me a hug. His was often the quiet, calm voice inside me, reassuring me and telling me I was stronger than I thought.

'Yes,' I replied, truthfully. 'Go to sleep. I love you.'

'I love you too,' he replied.

It was at that precise moment I realized my father had to die. I knew that if I didn't kill him, he would kill *us*.

I climbed into bed and stayed awake all night knowing that God had failed me, my mother was powerless, the rest of the world was too ignorant and uninterested, and my brothers were far too young. I knew that in a few years' time Iain would have helped me to save us in any way possible, but I also knew that we didn't have much time left.

I imagined my father coming home one night, strangling my mother so as to make the least possible noise, then opening my door and grabbing my hair as he cut my throat, before creeping next door to do the same to Iain and perhaps even to Anthony, his favourite. I had no idea what he would do after that, but all the crime magazines I'd pored over seemed to have the answer – most of these men never waited for the police to arrive, so I guessed that he'd probably hang himself.

The decision was made: I was going to kill him – that, I knew for certain. But how? There lay the new and burning question that would virtually consume my every waking moment and even my dreams for the next few months.

How could I kill a man with more physical strength and ferocity than anyone I'd ever seen in real life or even on the television? How could I do it and make sure that it was done properly? A mistake, even the slightest one, would definitely result in my death and almost certainly lead to that of my mother and brothers; there could be no error of judgement on my part, otherwise I might as well kill us all myself and save him the job.

Poison? For a long time it was my favoured method, but I quickly learned from my secret readings that to guarantee success I'd need access to the right materials that would do the job properly, without alerting him to the fact that a lethal substance was in his tea. Arsenic seemed to be the perfect answer, but how could an eleven-year-old get his hands on the stuff?

A knife in the heart? Well, even vampires died from that and my father could often be found slouched in his armchair, seemingly dead to the world. Surely I could make that a permanent situation? But what if I wasn't physically strong enough? What if I lost my nerve or momentum halfway through the thrust and it didn't go deep enough? I imagined him screaming out in pain, grabbing the knife and pulling it out of his chest, blood coursing down his body as he launched himself at me, plunging the weapon into me over and over again.

I even considered rewiring his electric blanket, and carried out experiments after reading a book on home electrics that warned of the risk of death when touching live wires. I took a plug, wired in an electrical lead to live and neutral, and touched the live wire to test the theory: it almost threw me across the room. Once I'd recovered, I examined my hand and discovered it had turned a beautiful shade of black on one side. Here indeed was a possibility and I held on to this final solution for a long time until I realized that the wires in an electric blanket weren't exposed. From science lessons at school – in which I'd become an eager student overnight – I'd learned that water was a great conductor, and so I visualized myself turning on the blanket as he slept and then pouring water all over him. Again, I saw him scream out, roll out of bed in agony and then turn to face me, to make me pay the ultimate price for my failure.

All of my dark secret plans, carried out in the controlled environment of my imagination, were flawed and incompetent. I knew I needed help in this matter. I had the resolve all right, but I was an eleven-year-old amateur and I couldn't reply on beginner's luck – there was too much at stake.

So many times I almost introduced Iain to my plan, but I was afraid to get him involved in a crime that could have left us both locked up in a unit for juvenile offenders. I applied the same principle to my mother. I couldn't bear the thought of her ending up in prison. Every other person I considered was crossed off my list either for being too young and feeble like me, or too adult and stupid, and therefore liable to report a potentially homicidal youngster to the police.

I didn't know which way to turn, and for a while it really felt like we were doomed. I knew that it would take a minor miracle for me to kill him all by myself and save my family, but I was also realistic enough to know that miracles could only be found in the somewhat suspect pages of the Bible.

Yes, I needed help from someone, I concluded, but who was out there who might be capable of assisting a murder?

I carried this question around with me for several long months until the answer came from the last person I'd considered on my extensive list of possible accomplices, who'd been under my very nose the whole time.

# 8 | *Horror Story*

---

STARTING SECONDARY SCHOOL in autumn 1979 was one of the most exciting times of my childhood. Ignoring Joey Longworth's warning that if you couldn't do joined-up handwriting the teachers made you stand naked in the school playing field, I joined the steady march of new pupils, early one September morning, in our crisp new uniforms on the way to Bulmershe School, and hoped that I wouldn't be the only one freezing my little knackers off on the football pitch.

I would often make the journey to school with one of my best friends, Alice, who lived close by. Something of a tomboy, she would usually respond to my endless teasing by giving me a karate chop or trapping me in an inescapable headlock. Although she exuded a carefree nature, there were days when her moods would swing wildly, though I never knew why. Nevertheless, she was great company most of the time and helped to take my mind off the traumas of home.

Bulmershe was one of those schools that you forever look back at and thank whatever unseen forces put it in your path. At its helm was a headmaster who, despite inspiring a certain fear in the early days, as time went on revealed a warmth, generosity and wisdom that inspired more respect from me than any man had ever managed before.

Mr Hadfield was from working-class Lancastrian stock and was as solid as he was uncompromising. On our first day we were all assembled in front of him for our introduction into 'big school'. Despite his short stature, he seemed like a giant of a man, and although I had a natural aversion to short men who puffed themselves up, it soon became apparent that there was no affectation on his part. He exuded a passion and a zeal for his pupils and was determined that we should all make the best of ourselves. We learned that he'd come from a less than privileged background and was destined for a life working down the mines, but through sheer hard graft and unwavering determination, he had gone on to university. He was a man who seemed able to peer into our very souls and told us in no uncertain terms that we should never accept anything but the best for ourselves, that anything was possible. To my astonishment, I found myself believing him.

He was like an evangelical preacher when it came to the subject of education and had a hardened belief in every pupil's ability to shine. He also spoke about the value of the arts in the world and that not to pursue at least one artistic endeavour was a crime. It struck me as odd to hear a man with a thick Northern accent espousing the importance of music and the arts, but it gave him an extra dimension that made him totally credible in my eyes.

He could also be fearsome man when it came to discipline and respect for school rules. Woe betide anyone whom he spotted dropping litter, and if he caught you sprinting down the corridor, the sound of his voice booming out 'Stop running, laddie!' would freeze you to the spot. In fact once I saw another teacher stop dead in their tracks until he realized Mr Hadfield was addressing a student.

He naturally inspired respect from every single pupil in the school and understood the importance of letting the kids express their feelings and talents in any way they could, as long as it didn't involve any sort of 'nonsense'. This stewardship seemed to filter down to almost every teacher in the school – even the average ones weren't so bad. They had a lot to live up to and almost seemed as much in awe of the headmaster as the children were.

I quickly made friends with a cheeky kid called Gareth, who looked very professorial in his glasses, but was every bit as wayward and impudent as me. We got on well and had a lot of fun entertaining each other during classes, but it wasn't long before our teachers began trying to separate us. When they weren't looking, we'd slip back next to each other and so eventually they gave up. We didn't make trouble as such, because we both enjoyed our classes too much, but our ability to reduce each other to fits of laughter could sometimes be distracting.

I'd go to Gareth's house after school and listen to 'Frigging in the Rigging' by The Sex Pistols at full volume, singing along as loud as we could. His sweet parents, who would give us fizzy drinks, were pretty tolerant people I thought; my mother would have had a fit if she'd heard me singing ''Cos there's fuck all else to do!' at the top of my lungs. We'd often spend time performing comedy routines from *Not The Nine O'Clock News* and I don't think I'd laughed so much in all my life than during those great afternoons spent in his company. He brought me out of myself by making me laugh so heartily and I returned the compliment.

I'd always avoided inviting friends to my house as the thought of any of them bumping into my father filled me with the utmost dread, but one day, when Gareth came to visit unannounced, my father happened to be at home. He led Gareth inside, chatting away to him and asking lots of questions in that sickly charming manner he could turn on at will. Sitting in the front room with them, I watched as greasy, fake pleasantries poured out of him while he joked with my friend.

I found myself biting my cheeks until I tasted blood. Gareth totally fell for it and even laughed along with my father, blissfully unaware that only a few hours before he'd been kicking me across the kitchen. I wanted to reach over and punch Gareth as hard as I could, but instead I sat there in silence, saying nothing and hating both of them.

When my father got up to leave, cracking another joke about us not getting into too much trouble, Gareth turned to me and told me how cool he was. I was expecting it, of course. I'd heard how wonderful my father was too many times before, but I still felt betrayed – I'd hoped for more from Gareth, which was stupid. He had been blinded by my father's charm like so many others.

By then I'd had a lot of practice in dealing with the knot that tightened inside me whenever anyone told me what a great father I had. I was so close to screaming out the truth about my father to Gareth, that he was a psycho and was going to murder us – but I couldn't, even if I'd wanted to. The reality of my home life had become a conditioned secret from everyone, and that included my best friend. When we left the house I was a complete bastard to Gareth for the rest of the day, until he had had enough and went home, leaving me to come to terms with the depressing truth that my best mate had fallen for such a fake.

I'd only been at secondary school a short while when, on account of my church choir experience, I was asked to take part in the Christmas production of *Joseph and the Amazing Technicolor Dreamcoat*. As I settled further into the daily routine and hung out with kids in my class, it seemed that things were as good as they could get. Life at home, of course, was far from rosy, and reminded me that the real world I lived in wouldn't be improved by positive things happening elsewhere. And so it was that yet another trauma was to be added to my already difficult circumstances.

The recurring nightmare that was to last almost two years invaded my sleep from the very first night I moved into my new room. As the weeks and months went on, I became completely convinced that both that room and I were cursed. There were two bizarre features concerning this nightmare, which separated it from being a mere bad dream or in any way comparable to the sleep traumas of my early years. First of all, I could never remember a single detail of what had caused me to wake up screaming. This was unusual because my memories of dreams, whether good or otherwise, had always been clear and easy to recall. The second odd aspect of the nightmare was that it only ever occurred when my mother was working the early shift, and thus she would always be downstairs whenever my anguished shrieks signified the climax of my night terrors.

This bi-monthly saga was always exactly the same: I'd wake up screaming at the unremembered or unimaginable horror that I'd witnessed in my sleep, shoot out of bed and pelt down the stairs, rushing headlong towards the front door where, just to its right and directly at the foot of the stairs, there was a half-length pane of glass waiting to cut my face to shreds. My mother would hear my screams and rush to the bottom of the stairs to catch me before I smashed my head through the glass.

I don't know who was more terrified during these spells – me from the nightmare or my mother, for fear that one night she might not be there to catch me. She didn't have to worry, though, because when she was working the late shift and my brothers and me were either by ourselves or with our father, I was safe from its clutches; it was as if the nightmare only wanted to scare, not scar me.

In the mornings after the event I'd have dim recollections of something I wanted to forget, but not much more than that, which suited me perfectly. I had a strong feeling that if I remembered the dream I'd probably never sleep again.

Yet however frightened I was deep down, I knew I had no choice but to stay strong mentally, because to buckle under the weight of everything would have left my mother and two brothers all alone. I felt an immense responsibility to them, though they never outwardly demanded anything from me. Perhaps being the eldest I naturally assumed that the onus was on me to try to make everything right. I lived with that inner sense of duty in much the same way I accepted the practical truth that my father was someone to fear greatly.

I had spent most of my childhood and early adolescence in total denial of the intense mental pressure I was under. Masking my true feelings from the outside world had become as much a part of my daily life as enduring the violence at home or seeing ghosts by my bedside. It wasn't so much a question of not having the 'luxury' of insanity, as being unprepared to admit that I was floundering, so I adopted a wild and extrovert character that deflected outside scrutiny. It seemed to work and so I honed it to near perfection.

All the while I was still seeing the ghosts who crowded into my bedroom at night. It's true to say I now have more belief in what I saw then than I did as a child, thanks to the benefit of knowledge hard won in the years that followed. All the pieces that fell into place, however incredible or inexplicable, forced me to confront and accept what, for so many years between childhood and late adolescence, I had denied and made rational excuses for.

In moments of extreme stress, or mental collapse, gates are opened up – which are normally tightly closed – sometimes for good reason, but other times because we're simply too scared to look under the bed and see what's there. Perhaps we'd see ourselves staring back at us – a terrifying prospect for many.

In my case, these doors to other hidden senses swung open because of the intolerable pressures I was under, but rather than helping to shed light on the situation, they made it even murkier and dropped me ever deeper into a confusing maze from which I could see no escape. As a child I simply trusted that everything would somehow be okay, as if some far-off voice was whispering that all I had to do was hang on in there.

So I did. I made my mother my North Star and took every bit of light she was able to give out. It kept me sane and was the crucial counter-balance to the pull towards what could have been a very dark world indeed. Her gentleness and humour shone through unabated, despite the escalating violence, and to me she was a fount of unconditional love, never waning nor withholding no matter how tired she often looked or how slowly she sometimes moved.

Inadvertently she taught me the art of concealment. Her brave face, despite the bruises, showed me that it was possible to smile and laugh even while crying inside. If she could do it, why couldn't I? In fact, she had no choice in the matter. She had to be strong, and knew that if she slipped and fell in her efforts to show us a different world, another side to human nature, we might all be lost in the future to the potentially endless cycle of abuse to which my father was inextricably chained.

The fateful decision I'd taken to kill my father put paid to my relationship with God. He hadn't given any sign that He was listening to my frantic prayers about getting rid of him; in fact things at home had begun to get worse. Now my father didn't even need to be drunk to get dangerously violent, and so I came to the natural conclusion that God clearly wanted me to suffer as much as possible.

Time dragged on and my prayers to Him became a litany of compromises and begging for scraps: send my father away for a while; stop the beatings to my mother; and then, pathetically, please cut the beatings to just once a week. God was having none of it, however, and rewarded my willingness to settle for anything other than the star prize of a grisly end for my father by sending him into my bedroom late one night, shortly after my eleventh birthday.

It's strange how, under certain circumstances, innocuous noises can take on a whole new meaning. The key turning in the lock at night became a shotgun firing in the downstairs hallway, a warning blast from a hunter's twelve-bore – run rabbit, run, run, run. There was nowhere to escape to, though, and so when the front door banged behind him, it also slammed shut on my nightly prayer that someone might have killed him that evening, because there he was, very much alive.

I clutched my duvet tightly and went through the usual motions of squeezing my eyes shut, grasping at the desperate wish that if he crashed into my room he'd presume I was asleep and leave me be. Though I might have abandoned divinity, I hadn't given up on a child's futile hopes. I could hear things being broken downstairs and I wondered what was going on. My mother was on the late shift, and definitely out of the house. I couldn't hear any voices, so I was sure he was alone – until I heard the terrible scream of one of our cats.

My mother told me that when Dino was a kitten, my father seemed to adore her and spent ages playing with her, but by the time she was a year old he'd started to kick and throw her across the room if she got in his way. We all worshipped those cats and it was heartbreaking to watch him treat them like rag dolls. Whenever he inflicted any mindless brutality on them, I'd imagine doing the same to him when I was old enough.

Listening to her awful howls that night split me in half, and the tinnitus, that uncontrollable defence mechanism, kicked in even harder until I couldn't tell the screeches of the cat and the downstairs crashes from the noises originating in my inner ear. Suddenly, the bedroom door was kicked open.

'Get downstairs, you bastard.'

I kept motionless and carried on feigning sleep, praying he'd give up. There was always that chance. A hard slap broke my pretence, and I got up and mutely followed him down the stairs.

To my horror I realized he was holding the kitchen carving knife. Was this it, I wondered? As soon as I concluded I was finally going to meet that useless God who'd dumped me in this madhouse, a strange, almost surreal calm washed over me.

I followed my father into the kitchen like the proverbial lamb. 'Get in the sink,' he snapped, and I obeyed. It struck me that there was nothing odd about the request because I'd come to expect the unexpected where he was concerned.

In fact, I thought, as I squeezed myself into the old, blue, plastic washing-up bowl, it was quite a sensible thing for him to ask; the blood would gush into the bowl and not make a mess in the sink – it was quite a domestic consideration on his part. I remember hoping fervently that whatever happened, I didn't want it to hurt.

He lifted up the knife, but instead of pointing it in my direction he held the blade in his hand and offered me the handle. 'See this knife, son?' he said in a dangerous low voice. 'You take this, kill that fucking cat and bring it to me when you're done. If you don't, I'll kill you – understand?'

All this was delivered calmly, logically, as if it were the most natural thing in the world. I couldn't see anything except for his face, and for a moment he hypnotized me into believing I was going to do nothing more than slice a loaf of bread.

Then everything went black as a hard smack around the side of my head sent me crashing into the plates and cutlery on the draining board. My father's face came back into focus. 'You stupid cunt. What are you doing in the sink? Get out and find that fucking cat or you're dead.' He thrust the knife in my hand, strode off into the living room and left me to climb down on to the kitchen floor as the reality of the task sunk in.

I didn't know what to do or where to go, except that I knew I had to find Dino as quickly as possible to save her from him. I'd faced up to the very real danger of being killed by my father, and was emboldened by the fact that I almost wished he'd stuck the knife in and got it over and done with.

I crept into the storage room that led to the back garden – one of the cats' many hiding places from him – and softly called out her name. Neither cat seemed to be there, amongst all the piled-up junk, and I became distraught. If Dino wasn't there, she might have been in the front room – where he was now – hiding behind the sofa. If that was the case then there was no hope for either of us: I couldn't so much as pluck a hair from her head, let alone do what he'd asked, and so if he found her he'd deal with me then do the job himself. At least, that's the way I saw things happening in my head at the time.

I walked back into the kitchen and prayed she was there, somewhere, but amidst the crockery and cutlery strewn across the draining board and floor she was nowhere to be seen. Holding my breath, I walked into the hallway where the living room door was half open and craned my neck to find out whether my father had beaten me to it and had quietly strangled her in my absence. I could just see the top of his mousy balding head over the back of his armchair. He seemed to be sitting still, waiting for delivery of a dead cat.

Relaxing a little, I realized there was still a chance I could work something out. I made soft noises with my front teeth and lower lip to call Dino, over and over again as quietly as I dared, my heart pumping wildly lest my father heard me. Then, to my absolute joy, I could see her head peering into the hallway from the front room where she had been hiding all along, and she slowly slunk over to me. She was a mess. He'd thrown some kind of liquid over her, and her fur was sticking up in different directions, making her look like a strange new breed. I lifted her up and quietly opened the front door to let her out. She shot off into the night and I wished I were a cat too.

I returned to the front room, holding out the knife in front of me, and readied myself for what was going to come.

'Dad, I couldn't find her.'

No reply.

'Dad?'

I emerged from behind the back of his chair and meekly stood before him. To my relief, he was out cold. His mouth hung open in a dead sneer and white gunk coated both his lips, making him look like a sleeping rabid dog.

I stood in front of him, examining this abominable creature in a way not previously possible. My trance-like state of a few moments ago had vanished completely, and my senses were sharp and alert as I considered how this short, skinny, stinking alcoholic with spittle-coated lips seemed like the most ridiculous thing I'd ever seen. Was it possible that this was the same monster that roared at and regularly overwhelmed a grown woman and three boys, and was the sole cause of so much misery and terror?

For years I'd find it impossible to describe precisely or adequately how deranged he was during such fits, until I watched *The Shining*. Though critics knocked Jack Nicholson for overacting, to me he was utterly convincing, and in the role of Jack Torrance he nailed all the characteristics of a violent psychotic.

I carried on looking at my father, feeling nothing but burning hatred as he slumbered on, snoring heavily, a thin river of dribble running down his chin. I knew this was my moment. I closed my eyes and saw a small boy raising a knife high above his head. 'Go for the heart,' another voice seemed to say, and a wonderful feeling of peace welled up inside me as I saw the flash of steel rocket past my eyes as the knife plunged deep into his heart.

But when I opened my eyes, there he was, and there I was. Knife hanging limply by my side, fuming at my cowardice, while he remained fully alive and doubtless dreaming of more ways to further torture his family.

I put the knife back in the cutlery drawer and went to my room.

All my dreams, prayers and preparations concerning his

mortal exit had finally come to nothing because I didn't have the guts to do anything about it. I knew deep down that I would never have the nerve to finish him off. I'd had my chance, I'd blown it, and now I deserved everything I got. I went to bed and told God that the deal was off. From now on I belonged to the Devil. I'd do everything in my power to shut God out of my life for ever, do everything against Him, and if that meant selling my soul to his enemy, then so be it.

The next morning my father acted as though the previous night had never happened and he didn't say a word to me, which is how he usually was when he was sober. I wondered if he was in denial or whether he'd got so wasted the night before that he'd completely forgotten. I remembered it all, though, especially my vow to that limp-dicked God who'd chosen to let me down so badly.

On leaving the house, I set out as if to go to school, but instead took a detour to the Little Park and sought out the local electricity generator shed. The neighbourhood kids called it simply 'The Danger', in deference to the huge red sign of a skull and bold letters that read 'Danger – Risk of Death.' To me the notice translated as, 'Come in, Andrew.' I climbed over the concrete wall and took out a small penknife that I'd swiped from a local shop. I cut into the palm of my hand, smeared it on to one of the gun-grey metal blocks humming with thousands of volts, and swore my soul to the devil. I vowed to Satan that if the price for my father's death was my soul, then it was his, there and then.

I went to school as if nothing had happened, but inside I felt something terrible and wonderful. If my secret life at home, my petty thefts and the ghosts were things I had to keep hidden from the outside world, this was one secret that I clutched to myself with glee, as though it were a precious stone I didn't want anyone else to be dazzled by, knowing that it went against everything good, decent and 'normal'.

I wanted to continue with choir, because I took any chance

I could get to sing, and only when I was immersed in music could I shut out the terrible thoughts that normally plagued me in moments of solitude. Those thoughts never stopped telling me what a useless and wicked child I was: I deserved everything I got because I was as evil as my father; did I really think that all this was happening by mere accident? So, between the self-hatred and the tinnitus, my attempts to fall sleep at night were as futile as they were agonizing.

It wasn't as if I went about sacrificing small creatures to Beelzebub or danced naked under a Walpurgis moon, even though such practices seemed quite thrilling. If I'd chanced upon a witch or warlock in those days, then things might have been very different. Essentially, it came down to my simplistic views of good versus evil and my resolve to take a different route. I now viewed God as my enemy and followed the logic that God's enemy must be my ally, and so I'd do well to explore all the options available.

I did, however, start taking a more studious interest in the occult. Over the course of time I amassed a small, but fascinating, collection of books on the history of witchcraft, ancient religions, and even one on black magic which I'd swapped for a stack of Corgi toys with a boy at school who'd taken it from his father's bookcase.

I'd draw pentagrams in my bedroom and read aloud from books various phrases that meant nothing to me, but because I was desperate for help from any quarter, if it meant spouting slightly silly names and incantations to demonic forces, then I had no hesitation in giving it a try.

A short while after this I scratched an inverted crucifix into the choir vestry, thinking it would at least endear me to the Horned One or perhaps get his attention, but all I got was a slap from one of the older boys who saw me doing it and told me that I was going to Hell. Big deal, I thought. I was halfway there so I might as well make the full trip.

★  ★  ★

By the time I was twelve, the early-morning wake-up calls my father had been so fond of were becoming more frequent and more savage. If he wasn't taking out his inner demons on me, then he was forcing me to watch him do it to our mother. Things took an even worse twist when he started to pull Iain out of bed to watch, and through blurred vision, as I fought to hold back the tears of anger, I'd see Iain standing there, unmoving and seemingly unperturbed. As I watched more closely, though, I could see that it was as if he wasn't really there. It wasn't so much that he'd gone into deep shock, so much as he'd managed to remove himself to a place far away from the unbearable scenes before him. It was an enviable skill that I wished I could learn for myself.

One night, shortly after Iain's introduction into the mix, after trying my best to fall sleep over the racket of tinnitus playing distorted electronica in my head, I got up to use the loo. As I took a few steps past my opened bedroom door to the toilet that lay directly ahead, I froze.

Standing there, unmoving and expressionless, were two dark figures. For a split second I thought they were my parents, but as I looked more closely I could see they were much older and far taller than either of them. Rigid with fear, I found I couldn't move. This wasn't part of the deal, I thought to myself. The ghosts were only allowed in my room while I was sleeping and they always had to disappear when I hid from them, but here they still were after I'd closed my eyes, counted to ten and opened them to find their continued presence on the landing. My initial shock and fear receded a little when I realized that they weren't looking at me, but staring straight over my head at the wall behind me. My heart still crashed wildly, but I felt my legs unfreeze and my eyes relax.

They were both in their late forties, at least six feet tall, dark-haired and dressed very drably. Long ringlets of dark, curly hair hung down on to the woman's shoulders, which were half covered by a cream-white, lace shawl that stood out against her long, plain, brown dress that reached the floor. He was of similar age, possibly older and almost dressed to match her style, in a long dark-brown coat and waistcoat. Initially I assumed they were Victorian, but on closer inspection I decided they were early Edwardian. Their facial characteristics were so similar that they could almost have been brother and sister.

Then the man said, pitifully, 'We're so hungry.'

A sudden inner screaming rang out and a fearful voice shot through my brain: he wants to eat me. Fortunately, the feeling of extreme terror soon passed, and a voice of reason told me not to be so stupid and to look more carefully. I stayed frozen to the spot, trying and failing to take in the reality of the situation.

As I looked at the man's face with the little composure available to me, I realized that I had never seen such sadness in all my life. His eyes were two blurry pictures of a terrible tragedy. At that point I suddenly knew, without a doubt, that they'd starved to death. I turned to my left to look at the woman, but she hadn't moved an inch and continued to stare expressionlessly ahead of her.

I didn't know what to do or how to get away, so I blurted out, 'I'll go downstairs and get you some food.' I hoped and prayed that they'd believe me, because I wanted nothing more than to be as far away from them as possible.

Suddenly I could feel my legs again. I fled back into my room, slammed the door and dived into my bed. I pulled the covers over my head and tried to blot out the unfathomable scene I'd just witnessed. 'Never again,' I angrily spat into the bed sheets. 'Never again – I will never see them again.' I said it repeatedly, until eventually I heard my mother getting up at seven o'clock.

Tentatively, I opened my door an inch at a time to check that they'd gone. When my mother emerged from the bathroom, I rushed to her and clung on for dear life. She thought I'd had a nightmare, but when I explained what had happened all she could do was reassure me that it must have been a dream. I refused to be fobbed off, however, and told her every detail. She acknowledged it might not have been a dream, looked at me as though she'd seen her own ghost, and told me to help her with the breakfast; it would make me feel better.

The curse of the adult. After everything I've seen in my life and all the inexplicable experiences that have taken place, there is still the distant voice of logic and reason that tries to explain away the ghosts on the landing as symptoms of trauma and mere figments of my imagination. Though it's true I experienced daily trauma, to me it acted as an open door through which certain energies took on specific forms. I was always wide awake and aware of every single sensation and detail. Since my younger days I've had enough self-induced hallucinations to know the difference, and am certain these people didn't exist within the realms of my imagination.

There was one tangible outcome from my experience with the unknown couple: throughout the rest of my childhood, I never saw the ghosts again. I never woke to find my room full of strangers, and I never saw sad-eyed men or women on the landing. As I grew into my teens, I remembered all my visitors and had the strangest feeling of missing them; in later life I even wished for their return, to let them know that I wasn't afraid any longer, but they never came back – their time had passed.

The incident of the sad-eyed ghosts coincided with the visit of my father's older brother, our uncle Tony. At nearly six foot seven, he was a huge man, and although I was always wary of anyone related to my father, Tony seemed to me like a gentle giant, speaking softly and moving carefully as if afraid that one wrong step could demolish a wall and bring the whole house down around us.

Unlike one of our other uncles, Charlie, who once visited when I was very young, and turned my father into a bag of nerves for the duration of his stay, Tony seemed to bring out a more relaxed side to him – or at least where his brother was concerned, because his presence changed nothing for my mother.

One morning Tony found a strange black pile stuffed behind the toilet cistern and took it to my mother to find out what it was. She turned around and showed him the blistered and bloodied bald patch at the back of her head where, the night before, my father had grabbed her violently, twisted round a thick rope of her long hair and yanked it right out. If we thought that this giant of a man would set the world, and my father, to rights we were sorely mistaken. He looked at her, said nothing and simply went about his business. How he could have been any different? He had had the same brutal upbringing as my father and had doubtless developed the same type of unfeeling attitude.

# 9 | *The Sins of the Father*

HOW MY FATHER made his money was a mystery to us all. Although he was a bricklayer and builder by trade, it was rare to see him don his old work clothes and boots in the morning, or return home in them at the end of the day. Usually, the crisply pressed suit he'd worn when leaving the house would have turned into a dishevelled, whisky-sodden mess by the time he'd staggered through the door in the wee small hours.

On the days when he was pursuing his alternative profession, whatever that was, he'd spend ages smartening himself up in his suit, combing every last hair into place and giving the mirror admiring glances, for he was as vain as he was good-looking. Although he didn't think twice about causing mayhem throughout the house, throwing plates and furniture around at will, and leaving my mother to clean up, he was meticulous where his own appearance was concerned. I'd secretly watch him from one corner of the room as he prepared for what looked like an office job, and wonder where he went when he wasn't masquerading as an honest worker on a building site.

Asking my mother was pointless. She had no idea what he did or where he went, and she knew better than to question him on the subject. All she did know was that however much he was paid for his secret work, she never saw a penny of it.

As well as being a serious drinker, my father also gambled heavily. Sometimes he'd win, but more often than not he would lose, judging from his reaction when he was at home watching his beloved boxing on TV. If I saw his expression start to turn black and shrink into itself, I knew that he wouldn't be the only one to suffer that night.

On one or two rare occasions, while I endured my usual late-night or early-morning hot seat, he was unbelievably joyful – blind drunk and incomprehensible, perhaps, but in a scarily good mood. He'd empty his pockets and wads of twenty-pound notes would fall to the floor amongst all the betting slips. He'd slur about this or that, slap me on the back good-naturedly and thrust large amounts of money into my hand telling me to 'buy some sweeties'. He'd always pass out on those nights, sometimes mid-sentence, and I'd shoot upstairs, count the money and wonder how many penny chews I could buy with £100.

In the morning, though, I'd always give it back. I knew he'd never remember giving it to me, but the money stank, literally, and I didn't want a single thing from him. Perhaps I should have kept it and passed it to my mother, but I was convinced that the money was somehow infected, that to touch it could mean catching whatever strange illness he had. Furthermore, there was still a chance that, halfway through the day, he'd suddenly remember giving me the cash the night before, and so the risk was far too great to take.

The closest I got to finding out what he did on those suited and booted occasions was when one night he snarled at me about all the sacrifices he was making for us. After calling us 'ungrateful little bastards who had no idea about anything,' he looked me in the eyes and said, 'You know what I do all day, son? For you lot?'

I stared blankly at him, wondering if the question was of the rhetorical variety or whether I was supposed to proffer a reply. Though I could have faced severe punishment for my response, I opted for a small 'No,' despite having bad feelings about what he did for a living.

'I fuck people, son,' he replied, his voice low and calm as he bored his menacing lasers into my own little windows that I wished had curtains to shut him out. 'I fuck them so they don't fuck me. You understand?'

I answered that I did, even though I had no idea at all. The overriding feeling I had was that to know any more would not be a good thing. He looked at me, holding my gaze as if he were interrogating a prisoner – which, of course, he was. He snorted, turned away from me and spat out that I didn't know anything and was a 'wee queer'.

Any thoughts he might have had about my following in his footsteps as a 'fucker' of people were mercifully prevented by my poofery it seemed. In reality, I was failing rather miserably on my mission to wear that label with pride; it was simply too silly for me to contemplate kissing boys when girls were obviously much more suited for it. After Paula Jefcut's wonderful instruction in the joys of the unspoken French language some years before, kissing had become my number-two hobby after music. If my other friends thought I was a sissy for hanging around with girls so much, then that was their loss; they didn't know what they were missing. My tongue seemed to have taken on a life and consciousness of its own, demanding that it be exercised at every available opportunity. After a marathon summer of licking the tonsils of every girl I fancied, and with my father's worst fear still a matter for fulfilling, I determined to get the issue of my homosexuality back on track, despite the stumbling block of finding boys both unappealing and rather stupid.

The opportunity came my way when, one day, while playing soldiers in my room with a neighbour, John, we decided to hide from Iain and jump him when he wasn't expecting it. We had just squeezed into my wardrobe, trying not to giggle and give the game away, when a small hand reached out and grabbed me between my legs. I wasn't at all shocked or taken by surprise and decided it felt quite good. Within a few seconds we were shaking around in the wardrobe, groping and touching each other, still trying not to laugh. As the moment had come to achieve that exalted rank of 'poof', I stuck a huge kiss on him and we snogged each other for a few minutes until it started to seem a bit pointless and boring. It had been great at first – exciting and forbidden – but a boy didn't taste anything like a girl, and besides, Iain was sure to hear the wardrobe rocking from side to side and I didn't want to have to put up with him calling me a 'bender' for the rest of my childhood, despite knowing it to be partially true.

I left the wardrobe, though perhaps not the closet, quite chuffed with myself, and sure in the knowledge that one day I'd be big enough to look that snarling homophobe straight in the eye when he asked me if I was a poof, and reply, 'Yes, as a matter of fact I am', in my best Quentin Crisp voice.

John seemed keen to play hide and seek with me in my bedroom quite often after that, but it didn't hold much interest for me. It was okay at first, I thought to myself, but if I had to compare him to the average girl, he came a very poor second.

I had achieved what I'd set out to do: to fulfil my father's worst nightmare. I was in raptures. After my wardrobe experience, every time my father accused me of being a 'queer' or 'poof' I'd inwardly dance with glee, all the time looking down at the floor so he caught no hint of the truth behind his accusations. Deep down I felt I was capable of anything now and it was a liberating feeling.

The bizarre spectre of homosexuality seemed to be a permanent fixture in our home. If it wasn't me trying my best to provoke my father into calling me a host of related epithets, it was his constant preoccupation with me or Iain being homosexual. However, on the day that my father decided to teach us both how to box, he stopped worrying about Iain on that score. Despite one of his nicknames being 'Bones', on account of his skinny physique, Iain proved more than a match for our father.

While I limply flung out my hands to his shielded face and he threw a sharp jab to the side of my head that sent me sprawling, Iain was remarkably fast and strong. When my father threw a few short jabs to Iain's face, Iain blocked them all seemingly effortlessly. My dad lowered his hands, beaming at his tough and manly son, and suggested he tried to take a swing at him to see if he could get past his defences. Iain didn't even wait for him to finish his sentence – or indeed raise those defences.

It was surely years of bottled-up rage and fury that powered the punch that sent my father's head reeling to one side. If I hadn't thought he would have taken it out on me, I would have burst out laughing at the dazed and shocked look on my father's face as he struggled to regain both his composure and pride. He shook his head a few times, rubbed his face gingerly and muttered, 'Ya wee bastard . . . well done . . .'

The boxing lessons ended somewhat prematurely as he shot off to put ice on his red, swelling face. I looked over at Iain, totally stunned by what I'd seen. I'd never seen a bigger smile on his face than the one that beamed back at me, and I threw my arms around him as though he'd won the world title.

There were no more boxing matches after that. I think that the crafty Glaswegian suspected that Iain could be a force to be reckoned with, and if he were taught how to employ his hidden strengths properly, future retribution might well come from that silent, aloof figure to whom he'd paid little attention until that point.

The reality of what could happen to me if my father discovered my wardrobe antics with John was brought starkly to my attention when, one night, I was roughly woken up by my father who was pulling me out of bed as if there were an emergency of some kind. At first I thought there must be a fire, because he seemed agitated and nervous as he whispered frantically, 'Get out of bed, son.' Something was definitely up.

I looked around to see if Iain and Anthony were being evacuated with me, but their door was shut and no flames were racing up the walls or stairs. It was him leading the way and me following as he ushered me into the kitchen. He said nothing, but thrust his suede boots at me and told me to wash them. I thought nothing of it, of course. It was one of the least odd requests he'd made in all our twisted father-and-son communions, and I naturally obeyed, still dazed from the speed with which he'd pulled me out of bed and sent me downstairs.

I put the boots on the draining board and as I started to fill up the sink I noticed him peering out of the kitchen window, through the net curtains. His mood was different from usual. He was nervous about something, possibly even scared. I shrugged off my tiredness and grew curious about his strange behaviour. I saw that he was barefoot and as my senses tuned into what was happening, I realized I could smell something burning.

Distracted by his puzzling demeanour as he stood staring out of the window, I must have been lost in thought because he landed a slap on me and told me to hurry up. As I went to pick up the boots I sensed that something wasn't quite right, and taking them in my hand it soon became clear what was wrong. The normally light-brown boots seemed to have changed colour and were now almost black. As I gripped the upper fabric to plunge them into the sink, my hands slid over the material and I almost dropped them on to the floor: they were saturated in blood. It coated my hands, and as I held the boots above the water, little red droplets fell, fading into pink streaks in the sink.

I didn't dare waste any time feeling shock or disgust. I'd been ordered to do something for him and, as far as my father was concerned, questioning him – either inwardly or otherwise – was a cardinal sin.

As I set about the task of removing the sickly liquid that seemed to have soaked every fibre of his boots, all the while my father waited at the window, barking instructions in a low voice. 'You tell anyone that asks that I was here all night, you understand me, son? If the police come, you swear to them that you were up all night watching telly with me. Got it?'

I got it all right and realized that so too had some unfortunate soul who'd dared to incite my father's wrath. I wondered whether the blood I was trying to wash out had been his victim's last few drops or whether it was possible that someone could have survived such excessive blood loss.

Although I washed and scrubbed those boots for nearly an hour, it was no use. Even when the water eventually seemed clear, the boots remained tattooed with the evidence of my father's violence. The stain seemed permanent, as the original light tan was now black. For some strange reason, I felt guilty.

After I'd finished my bloody chore, I was dragged into the front room and told to stay put while my father stuffed the soaking boots behind the cushioned seats on the sofa. I felt a bit sick. I thought I might throw up, but I knew that if I did there'd be hell to pay, so I sat there, sitting on my hands, too terrified to check whether I had washed off all traces of blood.

We sat there in silence for an age. He didn't say a word until eventually, he looked at me and said, 'Son, there are people in this world who shouldn't be here. You see a queer, son, and you fucking kill him, understand?'

I nodded, as was expected, and then he told me to come out into the front garden. The night was almost over and using a battered old axe he began to lever off the huge manhole lid that covered the drain in the centre of our little garden. I didn't know how he managed it because the cover weighed a ton, but after a while I heard grating and a little thud of metal on the grass. At that point he whispered to me to go and get the boots.

They were dropped into the hole below and with great effort the cover was manoeuvred back into position.

I was ordered to go to bed and to remember the story I'd been told if anyone asked me. I shot upstairs into the bathroom to scrub my hands, but I felt sure I could still see pink stains in between my fingers and under my nails. I grabbed the Vim powder that we used to clean the bath and scrubbed furiously until I couldn't stand the smell any more.

As it turned out, no police ever called and no one ever asked me a single question about bloodstained boots and queers, but the memory of that night haunted me for many years after. Often I'd wake up bathed in sweat and for no good reason I'd raise my hands in front of my face, expecting them to be dripping with blood. Then I'd remember those boots, and his chilling verdict on queers, and wonder if in some way I was an accomplice to murder.

For years I imagined that the boots were still stuck at the bottom of that yawning drain, but I found out recently that he'd reopened the drain some time after and ordered Iain to help fish them out. Presumably he later burned them, just as he must have done with his socks, while I was washing the boots.

If I thought that my complicit actions that night might have endeared me a little to my father, then I was sorely mistaken. Perhaps he'd seen the revulsion and fear on my face, and realized that if the police had turned up I would have been the worst liar ever to make sure he'd be put away for good. I'd already rehearsed in my mind what I'd do if I was questioned: I'd be convincing enough with my version of events if my father was present when they called and then, as they left us, I'd see them to the front door, tap one of them discretely and nod toward the drain right in front of them.

It never happened of course, and so I didn't get my chance to see him off via the legal route. It was back to the alternative plan, which had never really left my head anyway. Clearly it was hopeless to imagine he'd ever meet his match and drop dead at the hands of a rival – he was too fearsome and clever to be outdone by anyone, it seemed, and too untouchable even to be suspected of whatever injury or murder he'd committed that night.

And so on he raged, his obvious feelings of invincibility reaching a crescendo and turning the house and my mother upside down. My beatings remained confined to once or twice a week, which I could deal with quite easily, but as far as my mother was concerned he never let up. The weeks turned into one long crash and scream that I'd do my best to block out, but there never was any escape from it. Iain and I would often be hauled down to witness his disease in action and always, deep down inside, I'd feel an elastic cord being stretched and pulled with every punch and kick he left on her body, and I knew that it was only a matter of time before it snapped and so did I. Sometimes I wonder if he could see that in me.

In a corner of my mind remains the possibility that somewhere locked within him, in a far-off place he didn't even know existed, a voice screamed out for someone to stop it all, either before he beat my mother to death or he cut our throats exactly as he'd promised.

# 10 | *Nightmare at Christmas*

CHRISTMAS 1979 witnessed a period of escape and real fun in the shape of the school musical, *Joseph and the Amazing Technicolor Dreamcoat.* I was chosen to play Benjamin, the youngest of Joseph's brothers – the visual joke being that at twelve years old and the youngest in the cast, I was at least a foot taller than everyone else and stuck out like a sore thumb.

Our dashingly good-looking PE teacher Mr Pritchard was cast as Joseph – which was slightly odd as it was meant to be an opportunity to show off the talents of the children rather than the teachers. However, he took it all very seriously and made a great leading man, despite his bushy moustache looking a little out of character. He leaned back in true Neil Diamond style, with one hand sensually clutching the microphone and the other outstretched either to the sky or audience, which seemed to consist mainly of adoring mothers and female teachers. After one of his big songs I was sure I saw him give a crafty little wink to his fans. In fact I was surprised he wasn't showered with underwear at the end of 'Close Every Door'. Even my own mother wasn't immune to the Pritchard sex appeal and afterwards, much to my disgust, commented that he was 'a dish'.

As the curtain fell on the production, so reality brought me back to my senses, and with it came the worst Christmas yet. My mother had always made sure that every year she'd saved up enough money, over many months, to make it both a magical and memorable time. Even though she couldn't compete with the more expensive gifts our friends would show off, somehow she always succeeded in buying us wonderful presents that meant a lot to us all.

My father seemed to understand the basic principle that Christmas was a time for families to come together, and consequently he made sure that he stayed away. This made the time of the year even more sacred, truly special, and one that filled us with anticipation. There would be no screams, cut lips or broken noses. In my father's absence, my mother exuded all the radiance of the Christmas fairy, setting out decorations and dressing the Christmas tree in such a way that it felt as if we were in the middle of an enchanted world. Even though we'd grown too old to believe in Santa Claus, we'd still write our unrealistic demands of him, then throw the pieces of paper on the fireplace and watch as the sooty flakes floated up the chimney and out into the ether. My father's non-appearance over the Christmas period was probably the best gift of all, as it was the one time of the year we could feel truly safe together.

Over the last few years I'd been taking part in the Midnight Mass church service, my favourite event of the whole season. The proceedings would begin on the stroke of midnight in front of a huge congregation and the whole church would be illuminated by hundreds of candles that cast dancing shadows high up on the arches and stained-glass windows as we sang carols. It was the only aspect of Christianity that I could really accept. Although I had abandoned all faith in the notion of God, especially one so invisible and ineffective, I still couldn't deny the strong inner feeling that this amazing person, Jesus, really had existed and had tried to teach us about ourselves, but we were too ignorant and greedy to listen properly. So, with that in mind, and combined with the rare peace at home, I'd abandon myself to the festivities, and all the dark thoughts with which I was normally consumed seemed to leave me alone for a while.

Every Christmas Eve I'd arrive home from Midnight Mass in the early hours, after being ferried home by Mr Turner in his camper van, affectionately known as 'The Turner-Mobile'. My mother and I would sit talking for a while until it was time to grab a few hours' sleep for the big day that lay ahead. Where my father went or what he was doing didn't concern any of us – the fact that we knew he wasn't going to be around was all that mattered.

That particular Christmas I came home in a great mood, as usual, still with the peal of bells and descants ringing in my ears, and looking forward to spending time with my mother. But when she opened the front door, I knew it had all gone wrong. Her face was red and swollen, stained with tears, and she could barely meet my gaze. I heard my father scream out something from the front room and it felt as if my whole world came crashing down around me. This wasn't meant to happen. Christmas was for us – it didn't involve him at all.

My mother led me inside and whispered that I must run up to bed quickly. I stayed where I was, an immense anger building inside me, alongside an acceptance that I'd take whatever was coming to me as long as I could stop him from laying another finger on her. My father shouted out again, this time telling me to get into the front room. I felt the joy of Christmas vanish into the menacing atmosphere; now it was a night like any other for me and my mother, only this time was worse than anything I could remember.

I was pushed on to the sofa and told to watch everything – if I closed my eyes my father told me he'd kill me. I couldn't even understand what he was screaming at my mother, but it didn't matter; there were never any valid reasons or triggers, other than alcohol, that brought on one of his fits.

He grabbed my mother by the hair and threw her across the room. As she fell dangerously close to the French windows, he took hold of her again and started to punch her about the body. I couldn't take it any more and yelled at him to stop hurting her. His rage intensified, and a volley of punches rained down on me, but all I was aware of was my mother begging and pleading with him to leave me alone.

Eventually, he seized me by the throat, pushed me out of the front room and told me to fuck off to bed. I did as I was told, but I couldn't even attempt sleep: the beating downstairs continued for my mother and the only way I could blot any of it out was to focus my mind on how I was going to get rid of him, once and for all, and what I could do to make it as painful as possible for him. Those desperate thoughts carried me into a short spell of disturbed sleep until I was woken up by Iain and Anthony excitedly shouting 'Happy Christmas!'

Of course there was nothing happy about Christmas 1979. My mother did her best to pretend that everything was fine – despite her swollen face and cut eye – and she kissed and hugged us as usual, but every time our eyes met we communicated the knowledge that it had all fallen apart and that nothing could ever be the same again.

My father sat defiantly in his chair as if to say, 'I fooled you!' And as I clutched the Tonka toy my mother had bought me, I imagined the delicious sight of that metal truck being rammed into his face – it would be worth the repercussions just to cause him some pain. But, as ever, lacking my own inner mettle, all I did was to make sure that we all played with our new toys upstairs and out of his sight, in case he sprang into one of his unprovoked rages.

My father had spray-painted a huge black smear over our Christmas. He stuck fast to that chair like a scowling limpet on the day itself and remained there throughout Boxing Day as well, even though I was sure the pubs would have been open by then.

As if ruining the whole of Christmas wasn't quite enough to make his evil mark, on New Year's Day he celebrated by punching my mother repeatedly in the ear. The damage was so bad that she had no choice but to visit the doctor, a cheerful Irishman, who up until that point had merely sighed at my mother's lame excuses regarding the source of her injuries. On this occasion, however, he knew she had been beaten and also who had done it. He kept his other patients waiting and wouldn't let my mother leave until she'd told him what had happened. After she'd explained a little of what was going on, he took her by the hand and told her she had to get away from her husband as quickly as she could. In his opinion, my father was pathologically violent – she was in great danger and needed to take herself and her boys to a police station immediately and get help.

If it had been that simple, my mother would have taken such steps a long time ago; but it wasn't. The law at that time effectively protected the abuser, and anyone who had been abused back then would rarely have been in the correct mental or emotional state to contemplate the challenges and pressures of what was needed to launch a prosecution. The fact that my mother had been reminded regularly for years that if she ever left the family home she and her boys would be found and killed was enough to convince her that she could never contact the police.

At this stage my mother's mental state was close to breaking point and she didn't even know it. I'd find her crying in the kitchen, even though my father was nowhere to be seen, and knew that her spirit was slowly being crushed. She always looked so tired, pale and drawn, and her smiles seemed to be drying up, even though she would always try forcing one. In reality she was in the middle of acute depression and although I didn't know that at the time, I knew we were somehow losing her. Sometimes I'd come home to find her staring into space, unaware that I'd even entered the room.

In my young mind I blamed the ruined Christmas for what was happening to her and not the accumulation of mental violence, which was every bit as bad as the physical abuse she had suffered for so long; bruises and broken bones heal quickly, but the scars caused by mental abuse can take a lifetime to disappear.

With what happened several weeks later, all the Decembers that followed would flick a switch inside me. I'd feel as if I were sinking into a pit that I couldn't climb out of, as if the month itself were somehow responsible for everything and had to be circumvented by any means possible.

# 11 | *Crossing the Line*

B Y THE TIME I was twelve years old, it was clear that two runaway trains were set on a devastating collision course.

My father's was completely out of control: it rushed about madly in all directions; other people were like leaves on the line that he ploughed through without a thought. If he appeared to be on a downhill stretch and seemingly unstoppable, it was perhaps because we hadn't thought, or rather, hadn't had the courage, to put anything in his way.

Unaware of the power of intention, I had set my own small train in motion as well. Even though there was a fog in front of mine and my course was the more directionless of the two, with a mere child at the controls, there was no stopping me either.

Although my father appeared to be in total charge of his world and passengers, he had sorely underestimated what was going on around him. If he had only glanced round to take stock of his crazy ride and looked out of the window at the track ahead, he'd have seen me there, coming to head him off at the junction with terrifying intent.

★ ★ ★

March 1980. It was cold outside on the night that would change our lives for ever. I only remember this detail because I would later find myself outside in that freezing night air, breathing in the bitter chill of a nightmare and remaining trapped there for many years to come.

The night that Iain and I found ourselves in the midst of our father's late-night theatre of kicks and punches was initially like all the rest. We were dragged out of bed at about two o'clock in the morning, and told to stand in the corner of the room and to watch and learn. I made the mistake of averting my eyes from the scene unfolding in front of me, until a punch to the side of my head reminded me of the rules.

We both stood powerless and in a mutual state of shock as we were ordered to look at the 'useless cunt' who sat sobbing on the sofa in front of us – our mother. Through her tears she begged him, as she always did, to let us go to bed. Normally he would scream abuse at her for daring to tell him what to do, and more violence would often follow, but sometimes it could encourage him to calm down a little, after he'd punished her insolence. It was almost as if a tiny voice of reason, from the depths of his psyche, confused and shook him momentarily into an act of mercy.

This time, though, the distant voice of reason either wasn't heard, or my father was too far gone to acknowledge it. I'd seen and heard my mother being beaten more times than I could remember, but the ferocity I witnessed that night shocked me into believing that it could only be a bad dream. He began his mindless assault by screaming at her that she was a 'fucking whore murderer', before turning to Iain and me and telling us that she'd strangled our half-sister shortly after she'd been born. At this, my mother's sobs intensified and although I thought I was ready for his likely response to this interruption, nothing could prepare any of us for the explosive reaction that followed.

He grabbed her by the hair and threw her to the floor, raining punch after punch on her face and body, his ferocious boxer's arms moving with such speed and rage that I knew she wouldn't be able to survive much more of this. Then, as she curled up into a ball, desperately trying to protect her head, he switched to kicking her body repeatedly, until I knew that she would be beaten to death right in front of us.

I heard my voice scream out, 'Stop it!' and then it was my turn. I have no idea what he did to me, because I felt so numb from what I'd witnessed him do to my mother, and still the feeling persisted that it was all an awful dream.

The next thing I knew, my father had gone. He had done his work and disappeared upstairs to bed; the stench of whisky that still clung to the air and our mother's small sobs were the only reminders of the brutality he'd inflicted minutes previously.

I looked over at Iain, who was almost frozen where he stood. It seemed as if two wires were protruding from his body and someone was sticking the ends into the mains socket every few seconds. I had never seen him cry before, but tears streamed down his face as he jerked spasmodically at the unseen currents shocking his fragile frame. The perturbing sight merely added to the unreality of the situation.

I helped my mother to the sofa and stroked her hair, trying to discover what damage he'd done to her face, but also terrified at what I'd see hidden behind the long black hair that obscured her injuries. She wouldn't look at either of us and kept her face shielded as she softly wept.

I told Iain to go upstairs to bed, but he remained standing there, unable to move and powerless to stop the flow of tears that rolled down his face. A dam had been broken inside him and he didn't know how to deal with it. 'Go to bed, Iain,' I repeated. 'I'll be up soon.'

Through his tears he asked my mother whether she was all right. She calmed him a little by mustering her strongest voice and told him she would be okay and that he should go to bed. He didn't move immediately, and stood there for a while longer, not quite ready to believe her, yet reassured by the fact that she could still speak. Then, when he felt ready to move, he reluctantly left us to go upstairs.

Surely it was all just a dream? The three of us had been frozen, and reality had slowed down to give the impression that time no longer existed. We all knew exactly what had just taken place, but none of us could imagine what would happen next. We all knew that something would, though; it was in the air, thick and definite.

Alone, just the two of us, I realized that I was indeed awake when I eventually persuaded my mother to look at me. Her lip protruded, red and swollen, in a way I hadn't seen for a long time; her right eye was inflamed and disfigured, and a thin stream of blood ran from her nose, which she tried to stem with a tissue. But it wasn't her horrific injuries that finally snapped the unseen, stretched and heaving chord inside me: it was the look in her eyes.

I had never seen real despair before, and have only ever seen it since in the eyes of famine victims or people trapped in war zones, cradling dead children and relatives. It's the look of complete and utter resignation to the awful fact that all hope is gone. Her eyes, those loving and gentle brown eyes that normally sparkled and beamed out laser lights of love no matter how terrible things were, told me that everything was lost, that there was no way out and no one to help us.

And then it happened, just as I knew – and possibly hoped – it always would. Inside, I felt a blast detonate. It wasn't metaphorical or subtle; it exploded inside me to the extent that I thought I was having a fit or a heart attack.

The last remaining threads that had kept me chained to the belief that I was powerless to do anything finally snapped. It felt as if an old and useless skin had been cast off suddenly. The room became brighter, an unknown strength and knowledge filled me, and as I continued staring at my mother, trying to understand what was happening, I heard a man's voice, loud and clear, from the distant past: 'Take this, son, and go hit your mother in the head.' I saw my father handing a small child the hammer that he wanted me to use on my mother, but when I saw myself holding the implement, I realized that it wasn't a hammer at all; it was something quite different.

I'd spent so long forming my internal pleas for help about how to stop my father, yet the answer had been there all the time. I simply hadn't realized it until I revisited that bitter childhood memory and had the vision of gripping an entirely different tool. Up until this point, my whole life had been one perplexing jigsaw puzzle, missing all the crucial pieces. But now I'd found what I'd been searching for. It had been there in front of me all along and had only been waiting for the right moment to be discovered.

I held on to my mother and told her not to worry, assuring her that everything was going to be fine and that she had to listen very carefully to what I was about to say. I could tell from her expression that she sensed something had shifted inside me, and if she was shocked as I revealed my intentions, she didn't show it.

'I'm going to go upstairs and kill him. You'll have to phone the police, but wait until I've come back down. You'll tell them what he did to you and that you didn't see I'd left the front room. The next thing you knew was that I was back down here, not saying a word. I'm going to tell them I don't remember a thing about what I did, and that I only recall seeing him dead in front of me.'

My mother stared back at me, knowing that nothing could stop me, but also struggling with the reality that her choirboy son, who had never hurt anything in all his life, was intending to murder his own father. I read her thoughts as clearly as my own. I saw a glimmer of resistance and quashed it.

'If I don't do it, he's going to kill you – and you know he

will. With all the police records on him and your hospital records, there's no way I'll end up in prison. Everyone will see what a lunatic he was. Perhaps I'll be sent away to a loony bin for a while, but we both know there's nothing wrong with me. I'll make a quick recovery . . .'

I tried to smile, to let her know that everything really was going to be okay. I could tell she wasn't convinced, but we both knew that she had no say in the matter and that my sudden departure from the innocent world of a child to the reality of being an adult and killer was running its own course. Even if I'd wanted to, I couldn't have stopped the events that were now in motion. The real truth was that I'd waited a lifetime for this moment to arrive and nothing on earth could have distracted me from my quest. I wanted it too much and the thought of ending his life filled me with nothing but satisfaction; even a sense of completion.

I went into the kitchen passageway and opened the door to the small storeroom to find what I was looking for. I pulled apart old boxes and pieces of junk, searching desperately, with my heart racing faster and faster at the thought that it was lost or had been thrown away. I scattered a pile of newspapers wildly across the floor, a rising panic starting to build at the notion that my plan had been thwarted.

Then, suddenly, there it was, waiting for me in the darkness, ready to be used for its true purpose, and not to bury any more pairs of bloodied boots in the front garden. I picked it up and held it, feeling its weight, before running my finger along the sharp edge of the blade.

What we had always called an axe was, in fact, a strange hybrid of axe and machete. It was about a foot and a half long, and fashioned from black steel. The wooden handle had vanished or been broken off many years previously, and all that was left on the handle was a spike, which made it difficult to hold and was the reason it was hardly ever used. It was quite useless for chopping wood, but perfect for something else.

I stared at it for a moment and followed the line of the blade. There were small pit marks and a chip along its edge where it had been misused, but the only thing I was interested in was the strong outward curve where the thick outside edge met the blade, which formed a menacing and sharp point. I needed two hands to grip it properly, as the spike was no longer than four inches, but it was definitely wieldable, and I knew that, provided I held my nerve, it would definitely finish him off once and for all.

I made my way to the foot of the stairs and glanced into the front room. My mother was sitting in a state of shock, staring at the wall. I closed the door and quietly made my way upstairs, a curious burning sensation filling every part of me as I contemplated killing the bastard who always managed to sleep so soundly after even the most violent of attacks. I clutched the axe tightly in one hand, knowing that I couldn't afford to make any mistakes – even the smallest error could result in the deaths of my entire family if he survived.

I didn't bother to open my parents' bedroom door with any stealth; if he woke up I'd be on him before he even knew what had hit him. But nothing could have roused my father that night. He hadn't bothered to draw the curtains and I could see him lying in bed, dead to the world and snoring low grunts into the pillow. The fact that he could sleep like a baby after inflicting all that damage on my defenceless mother made me hate him even more. Nothing went through my mind beyond that. I'd come to do a job and no more.

Clutching the axe with both hands now, I raised it high above my head, paused for a moment to check my grip and brought it down as hard as I could.

At the precise moment of impact, another explosion tore through me. A split second after the dull and sickening crack of the black steel hitting skin and skull, a low and terrible groan escaped from his lips, and through the half-light of the open curtains, his eyes opened wide, bleached white and larger than

I'd ever seen before. I struggled to pull the axe back up, even though it wasn't embedded in my father's skull, but instead had bounced back in a recoil action. My hands were suddenly soaked in sweat and the weapon slipped from my grip as I staggered back. Somehow I managed to keep hold of it, but not myself.

The whole world seemed to be collapsing around me, spinning wildly and out of control. Everything started to go black and the next thing I knew I had reeled backwards out of the bedroom, all my former strength and sense of purpose retreating rapidly and being replaced by confusion and stark fear.

As I fell out of the bedroom and on to the landing, somehow still clutching the axe in one hand, the floor and ceiling seemed to swap places, and I had no idea if I was up or down. Then the terror hit me, full force. The reality of what I'd done smashed me into a thousand little pieces of individual screams and before I knew what was happening, I found myself rushing down the stairs.

The stairs.

At this point I feel everything going into extreme slow motion.

I bolt down those stairs as fast as my legs can manage, but the air is thick with glue and invisible restraints that won't let me escape. This can't be happening, I think to myself. I know I'm awake, but the shocking circumstances suggest otherwise.

I am in the middle of my recurring nightmare, but I know that this time the sequence of events is real.

A wall inside my mind comes crashing down as the realization dawns and the horror is released. I'm sure that I'm rushing at breakneck speed down those familiar stairs, but every step takes a lifetime and each breath promises to be my last.

I see my mother slowly, so very slowly, turn the corner from the front room along the hallway to the bottom of the stairs. Her arms open to catch me, to stop me from flying into the pane of glass, just as she has done so many times before, but I know that this time I will never reach her – she's too far away and time has ground to a near halt. I am meant to be trapped here, it seems; imprisoned for ever in my nightmare.

I think I am screaming, but I can't hear anything, and I know that if my mother doesn't reach me soon, I will die. But then she is there, arms around me, holding me tightly and stroking my head, just as she has always done when the dream was just a dream.

A terrible and low groan comes from high above us and we both turn to look. My father stands at the top of the stairs – but it's not my father. It's a monster with a bone-white face streaked in thick lines of blood that gush from somewhere in his head, and it's groaning about being shot.

As my few remaining walls start crumbling away, I remember the recurring nightmare in all its glory at last, and everything falls into place – but the solved mystery only sends me even further over the edge.

A curtain parts somewhere far away in a distant corner of my memory. I see my father, bathed in a sickly orange glow, his head split in two, blood coursing down his ghostly face, and he's crying out to me as I run into blackness: 'Why did you murder me, son? Why did you murder me?'

The next thing I remember, I was spread out on the front lawn, pushing my face into the sweet-smelling grass and trying to suck the dew from the small blades pressing against my cheek. My left hand rested on the cool metal of the drain cover where, not too long ago, I had helped my father to bury his blood-soaked boots using the same axe I'd just brought down on his head.

I felt strong arms wrap themselves round me and half-carry me inside the house. I struggled to break free – it was the last place I wanted to be. But a soothing, persuasive, familiar voice called my name over and over again, until I realized that it was my mother who was leading me into the front room.

I sat there, shivering, as she held me by the shoulders and I felt her strength course into me. It took me a while to understand exactly what she was saying as I was still in shock, but she kept at me until I partially came to my senses.

When I did, the first thing I tried to do was to run out of the front room, but she caught hold of me and told me to breathe deeply and relax. Sitting me back down she explained that my father was back in bed and he was still alive. She'd called an ambulance and told me to listen carefully.

Our roles were reversed once again. Only minutes earlier I had felt as though I were the adult and she the child, but now we were back in more familiar roles, and I took a great deal of comfort from that knowledge. She seemed stronger and more sure of herself, and made it seem possible that we could get through this ordeal. As she spoke, telling me what we were going to do next and what we would say had happened, I could see all her inner strength come rushing to our aid.

Again and again, she repeated the same mantra: say nothing to anyone about the evening's event. When I blurted out that he'd come after us all and kill us, she calmed me down and said he didn't have a clue what had happened to him and never would. Though I believed her faithful assurances, the fear that he'd remember the next day was a thought that wouldn't go away. I could picture him coming at me with the axe, saying, 'Okay, son, now it's my turn . . .'

Then I remembered the axe – where was it? I had no idea where I'd dropped it and if it was in the front garden, where I'd fallen, it would be discovered. To my relief, my mother told me she'd taken it from me as I'd crashed down the stairs and had hidden it in the coal bin in the back garden.

Iain and Anthony, aroused from their slumbers by my father crying out that he'd been shot, kept calling out from upstairs, so my mother shouted up to them to stay in their room until she'd made certain I was all right.

The ambulance came and took my father away while my mother stayed at home with her three frightened sons. Amazingly, I slept after they'd gone. There were no bad dreams, no ghosts, nor even any regrets over my actions; my conscience seemed strangely untroubled.

A few hours later, my mother woke me to tell me to get dressed – the police were downstairs and they wanted to talk to me. It took me a few seconds to work out why they were here, until the events of the night came back into ugly focus.

Downstairs, seated at the table in the front room, were two men in suits and not the uniformed policemen I'd expected to find waiting. As an avid fan of television cop shows, I knew that plain-clothed police only dealt with serious stuff and I felt my legs wobble as I approached them. I sat down and was asked what I remembered about the night before. I tried to recall our story, but feeling pressured by their scrutinizing gaze, I faltered and stammered out a confused version of events.

The story I was supposed to tell was that we'd all been fast asleep when we had woken to hear my father shouting out from the bottom of the stairs that he'd fallen over and hit his head outside on the gatepost. My mother had led him upstairs to lie down and had called an ambulance – and that was all that I knew.

What I didn't anticipate was having to go through my account again, but this time from a different angle: what had happened while we were waiting for the ambulance? I was clearly the world's worst liar. I knew it and they knew it, and suddenly I was rambling. Without knowing quite what I was saying, I'd told them that I saw my father covered in blood at the top of the stairs – but from the perspective of being downstairs.

They looked at each other briefly and one of them carried

on scribbling into his little book. The one who'd been doing most of the talking said, 'But, Andrew, you told us that you were upstairs in bed when your father came home . . .'

I froze. They knew. I didn't dare to look at my mother for help; I'd failed her – yet again. I'd been found out and now I'd be sent to a home, my father would return to the house knowing what had actually happened and life really wouldn't be worth living any more. I stammered, 'But . . . but . . .'

There was a brief silence. Both detectives looked at each other and then at my mother – her eye blackened, her whole face swollen and covered in bruises. Without meeting their gaze she mumbled that I must be confused and in shock.

The detective who'd been doing all the writing put down his pen and closed his book. Looking at me, he said gently, 'Don't worry about anything. Everything's going to be okay. I think we've got all we need.'

As they both got up to leave, the questioning officer placed a hand on my back, softly patted it and told me to look after my mother. They never called again.

It was undoubtedly obvious that no gatepost could have caused my father's injury: there was no blood on the gatepost itself; there were spatters of blood decorating the bedsheets, which suggested that the injury had taken place in the bedroom; and I had 'guilty' written all over my face, but my mother had 'victim' emblazoned across hers. Despite our great fear that my father would call to mind what had really happened, my mother was proved right – as with all his heavily drunk moments, he could remember nothing.

I am in eternal debt to those two policemen and their instant understanding of the situation. Even if they didn't know the exact details, they didn't need to. All they knew was that here was a beaten woman and a frightened child, and the man responsible – with a long criminal record for theft and violence – was lying in hospital with head injuries, and unable to remember a thing. Perhaps they felt that a certain justice had been served that they wouldn't have been able to deliver themselves.

After they'd left us to consider alternative endings to the night's horrors, we sat there in silence for a long while until she opened her mouth to utter the words that would ring inside me like a noisy tolling bell for many years after: 'Never tell *anyone* what really happened.'

I swore to her that I wouldn't and with that promise, I locked the door tightly shut on that night, hardly daring to believe that any of it had been real.

# 12 | *Watershed*

S EVERAL YEARS LATER, my mother filled in the gaps of what had happened in the anxious days after that night, for the trauma I suffered had rendered my memory completely useless. I could barely remember anything. In the hours after the attack, a huge door began to close slowly on me, shutting out the world and the next six months of my life.

Any memories during this time fell down a big black hole; my mind shut down to attempt recovery from that night and the waking nightmare of running down stairs of treacle, my father's red-and-white face at the top of the stairs calling out that he'd been shot, and the vision of his reflection within my splintered mind, pleading and crying out to me that I had murdered him.

I had vague recollections of my mother urging me to visit him in hospital to avoid suspicion; a flash of seeing him on a ward, wired up to tubes and bandaged up; a ride in a taxi with my family and staying with another family; a hazy memory of a visit to my grandparents' house; the sea crashing on to a beach of pebbles . . . All of these fragments seem like wisps from a dream that I only know happened because my mother told me so.

My father had been extremely lucky to survive. Were it not for the lack of a handle on the axe, his skull would have been penetrated completely, instead of sustaining a mere fracture. The angle of descent, as I swung the point downwards on to his head, meant that it had slipped slightly from my grip, and only the dull blade had met its target with nowhere near the amount of force I'd put into the swing. He'd sustained bad head injuries, but the skull fracture was only a minor one.

While he recovered in hospital, my mother served divorce papers on him and fled to safety, taking us to a friend's house where he wouldn't be able to find us. After contacting a good solicitor, an injunction was served and he was barred from entering the family home. We returned to the house two months later and were advised that if we caught even a glimpse of him we had to run to the nearest house and ask someone to call the police. For a long time my mother lived in genuine fear for her life, not knowing whether my father, or one of his associates, would visit us when we were least expecting it and carry out my father's repeated promise of murdering us all.

Not long after our return, he was spotted coming back on to the estate, and a friend ran up to our door to warn us. My mother told me to hide all the knives, but I remember nothing of this day, least of all him forcing his way into the house and coming after my mother with a meat fork. We fled from our home, apparently, then the police arrived quickly and picked him up before he could cause any serious trouble.

On one frightening occasion after my father had left us – though I have no idea exactly when – I recall seeing him in the shopping precinct at Woodley. At the sight of him I began running as fast as I could, and as I ran away, I heard his desperate pleas for me to come back – the tone of his voice conveying hurt and disbelief that his own son could be so afraid of him. I don't know where I was headed, but I remember being lost somewhere outside Woodley in a place I'd never visited before. In truth I never really stopped running until I reached the winter of that same year, six months later.

As I emerged from my cocoon of self-preservation, the first clear images I can remember were of my mother and her friend Tracey getting ready to go out to a disco. I recall Tracey telling a lot of rude sex jokes and it must have been during this saucy routine that I heard my mother laugh. I couldn't remember the last time she'd been capable of such a response, and I looked in amazement as tears of laughter ran down her face. I was so concerned and confused that I even asked whether she was okay, but she took me in her arms, hugged me and told me she'd never felt better.

The sight and sound of that laugh must have awoken me from my hiatus. From that point my memories become clear again, and I remember those days as being among the happiest we'd ever had. Not only had my father gone from our lives, but it also seemed he had decided not to fulfil his murderous promise — though we all remained on our guard out of habit.

My mother was changing into someone I hardly recognized, and it was a metamorphosis that I loved to watch develop. She was like a prisoner who'd been released after a fifteen-year jail sentence, and who had the freedom to do anything she wanted. Revisiting her lost youth, she looked, sounded and acted younger — sometimes quite embarrassingly so — and she exuded a natural energy that made those days seem electric. My brothers and I drank it all up — sometimes literally.

She'd throw parties where hip young things from her factory job would parade around in tight white trousers and sparkly tops and dance to dreadful disco music. Her sloshed friends would 'ooh' and 'ahh' at the three sweetly behaved children who were allowed to stay up until ten o'clock on party nights. Sexy women in low-cut tops would gurgle about how cute we were, kiss our cheeks and tell our glowing mother how lucky she was to have such darling boys. Iain and I would then compare notes to see who had managed to look the furthest down their fronts. Even the guys at the parties seemed okay and were friendly with us, though they sometimes reeked of the dreaded whisky. As soon as they'd got too sloshed to notice, we'd swipe their drinks, and by the time we'd all stumble up to bed at ten, we'd be half-cut on Bacardis and Cinzanos.

It was fantastic.

The sense of freedom we had during those times was like being on a cloud from which you never wanted to come down. Sometimes I'd make my way home from school and the old, conditioned reflex of feeling the pit of my stomach tighten and cramp would hit me, but then I'd realize that there was nothing to worry about any more – *he* really was gone. I'd jump and give huge whoops of delight as I danced home. Neighbours and passers-by might have thought I was a bit soft, but I was happier than anyone could even begin to understand and didn't care what I must have looked like.

My mother's liberation took many forms, most of them positive, but the one thing that caused me most distress were her jeans. With every month that passed, they seemed to be getting tighter and tighter. I was amazed she could even put them on, never mind walk in them.

At one parent-and-pupil evening at school, my mother showed up wearing the tightest pair of jeans I'd ever seen, sporting two patches sewn on to the rear pocket. To my horror, I noticed that one of them featured an outstretched middle finger.

'Mum, you can't go in there with that on your bum!' I complained. I pictured the faces of my sweet, conservative teachers and friends' parents as they got an eyeful of my mother's rear end and groaned to myself. She laughed out loud, hugged me, and told me not to be so uptight. We went into the school hall where all the other parents, teachers and kids were milling around and I looked for some seats, hoping that if I kept her in a sitting position for the rest of the evening, I could conceal her rude behind. But before I could find any chairs, she had made a beeline for Mr 'The Dish' Pritchard. They both stood uncomfortably close to each other and seemed to laugh far too loudly at each other's jokes. I tried to find somewhere to hide, but instead got cornered by my music teacher, Mr Gorman.

I really liked Mr Gorman. He had huge, black curly hair, got me involved in everything musical at school, and put up with my antics with exasperated resignation. He chatted away to me about the upcoming school play and then asked me where my mother was. I lied that I had no idea. 'Ah no, look,' he said, scanning the room. 'There she is, with Mr Pritchard.' I prayed he wasn't looking at her arse.

My mother's obscene jeans patches to one side, the change in her was extraordinary and we did everything we could to encourage her – though we all agreed that hitting on teachers was definitely out of bounds.

For years, we'd had a Sunday treat of a bus journey to Reading, using the little money that my mother had saved up all week, rounded off with a trip to the Wimpy. They were special times for all of us and they continued even after the divorce. Sometimes she would allow herself the freedom to go out on a Saturday night with her friend Tracey, but as money was often quite tight, she couldn't always afford it. On one such occasion Tracey begged her to come out for a dance, but my mother was adamant she didn't have enough money, and didn't want anyone paying for her all night, even though Tracey had offered. So, it was down to Iain and me to convince her to use our Sunday money instead, to give her a break and let her have some fun. Eventually, after much persuading, she agreed, which left me and my brothers very proud of ourselves – not only had we given her a night out, but it meant we had the whole house to ourselves and could stay up late. A few burgers were worth sacrificing for that sort of fun.

As Christmas approached, along with the memory of last year's disastrous holiday season, for the first time I noticed how dangerous this time of year could be. All it seemed to involve was excessive spending, which put unnecessary pressure on people with little money to buy presents they couldn't afford, and resulted in a ridiculous amount of debt.

Our mother knew that all we had ever really wanted were bikes, but we never seriously expected her to be able to afford such costly items. Instead we were always content with smaller, more affordable gifts, which still put a large dent in her savings.

I later found out that she'd secretly started saving in January for the Christmas ahead and that little items she might normally have bought for herself throughout the year were sacrificed to help pay for our special Christmas gifts. If I'd known of her intentions I'd have intervened and told her not to worry. As far as I was concerned the greatest present she could ever give us was her own happiness.

This year she'd over-reached herself. Two heavy bills arrived simultaneously, requiring prompt payment, but she'd already spent all her money on our presents. Three days before Christmas I found her in tears in the kitchen and asked her what was wrong. She eventually explained that she didn't have any money for the Christmas food and looked at me as though she'd let us all down. An idea shot through my mind and I beamed at her not to worry. Everything would be fine.

I found Iain and Anthony and told them my idea – they loved it. That night all three of us walked the few miles to Sonning-on-Thames, knocking at every posh door we passed and singing Christmas carols. Of course, we weren't any ordinary little urchins, belting out half-remembered discordant hymns; both Iain and Anthony had incredible voices, and while they sang the main melodies, I hit the descants that capped off the final verses. Amazed residents would answer their doors and just stand there, smiling, not saying a word until we'd finished. Some of them even asked us to sing another.

As we approached one large house, Anthony opened the gate to start walking up the drive, but Iain and I stood our ground. I explained to Anthony that this was the house our mother had used to clean every day, where she was treated like the dirt she was expected to remove. They could keep their money.

We didn't count all the coins and notes we'd collected until we got home. We told our mother to close her eyes and when she opened them, she sat there staring at the large pile of cash in front of her. For a moment she didn't look happy. 'Where did you get this money?' she asked, in a small voice that made us wonder if we'd made a huge mistake.

I explained that we'd spent nearly three hours singing and walking miles around Sonning, and that everyone had been so happy to give us a donation. For a moment we were afraid that she was going to tell us to go out and return the money. Then she smiled, burst into tears and threw her arms around all three of us as we whooped in delight. She knew there was a time and a place for pride and this wasn't it – we'd worked so hard for that money and not a single penny of it was charity. It was simply fair payment for listening to three beautiful voices, and for being reminded of the true meaning of Christmas, which was often overlooked in modern times.

We had earned over £50 from that night, which to us was a small fortune. My mother kept saying, 'I can't believe it,' over and over again. Only one shop in Woodley stayed open on Christmas Eve, but it was stocked with enough goodies to buy everything we needed to make our Christmas a great one, and the last one I remember with any real sense of joy.

On Christmas morning we all got up and went downstairs to open our presents that were usually left under the tree. This year, however, there was nothing there. We looked to our mother, who returned our gazes sadly, and said, 'Sorry.' We tried our best not to appear too disheartened, but I remember thinking that she could have at least bought us a cheap gift each, and wrapped them up, just to give us something to open.

Then, as casually as she could, she asked us to fetch some coal from the back garden. She was the world's worst at trying to fool us, so we raced through the kitchen and as we hit the storeroom the sight that greeted us was unbelievable: three brand new bikes – and each one the exact model we'd wanted. During the year she'd dropped enough hints that this Christmas might be the one when we'd get the bikes we wanted, but none of us believed that it would happen because she had too little money to afford such expensive items. Nevertheless, there they were: a metal blue Arena for me, a Chopper for Iain and a Grifter for Anthony. We almost crushed our poor mother with our hugs while she tried to explain that they were next year's Christmas and birthday presents as well, but we didn't care about that – all we were interested in was giving our new toys a test ride and seeing if they would plough through the snow that was falling outside.

After giving her our own small gifts, which mainly consisted of kitsch ornaments of horses and dogs that she pretended to adore, we scrambled out of the house, jumped on our precious bikes and hit the icy racetracks of the estate.

Over the next few years we'd realize our mother's estimations were way off the mark: what she really should have said was that the bikes made up the next *five* years' worth of presents, because that's how long it took her to pay for them.

# 13 | *School Struggles*

THE CLOUD that carried us far and wide in the days after our father's permanent departure was a beautiful one indeed. It disregarded the past and the dark events that had created it, and on we rode, blissfully unaware that nothing lasts for ever. The euphoria of that freedom, which had raised us to great heights, could only last for so long – and the comedown would be harsh.

For almost a year after the night of my father's attack, I hadn't given the incident any conscious thought. I'd completely shut it out and more or less fooled myself into believing it had all been one bad dream; it didn't seem real anyway, particularly as things were so different and happier now. But doors are curious things. You think you've closed them and only you can open them up again, but nothing could be further from the truth. Some of them don't have locks and are apt to blow wide open when you least expect it.

Life at school had been going quite well. Despite my urge to perform in front of classmates, doing impersonations of various teachers and the infamous Frank Spencer, I was faring well in most subjects, especially English. I knew that for my age

I was good with words. I loved them and lost no opportunity in playing with them during creative writing lessons. In fact I would often find myself straying from a specific assignment as my imagination took the story or poem I was writing into a different realm altogether.

My English teacher was a fantastic man called Mr Beer. He always dressed in old-fashioned tweed and looked as if he'd stepped out of an Ealing comedy. I loved him. My impersonation of him crossed Magnus Pike, the dotty scientist, with Quentin Crisp, but it was done with the utmost affection. In fact I even showed him one day, and made him blush and laugh at the same time. During class he'd read out a passage of great literature, or a poem, and would throw his hands up in every direction at moments that excited him. I worked hard in his lessons and silently adored his bad dress sense, floppy hair and wild mannerisms.

Usually I'd spend a hasty fifteen minutes on homework for my other subjects, but for English I'd devote hours to my after-school tasks and be rewarded by a witty comment from Mr Beer, commending my audacity and ideas. I'd always get As, but I didn't really care about the grades – it was only if he didn't make a scrawling remark in my book that I felt I could have done better.

Then, one day, he wasn't there. No explanation for his departure was offered, despite the fact that he was one of the best teachers – if not *the* best – in the whole school and would be sorely missed. I looked with disappointment at the supply teacher who had replaced him; she was a young woman trying far too hard to give the impression of being a wise, experienced educator. When I asked her where he was she replied stiffly that she had no idea, she was merely temporary and that in any case it was none of my concern.

I felt as though I'd lost a friend when Mr Beer left us, and if that wasn't bad enough the next supply teacher who was parachuted into our class made things much worse. Young and inexperienced, she started off well enough and read aloud some William Blake poetry, which was amazingly beautiful and dark. For our homework assignment she asked us to write a poem about the seasons.

I was bowled over by the verses she'd read to us, as the only poetry I'd heard before was too flowery and gushing to interest me at all. So, inspired by the darker elements in Blake's poetry, I wrote into the night about the fires of summer giving way to dying in autumn. I knew I'd produced a good piece of work, but when I read it back to myself I thought it was probably the best thing I'd ever written.

We handed in our books the next day and I looked forward to the next English lesson with relish. When the day finally dawned, she explained that she would hand back everyone's homework books except for those containing the best poems, as they would be read out at the end of class. As my book wasn't returned, I sat in excited anticipation, waiting for my work to be recited. She picked up the last exercise book on her desk, which I naturally assumed was mine, and started to read, but the poem was someone else's. I sat there, confused and crushed; why hadn't she given me my book at the start of the lesson? At least then I'd have known my 'brilliant' piece of poetry was, in fact, simply average.

Then the bell rang and there was a mad scramble for books and pens as everyone got up to leave. She called out my name and asked me to stay behind. Relief washed over me at last. She didn't want to read it out because it was obviously too good; perhaps she was even going to suggest that I enter it into a competition or even get it published? My heart raced wildly at all the possibilities while the classroom emptied, and as I approached her she reached into her bag and pulled out my exercise book. As the door closed on the last pupil to leave, that was her cue to tell me what a little talent I was.

'Who wrote this poem?' she demanded.

At first I thought I'd misheard her.

'Who wrote this poem?' she repeated, accentuating every word as if I was being deliberately stupid.

'I did, Miss,' I replied, confused by her combative manner.

Her face darkened and she opened up my book, read out one of the words I'd used and asked me what it meant. I started to feel uncomfortable, and wondered whether she was stupid or illiterate. I gave her the definition she'd asked for, but still she wasn't satisfied and asked me for the meaning of another word. I complied once again. Her face tightened even more, her eyes squinted at my poem and she read out one of the lines, demanding to know its significance. My patient explanation seemed to make things worse. She became very angry and shouted, 'Do you know what a thief is?'

My legs started to shake. I knew what a thief was all right. I used to be one and had almost forgotten my horrible little habit. I nodded, dumbstruck.

'Good,' she responded. 'Then tell me who wrote this poem?'

I felt tears start to well up, but I fought them back and pleaded with her, '*I* did, Miss – I swear.' She threw my book at me, shouting, 'You evil child! You are a liar and a thief! Who wrote this poem? Tell me now, or I'll send you to the headmaster . . .'

As she screamed out the words 'thief' and 'liar' at me, I suddenly felt I must be both. I even wondered if perhaps I'd stolen the work without even being aware of it. I tried to picture myself copying the poem from a poetry book that I didn't even own, but instead saw myself sitting on my bedroom floor for most of the night, writing and rewriting ideas and images through words.

On and on she shouted accusations at me, her face red with rage. Finally, I'd had enough. Unable and unwilling to defend myself any longer, I grabbed my satchel, fled from the classroom and locked myself in a toilet for the rest of the day until the final bell rang.

I went to school the next day knowing I probably wouldn't be summoned to see the headmaster, even though I was desperate to expose the inadequacies of Mr Beer's pitiful replacement. Not a single line of that poem was plagiarized and I would challenge any teacher in the school to find another poem remotely resembling it.

For the next couple of days I obsessed about how I was going to make her pay for her humiliation of me and resolved to make her life as unbearable as possible. But when we entered the classroom for our English lesson, she wasn't there. Instead, there was another teacher in her place. Her disappearance didn't put an end to my raging anger and desire for retribution though. As a consequence of her maltreatment, I resolved never to put any effort into English again. At the time I didn't appreciate the irony that if she'd set out to screw me over, she'd succeeded with her first and only attempt.

Around the same time I was called to see the visiting hearing specialist, who kept a check on a few kids with hearing problems. She'd plug me into the 'bleep' machine, as I called it, and I'd plonk square blocks on to the table every time I heard it any sound rise above my tinnitus. Though I felt like a bit of an idiot, I enjoyed escaping from lessons for half an hour. After this particular test, she asked me a couple of questions and then folded her arms and squinted at me as though I was a specimen in a jar.

'I was speaking to you in a very quiet voice, but you heard every word,' she said, suspiciously.

I didn't understand what she was getting at, and looked at her dumbly.

'What I mean is that you seem to fail the tests with the machine, but you can hear every quiet word I'm saying. Can you explain that to me?'

I felt rather stupid for a moment until I saw the triumphant expression on her face, and it dawned on me that she was accusing me of faking my ear problems. I couldn't believe it.

Not only had I been doubted by my English teacher, but now it was the turn of the school nurse.

I'd been poked and prodded for most of my life thanks to various hearing problems, and here she was implying that I was making them up? I remained speechless while she declared that I didn't need any more hearing tests because she didn't think there was anything wrong with me.

I left the room in a daze. And again, I had a crazy feeling that perhaps she was right. Maybe I really was imagining it all, but in answer to such a stupid suggestion, my tinnitus reared its head and whined out its objection. By this time, having been told by doctors that there was no cure for the condition and that I'd have to learn to live with it, I'd practised pushing it into the background where it happily whirred without bothering me too much, apart from at night and during times of stress, when it did as it pleased.

I hid in the toilet next to her little room and waited with my ear pressed to the wall. Eventually I heard her door open and her footsteps clacking down the corridor. I left the toilet and slipped into her testing room, my heart pounding wildly but my ears howling their encouragement. My original intention had been to smash up her precious audio-testing apparatus, but after ripping the wires out of the back of the machine I decided to target something more personal, and so I picked up the handbag she'd carelessly left on the desk, tucked it under my arm, and bolted back into the toilet.

Recalling my old habit, I opened up the cistern and emptied the contents of her bag into it, watching spitefully as keys, a small notebook and other assorted items hit the water. I noticed a small purse slowly sinking to the bottom of the tank and fished it out. On opening it, I found some money, and I chewed my lip guiltily. I hadn't stolen anything for a long time, but looking at the cash was too hard to resist. I stuffed it into my pockets, pushed the cistern lid back over the tank and walked out, suddenly not feeling quite so sure about what I'd just done.

Half an hour into my next lesson, the door opened and there stood Mr Hadfield, the headmaster. I knew I was in trouble when he cast me a dark look and raised his eyebrows as if to say, 'Well? What the hell are you doing still sitting there?' I got up amidst the murmurs and stares of curious classmates, knowing full well I wouldn't be able to get away with my earlier actions.

Mr Hadfield didn't say a word to me as we walked to his office. A visit to his inner sanctum was very serious indeed. I'd never been unruly enough to warrant it before, but this time I'd crossed the line and here I was.

'Sit down, lad.' I did as I was told immediately.

'First off, where is it?' he asked.

I didn't even think about feigning innocence. I told him where I'd drowned her bag, then pulled out the money from my pocket.

'Stay here,' he said, and left me stewing in my boiling juices for what seemed like an age. Eventually, he returned to tell me I was a lucky child indeed as the nurse wouldn't be pressing charges.

Strangely, the idea of the police getting involved hadn't even crossed my mind. The only thing that concerned me was finding myself on the wrong side of the one teacher for whom I had the most respect and admiration.

Mr Hadfield looked at me and gave a huge sigh. 'Why did you do it, lad?'

I shrugged. I didn't know why – or at least I couldn't and didn't want to articulate the reasons for my actions.

'Yes, you do know why,' he replied. He wasn't about to be fobbed off and leaned back as if to say we had all the time in the world.

I explained in stammering tones what had happened during the test and swore that I wasn't faking any of my hearing problems. I told him how hard it was to sleep with my tinnitus, and how doctors had even suggested I wore a hearing aid, but I'd refused.

He'd stared at me intently the whole time I was talking, then looked down at the huge diary in front of him and said something I didn't quite catch.

'Sorry, sir?'

Mr Hadfield looked back up at me. 'Son, do you know what lip-reading is?' he asked. 'The reason you understood the nurse even when she was talking quietly was that you could see her mouth. You were lip-reading her words without even being aware of it.'

He was a genius. I was so relieved that he knew I was telling the truth, and almost grinned as the burden of being accused of lying was lifted. It wasn't quite over, though, as there was still the matter of my thieving to sort out. But he didn't seem keen to ask me the obvious questions I'd been expecting: didn't I know the difference between right and wrong; didn't I understand how bad stealing was?

Instead he asked me how things were at home. How was my mother? Was I happy? And then came the cruncher: 'How are things with your dad?'

'Good, sir,' I lied.

'Okay. Do you still see him?' he asked.

Until that point it hadn't occurred to me that anyone at school had known about the divorce; Iain and I had kept it quiet to spare our being the focus of unwanted sympathy and gossip. Besides, even having to mention anything at all about my father was unthinkable.

'No, sir,' I replied, squirming in my seat. Then, all of a sudden, he was no longer my feared and unquestionable headmaster; he was more like a close uncle who was keen to listen and offer thoughtful advice. He started to tell me about his own father and how because his dad was a hard man, it had made him even more determined to be better than him.

He explained how hard life can be when you're under the influence of other people, but that a man is his own man – he can be anyone he wants to be if he truly desires it. I sat transfixed by what he was saying, but much of it whizzed over my head. Then, he leaned right over the desk and said, 'You know what, lad? If you don't want to see your dad, then that's your right and don't let anyone try to force you, okay?'

I nodded, thinking that it was an odd thing to say out of nowhere, and he gave me a wise smile in return. 'You're a good kid, laddie, and all the choices are yours to make – never forget that.'

Those were his last words before he assured me that if ever I wanted to talk about anything, I knew where he was.

When I read of his death a few years ago, I'm not ashamed to say I cried. Although he had no chance of teaching or reaching me fully at the time – I was too far away and on a path I needed to tread – his canny understanding and insight had made a massive impression on me all the same. He had sowed a seed, albeit one that was slow in taking root.

Many years later, when I found myself watering that tree, I thought back to the stocky and intimidating Northerner who'd planted it and recalled the knowing twinkle in his eyes as he told me never to forget that life is nothing but choice. Perhaps he'd imagined I'd forget it the second I left his office, but I hope he had enough faith in me to believe that many years later it would bear fruit.

# 14 | *Unwelcome Reunion*

A WEEK AFTER I'd been advised that if I didn't want to see my dad, then I didn't have to, my father asked to see us. Naturally, my mother wasn't happy about it. She sat me down with my brothers and told us that he was exercising his legal rights to see us once a fortnight. There was little she could do about it, but she hoped that we'd all refuse to see him. Much to my amazement, Iain and Anthony revealed that they wanted to go.

'I'm a bit curious,' Iain said, as we sat in his wigwam in the back garden. 'Don't you miss him even a little bit?'

'Don't be stupid,' I replied, suddenly hating the fact that Iain and me were so alike. 'I hate him.'

Iain didn't say anything after that and neither did I. Normally we could argue all day about a difference of opinion, but on this occasion we knew we were both right. Our father still had a pull on us that, despite all we'd been through, drew us to him. It wasn't just genetics, it was a mixture of intense curiosity, the feeling of a heart-thumping drama and something else I didn't want to even think about.

But I had another reason for steering clear of my father –

one I couldn't share with Iain as we sat in the garden. I was terrified at the thought of him suddenly remembering the moment he opened his eyes to find me standing over him with an axe in my hand. Although I kept telling myself that it was impossible, because he was looking away from me at the time, I still had an irrational fear that he'd seen me from out of the corner of his eyes. Maybe he was choosing his moment to reveal that he knew everything – armed with a hidden carving knife.

In the end, however, I decided to go with Iain and Anthony, telling myself I had to be there to keep an eye on them in case he went crazy. The need to protect my brothers made me feel better about agreeing to see him, because the other reason – the fact that I actually missed him – made no sense whatsoever, and I hated myself for it.

The following Saturday morning, an old Saab pulled up outside the house. To our surprise our father was at the wheel, honking the horn and waving to us as we peered out of the front door. I hadn't even known he could drive, yet here he was with his own set of wheels. I tried not to feel slightly impressed.

My mother stood behind the door, out of sight, and commented that the car was probably stolen. Then she hugged us all and reminded me that at the first sign of trouble, we were to run away and call the police.

We got in the car and our father turned to greet us. I stared back, shocked, not saying anything. He had lost a lot of weight. Despite his smart suit, he looked dreadful and somehow years older. His face seemed more lined than before, and I noticed his lower lip sometimes shook, as if he were cold.

I started to feel a familiar rush to my head and took deep breaths to keep myself together. I hadn't seen him up close since the night of the attack, and looking at him now made me wish I'd stayed at home.

I tried not to let my thoughts run riot as he chatted away

and asked us the kind of questions he'd never bothered with before: how we were getting on at school, how were our friends, and did we miss him? All his efforts to be friendly merely worsened the guilt that was beginning to surge up inside me. I tried my best to concentrate on the car journey and the view outside.

No one had responded to his last question about whether we missed him, but I replied, 'Yes, Dad.' It sounded like a lie and everyone knew it, but deep down it was more truthful than I realized at the time. We fell silent for a while as we all tried to pretend that we were one happy family on a sunny day out.

We drove into Reading town centre and after taking us out for us some burgers, our father asked us what we wanted to do next. We all had different suggestions, including a visit to the cinema or the park, but he decided that the best idea was to haul us into a pub full of his cronies while he got drunk.

For the next two hours he drank cider, trying his best to act like a normal father whose sons loved nothing more than to be surrounded by small-time crooks and alcoholics. Every now and then he would notice my discomfort and ask me, 'What's the matter, son?'

The more he drank, the more his former self began to creep to the surface. A few drinks later and there he was, as large as life, snarling and eyeing us all through angry and bloodshot slits. 'Your mother's a fucking whore, boys,' he slurred angrily. 'She paid someone to try to murder me.'

We all sat there quietly, not knowing what to do or say. All I could think of was that he was on to me; even if he didn't suspect me directly, he was bound to discover my secret eventually, and I'd be dead. He ranted on and on about our mother being a prostitute and how he knew she was involved in trying to have him killed. We all looked at each other as he kept on repeating, 'Fucking dirty whore . . .'

I couldn't take much more of this, so I got up and told my brothers we were all leaving. My father looked dumbstruck, without the faintest clue as to why I'd want to abandon such a great family outing. 'What's the matter, son?' he demanded.

Iain explained that if he carried on calling our mother names, we'd never see him again, but my father told us not to be so stupid and to sit down. I looked at my two brothers for a consensus and we all sat down again reluctantly. Although he tried to think of small talk that didn't involve insulting our mother, he was unable to avoid the subject for long, and so we all sat there in an uncomfortable silence for the next half an hour. Eventually he announced that he had to go and do some 'work', and thrusting a bundle of cash into our hands, he led us to the bus stop to make our way home.

As I grew more confident that my father's memory of the axe incident would not reveal my involvement, we visited him a few times after that. He'd always start off in a positive frame of mind, but it didn't take him long to start on our mother. Each time we'd get up to go, he'd promise to shut up and would then drink so heavily that we couldn't understand a word he was saying. On our fourth meeting, the pattern was the same. Once again he started slurring out his unpleasant accusations and I prepared, as usual, to get up to leave, but Iain decided that it was time to speak out more forcefully.

'Don't you ever call our mother a whore,' he spat out in anger. 'If you ever say anything like that again, I'll never see you again.'

He stood there, much taller than I'd realized, and I braced myself for the inevitable fireworks. Instead, our father mumbled, 'Sorry, son,' and told him to sit down. I was stunned. Iain had always been the steady voice of calm, but here he was, red with anger and facing up to him in a way I'd never dared. I was deeply impressed and full of envy. His surprising outburst got results too, as it was the last time our father referred to our mother in this way. Occasionally he'd gear up for a rant, but when he noted our expressions he'd stop, and swear at the floor or into his drink.

Normally these father-son meetings would involve him thrusting large amounts of cash at us. Though I hated it, I never refused it. As often as I could, I'd convert it all to coins, abandon my brothers to him and spend most of it in the pub fruit machines. I'd played on them before, but never with quite the same feeling of satisfaction and escapism as I did when we were in our father's company. The more the reels rolled round, the more I felt my own inner wheels spin – click, click, click – which helped to block out my thoughts and the world around me.

My obsession with these machines was growing stronger. The spinning reels seemed to exercise a calming influence on my mind as if I was in a state of hypnosis. But what started off as innocent fun was fast developing into a classic addiction; while I played them, I hated them, and when I was away from them all I wanted to do was play them. I didn't do it to make money – no gambling addict ever does. They pretend that making money is the only reason they're doing it, when in fact the sole motivation to win is to have more money with which to carry on gambling. So, even when I hit the jackpot, the cash was always going to end up back inside the machine.

There still seemed much to escape from, despite the ghosts having vanished and the recurring nightmare now just a memory. Although new nightmares had taken their place, they were merely textbook bad dreams that didn't have me jumping out of bed in a blind panic. My insomnia, however, remained. The long nights in my room were spent battling the tinnitus and trying to avoid the gnawing feelings of guilt that were beginning to manifest themselves.

As a result of my father's absence from the family home, he'd lost the demonic persona of his former self, and all I saw now was the shrunken man who seemed so happy to see us every now and again. After a while, I couldn't face seeing him any more and skipped the visits, but even then I'd still feel compelled to meet with him. The money he gave me was feeding the growing inner monster of my fruit-machine addiction. I hated myself even more for taking it and would transfer that loathing to the spinning reels.

As I'd sworn to my mother that I'd never tell another soul about what had really happened that night, I was pretty much stuck with the secret. Even if I hadn't made the promise, there was no one to tell anyway. I had the crazy notion that if I mustered the courage to tell Iain, he'd disown me. I was convinced that if anyone found out what I'd done to my own father, I'd be exposed as the evil creature I knew I truly was.

It took me a long time to partially bury the memory of that night, and I realized that the only way to speed up the process was to avoid my father altogether; I stopped my visits and it seemed to work. But if I thought I'd succeeded in cementing over a dead body where no one would ever find it, what I hadn't appreciated was that weeds can still break through even the most carefully laid concrete.

In my early teens, music was on hand to help push away any unwanted thoughts. I'd spend hours listening to my Beatles cassettes, and dreaming of being on stage with them. My good mate Mark, who was also a Fab Four nut, would clear out his father's garage and we'd mime along to The Beatles, using tennis rackets as guitars. I was John, he was happy to be Paul, and soon another friend joined us to play George. We couldn't find anyone who wanted to be Ringo.

Such was my obsession with The Beatles that the news of John Lennon's death in December 1980 had hit me hard. I'd been collecting my books and bag from my locker at the end of school when a friend rushed up to me and breathlessly informed me that my musical hero was dead. At first I thought he was playing a sick joke, so I rushed home and switched on the television, still holding on to my disbelief. But within moments of watching the scenes from New York and the photo of Lennon's murderer intermittently flashing across the screen, I knew that something had changed for ever.

I had never given much thought to the outside world before, because life had always been difficult enough in my own little shell – I didn't need further complications or confirmation that life was cruel and that other people made it so. Now, though, I realized for the first time that the sickness we had lived with in the shape of my father was endemic and not just confined to our four small walls. It was a tough truth to accept, and as I watched the chaos in New York that afternoon, all my childish notions about there being a better world outside vanished.

Back on the domestic front, school plays had replaced the choir as the outlet for my musical urges. I'd decided to quit the choir after realizing that even the beautiful sounds we conjured up could no longer distract me from the growing cynicism I felt for the church and all those who were part of it.

The vicar's sermons sometimes dealt with issues that made me feel as though he were addressing me directly from the pulpit. I'd find myself sinking into the choir stalls as he softly reminded us the importance of leading good lives of non-violence and honesty. I grew increasingly uncomfortable and it became even harder to look him in the eye after one of these uncannily personalized speeches.

My body language must have been all too obvious, as one day the choirmaster asked me if I was happy there. 'No, not really,' I replied.

He looked sadly at me and said, 'You don't have to do anything you don't want to do.'

And so I opted to leave, and to devote my musical energies elsewhere.

During my last school play, *Smike*, I became good friends with two girls in the year above me. Maria and Sarah dealt with my precocity and prima donna antics as effortlessly as swatting a fly. When I once walked out of a school rehearsal because the music teacher had shouted at me, they ran after me and laughingly told me what a little sod I was, before mercilessly imitating the way I'd stormed out. They had me back at the rehearsal within minutes, much quieter and humbler than I'd been earlier. After that, they couldn't get rid of me – I fell in love with them both instantly.

Sarah was a great character who'd tease and impersonate me endlessly and Maria was . . . beautiful, in every way possible. She was the prettiest girl I'd ever seen with a short bob of thick dark hair, a light sprinkle of freckles and the most incredible brown eyes. I thought I could live in those eyes if she'd only let me, but I knew deep down she wouldn't. I was too young for her and she was far too beautiful to be seen with someone like me, whose strange-shaped face had been compared to an alien's by one girl I'd asked out. Maria had the softest, smoothest voice I'd ever heard with the slightest hint of an occasional lisp that made her sound even more entrancing. She always seemed to have an air of sadness about her, but I never knew why.

We'd walk to and from evening rehearsals and sometimes went to Maria's house to drink Pepsi. Not only did it feel very cool to be accepted by two older girls, but every time I looked at Maria, or whenever she opened her mouth to speak, stirrings deep inside me would rise up and turn me into an awkward and bumbling idiot. It felt wonderful.

Normally I wasn't shy with girls, having progressed from the shock of French kissing to tackling the impenetrable minefield of bra wire, but Maria induced an unusual coyness in me, which meant I was only able to gawp at her lovely face and stumble over my words whenever we spoke, and afterwards kick myself all the way home for being stupid. So, I suffered in silence and then revelled in the floating sensation of just being near her; strange waves of delight washed over me whenever she spoke in silky-soft tones, and I'd wish fervently I could kiss her precious lips.

I suppose she was my first love. Unrequited though it may have been, it was nonetheless wonderful. Though I suppose she was aware of my feelings, she was far too sweet either to lead me on, or to tell me to get lost. I loved her all the more for that. Looking back, I wish I could have told her how, for one brief moment in time, she brought light to my otherwise dark and troubled life.

# A New Start

MY BROTHERS and I didn't welcome men in our house, and so when our mother announced to us that she'd met someone and that he'd be visiting that night, we all went very quiet. She patiently explained to us that he was a really sweet person whom she'd met at work, and that we'd like him.

We sat there in silence for a while, pondering this big newsflash, until Iain asked to know the man's name. My mother pulled an odd face, preparing herself for our inevitable response. 'Dick,' she replied.

Anthony howled with delight and rolled around on the floor shouting out, 'Dick?!' Eventually all three of us were at it, delighted that we could say 'dick' as often as we liked and not get into trouble. We decided that anyone called Dick couldn't be that bad, particularly as his name provided us with an endless source of fun that we'd exploit mercilessly.

Later that evening, when the front door knocked, the three of us sat on the sofa trying not to laugh too much and whispering 'Hello . . . Dick!' to each other. Our mother told us to grow up, but I could see she was trying not to laugh herself. A few moments later, a huge man carrying a crash helmet and dressed in full body armour walked into the front room led by our mother. We were temporarily stunned, and stared at him in awe and wonder.

'Say hello, boys,' our mother urged, reminding us of our manners.

'Hello,' I said, trying not to look too impressed.

'Hello,' mumbled Iain, cautiously.

'Hello . . . Dick!' said Anthony, and that was it. We all spluttered hysterically into our laps and our mother looked down at the carpet as she stifled her own giggle. Composing herself a little, she shot us a look that told us to shut up or face the consequences. 'They're a bit nervous,' she explained lamely.

Clearly he'd had experience of kids our age before and was able to deal with our silly behaviour. 'Hello, guys,' he smiled.

He seemed really friendly, and so Iain and I calmed down a bit, trying our best to make it easier on our mother. I could still see Anthony out of the corner of my eye, though, shaking with laughter. His giggles were always infectious, so to calm myself I tried to act more grown up. 'Can I see your bike?' I asked him, completely forgetting that 'bike' was local slang for 'penis'.

My unfortunate choice of word pushed Anthony over the edge, and he let loose with such a mad laugh that even Iain couldn't resist sniggering. While our mother covered her mouth, I tried to look as innocent as possible.

Poor bloke. He took it all in his stride and didn't seem fazed. He took me outside to show me his Triumph 250 and it was awesome. I asked him if I could get on it, to which he replied, 'Sure,' then handed me the keys and let me start the engine. As it roared into life and I pulled the throttle back and forth, I fell in love with it immediately, and decided that anyone with a bike as cool as this couldn't be bad at all.

Soon after this first meeting, when I'd turned fourteen, our mother announced that she and Dick were going to get married. Naturally we were happy for her – she seemed to have found someone who really loved her and we got on with him well enough. She also explained that we'd be moving to his place, which produced mixed feelings in me.

The friends I'd made at school were very special to me, and the thought of moving away from them and joining a new school filled me with sadness. On the flip side, moving in with Dick would mean leaving our Woodley home. It was a constant reminder of past miseries and to be rid of it would mark the start of a new beginning, which was something we all needed.

On my final day at school I was given leaving presents from my classmates, and told that things wouldn't be the same without my jokes and entertaining. I also met with Sarah and Maria who made me promise to keep in touch and visit them – I assured them that they couldn't keep me away if they tried. Maria gave me the saddest look, and for one moment I thought she was going to reveal that she'd loved me all along and that I couldn't leave her. Instead, she gave me a small smile and told me to be good and not to forget them. I wanted to hug her so much and tell her how much I loved her, but instead I walked away and tried not to cry.

On the day of the move, we piled all our possessions into a van and took one final look at the house, the scene of so much pain and despair. My poor mother looked to be on the verge of tears and so we all gave her a hug. She sniffed, smiled at the house we were leaving for ever and said, 'Good riddance.' No one could agree more. But as we drove away from Woodley, I felt a sudden pang at the thought of leaving it behind. Though the house held many bad memories, Woodley itself – the people, the parks and the long summer evenings spent with some great people – was a different matter entirely.

In years to come I would find a time when I ached at the thought of all the good things that juxtaposed with all the shadowy times in that little terraced house: my first French kiss with Paula Jefcut; hiding in secret lairs in the ground; endless bike trips to Sonning; Mark and me miming to The Beatles in his garage; Maria and unrequited love; and sweet, peaceful days and nights as a choirboy.

All these things and many more were priceless. Perhaps without them the life that followed would have been very different.

Maidenhead, where Dick and his Triumph 250 lived, was a polarized mix of expensive houses and council estates. Our estate, in the council category, was much larger than the compact one we'd left behind. Sprawling over a square mile, all the houses were like characterless, identical red-bricked boxes, which created a maze of blandness that I instantly disliked. Thus, I braced myself for what Dick's house looked like on the inside.

Fortunately it wasn't that bad. It had 'single man' written all over it, though, and so our mother lost no time in getting to work on it. The next few months were devoted to making home improvements – decorating, redoing this, getting rid of that – and slowly the house was transformed into a family home.

I had my own room at least and spent most of it avoiding the endless activity downstairs. I'd listen to The Beatles or read and try not to think too much about the friends I'd left behind, whom I missed a lot. For some inexplicable reason I had a bad feeling about the house, the estate and even Dick. I tried to tell myself that I was wrong. He seemed like a good bloke, and hadn't given me any cause for concern. I tried hard to be nice to him, even though I couldn't shake off the feeling that I had to watch him.

I joined Altwood Church of England School halfway through the third year, and stuck out like a sore thumb. By the age of fourteen, I was a walking beanpole and had hit six foot one. My feet were huge and it didn't help that my mother had bought me a pair of black slip-ons that seemed to add an extra two sizes to my size tens.

At my first English lesson, I was introduced as 'the new boy', and did my best to avoid the inevitable stares and whispers that followed me as I sat down at my desk. The kid next to me gawped at me like he'd never seen a six-footer in clown's shoes before. He gave me a nudge and asked, 'How hard are you?'

'What?' I replied, in surprise. No one had ever asked me that before.

'You look really hard – are you?' he persisted.

'Er, no . . . I don't think so,' I told him, wondering whether he was a bit daft.

'Tough,' he said, and gave a low whistle. 'Everyone thinks you're hard, so you're gonna have a few people after you for fights later.'

This confused me. I'd had a couple of scraps in Woodley, but they were pretty silly events, and mainly involved rolling around for a couple of moments and then shaking hands and becoming mates again. I'd never even seen a proper fight at Bulmershe, but at my new school it seemed to be part of the curriculum.

The bell rang to signal the end of the lesson and to my complete amazement, one of the boys opened up the classroom window and dived out headfirst, while the other kids cheered. The teacher didn't bat an eyelid and carried on packing up her things. It was so surreal compared to the no-nonsense discipline of my last school that I wondered what I'd let myself in for.

Luckily for me, the fights didn't come. I kept my head down for the rest of the day and when the final bell rang I legged it out of the school gates. I was no fighter, that was for sure, and wasn't even curious to find out exactly how many eager kids were spitting on fists and getting ready to hammer the new boy.

When I got home, Iain and I compared notes. We were both amazed by the madhouse that was Altwood, but while I was being singled out for my fighting potential, Iain had been chatting up two fit girls in his class, and now found himself in a dilemma because he didn't know which one he preferred. I groaned inwardly and cursed the unfairness of life.

Fortunately, my classmates soon realized that a tough exterior was not always an indication of true hard-man material. Although word had got around that I looked hard, as soon as I opened my mouth it became obvious that I was anything but. Years of mingling with choirboys and my well-spoken friends back in Woodley had rubbed off nicely, which meant I avoided being drawn into any unnecessary bouts of physical combat.

In my second week at Altwood I discovered that classes were determined by a student's ability, and so I took the first opportunity I could to escape the crazy English class with its parachuting pupils. We were set an essay and I filled it with as many long words as I could manage. In the next lesson, the teacher returned my book exclaiming that I didn't belong in her group, before asking me, 'What on earth were you writing about?'

I replied that I didn't have the faintest idea. She sighed and wished me well in my new class. Mission accomplished.

My new English group was a great improvement. This teacher had much more control over her charges, and was able to discuss composition enthusiastically to a class that seemed to be paying attention, so I thought I'd be happy enough here.

I sat next to a skinny kid with freckles. When the teacher wasn't looking, he nudged me and asked me in a whisper if I was a swot. In response I picked up my ruler and flicked him in the ribs. From that moment we became friends and over time would become inseparable. Mark – or Oddie, as everyone called him aptly – filled me in on the way the school worked; whom to avoid, whom to tease, and which girls did it. It was a lot to take in, but as we'd share three years of friendship, there was plenty of time for me not only to fit into Altwood, but also to make an impression – though perhaps not in the best possible way.

# 16 | *Teenage Kicks*

A FTER A YEAR or so of living in Maidenhead, things started
to go wrong. The brand new beginning that my mother
had hoped for hadn't worked out as far as I was concerned.

Dick was a sweet enough guy, that was obvious, and I know
he tried his best to deal with the challenge of taking on three
growing boys from another family. Unfortunately, his best
would never be good enough thanks to his fatal flaw: his
temper.

Whenever we wound him up, which was often, he'd react
with displays of aggression that sometimes scared me, but mostly
which forced me to meet him head on. I'd sworn to myself that
no one would ever bully or lay a finger on me again – and that
included my stepfather. If there was one thing that was certain
to start a war between Dick and me it was the threat of
violence, and it came about six months after we'd moved in.

During an argument about what I had or hadn't done, he
started to shout at me. I can't remember what I said to him as
he verbalized his anger at high volume, but the next thing I
knew I was pinned to the wall, his left hand gripping my throat
and his right arm drawn back five or six inches from my face,

with his hand forming a fist. I stared back at him, my eyes full of hate, and feeling such a fury rising in me that if there had been any kind of weapon to hand I'd have used it. Instead, I shouted at him to carry on and hit me.

'Go on,' I told him, his huge hand squeezing my throat, making it difficult to speak. 'Do it! Just fucking do it!'

For one moment I thought he would. He puffed and panted as if he was having a minor fit, but then let go of me roughly and walked off. It was the beginning of the end. Even more upsettingly, my mother's reaction to my complaints against Dick suggested she didn't want to know nor do anything about it. I stared at her in disbelief. In my view, it seemed she didn't care that her sons were being threatened with violence – Iain had also been at the receiving end of Dick's uncontrollable temper. It soon became obvious to us that although our stepfather could be a lovely guy, he also lacked the ability to control himself.

With regard to my mother's disappointing response, I accepted that she loved her husband and needed to show him some loyalty, but to dismiss my fears about his temper so readily was a bitter blow, and upset me greatly. It made no sense at all. I felt abandoned, betrayed and alone, and the more I thought about it the more my anger grew.

The confrontations between Dick and me intensified, while my mother seemed to be living on another planet. To make matters worse, Iain and I had started to find ourselves at each other's throats constantly.

With the benefit of hindsight, moving in with Dick was always going to be a recipe for disaster. At the age of twenty-eight, he was too young and immature to handle tense situations wisely, without losing his temper. Though he never carried out any of his threats, it was still a frightening sight to witness him become more and more angry.

On one occasion, I told him that I'd kill him if he ever touched me again and I think he believed me. Like everyone else in my life, except my mother, he had no idea what I'd done to my father, but sometimes I came close to telling him, just to warn him that he wasn't dealing with any ordinary teenager.

What I hadn't realized, until some time later, was that my mother was being prescribed Valium. In my confusing and selfish adolescent world, I never once gave a thought to how the many years of abuse may have affected her, and I think that she made the same mistake with me; she'd closed her mind to the very real possibility that I was an accident waiting to happen. Although we had removed ourselves from an extraordinary situation and settled into a more normal way of living, we still seemed unable to come to terms with the memories of the life we'd left behind.

After one of my many fights with Dick, I sat in my room contemplating how life had gone downhill since leaving Woodley. I considered all my friends who were still lucky enough to live there, and as I thought of Maria, I knew we'd made a mistake coming here. I suddenly missed her terribly. I decided to give her a call, but there was no reply and so I tried ringing Sarah to find out how they were, hoping that they missed me too.

A small voice I didn't recognize answered the phone. 'Is Sarah there?' I asked, wondering if I'd dialled the wrong number.

'That's me,' the small voice replied.

I dived into a one-sided conversation about how bad it was here, how much I missed them, and that I was going to come and visit next week. There was a long silence at the other end of the phone before Sarah dropped a shocking bombshell that left me reeling. The previous week, Maria had been on her way to school when she suffered a massive brain haemorrhage; she died on the spot.

I can't remember the rest of the conversation or how it ended. After hanging up the phone, I went to my bedroom and sat there in a state of numbness.

So this was life. Mine was shit and now Maria, one of the kindest and most magical beings in the world, had lost hers. I couldn't make any sense of it. There were so many things I wished I'd told her, and now it was too late.

School remained something of a joke. Half the teachers seemed content to take the money and run, while the other half had all but given up, knowing they were fighting a losing battle.

My music teacher, Mr L, was particularly bad. At my first lesson, I'd proudly given him a letter from my previous school's head of music, which had been written to inform my new teacher that I excelled at the subject and had a number of musical talents worth nurturing. Mr L looked at it, then at me, ripped the letter into little pieces, told me I was as useless as everyone else and gave me a triangle to bang for the rest of the year. So much for nurturing my talents. Consequently there didn't seem much point in bothering with music any more.

By the fourth year I'd been skipping classes for quite a while and as no one ever pressed me for a reason for my absence, I took this as a green light to bunk off whole days of school. Oddie and I would sit in a nearby park, smoke cheap cigarettes, drink even cheaper cider and revel in the freedom of being away from that hopeless place of learning.

When we did decide to show our faces, it was only to entertain each other and to underline the futility of being a pupil at Altwood. On one occasion, we turned up drunk on red wine that we'd made ourselves using a kit. We staggered into one of the corridors, screaming our heads off, and were grabbed by a science teacher who called us 'little cretins', to which Oddie slurred in reply, 'No, we're not! We're pissed!'

The teacher let us go and said nothing. The next day we might have been expected to be hauled up in front of an angry headmaster, but we weren't – the only punishment we received was self-inflicted, in the form of a violent hangover from our hastily concocted home-made wine.

By the time we had got to our fifth year, the year that was meant to be shaping our futures, we were uncontrollable.

On Wednesday afternoons we had a double period of hated maths with a teacher who was a latent sadomasochist. His favoured form of discipline was to grab an offender's nipples between two fingers and twist as hard as he could, keeping him there until the groaning boy had either learned his lesson or the teacher had vented his kink.

One day I decided to postpone the perverse activities of our maths teacher by using the school payphone, shortly after dinner break, and dialling the main switchboard. I put on a heavy Irish accent and told them it was the IRA calling to say there was a bomb in the school.

The speed of their reaction was surprisingly impressive. The fire alarm sounded almost immediately and the school playing field soon filled up with nervous-looking teachers and excited children waiting eagerly for flames to consume the school buildings. When word got round that it was a bomb scare, the kids were even more delighted at the thought of everything going up in one big bang. Overall we lost about an hour of maths while the school was swept for non-existent explosives, which made the lesson almost bearable and meant that our deviant teacher didn't have the chance to satisfy his perverse urges that afternoon.

I did it again the next week. And the next. By the fourth time, the teachers trudged so slowly and wearily on to the school field that it seemed as though they didn't give a shit whether the whole place exploded or not. What amazed me was that my accent sounded more Cornish than Irish, and on my final call, as an experiment, I put on a heavy Indian accent and still they rang the alarm bell.

I didn't think I could get away with the calls for much longer, so I decided to stop. Instead I told my maths teacher that I thought he was a perv and I wasn't going to come to his classes any more. To my delight, he gave me a huge smile and said, 'Thank you,' leaving me wishing I'd been more up front much sooner.

As the year dragged on, my behaviour became more unpredictable and destructive. Once, a long time ago, I had loved learning, but at this school the teachers made no effort whatsoever to encourage passion for any subject.

I was also having a real dilemma with girls. In my year there were none as attractive as those I'd left behind in Woodley. In fact there were only two I really liked, but Zoe pretended I didn't exist, and Fiona only dated men twice her age – I expect my bad dress sense, acne and unfashionably long greasy hair didn't do me any favours either.

The Altwood girls were an advanced lot. One girl, whom I sat next to in biology, had fallen pregnant aged fourteen and was quite the expert in all things sex-related. I would listen as she launched into her own, highly instructional speeches about her favourite sexual positions, DIY vibrators and how taking it up the arse hurt like hell. I was shocked and enthralled. As the teacher droned on about the female reproductive system and showed us lame black-and-white films from the 1970s, my fifteen-year-old biology partner was telling me more about sex and how to do it properly than any science lesson could ever manage.

After a month of sitting next to her, and watching Fiona deliberately and seductively showing off her perfect long legs, I knew that if I didn't put this new knowledge to good use, I'd spontaneously combust.

I voiced my dilemma to Oddie one afternoon and told him that if I didn't lose my virginity soon I think I'd die. He nodded sagely and ran off a long list of potential candidates for the job, but none of the names were very unappealing. In fact I was scared of half the girls he mentioned. Instead I came up with my own list, but with each suggestion Oddie shook his head saying, 'No chance.' By the end of the discussion, we'd both agreed on a girl we knew went all the way after a couple of beers. The girl we had in mind was known as 'The Bike,' as everyone seemed to have ridden her on that brief and frantic pedal to manhood. I swore Oddie to secrecy.

Stacy wasn't all that bad-looking and had a wonderful body she enjoyed showing off, but she wasn't the kind of girl you took home to meet your parents, in case she ended up with your father. I knew that the best chance of losing my virginity was with her and so at one party I knocked back a few glasses of Dutch courage and asked her for a dance. Before too long we were swaying next to each other in time to Spandau Ballet's 'True'. Though she persisted in singing along throatily into my ear, which was pretty unerotic combined with the squelching of her chewing gum, she more than made up for it as she grinded her lower half against my crotch like an experienced Eastern dancer. The more worked up I got, the more I wondered how best to broach the subject of taking things further. Fortunately, she took the lead; squeezing my arse tightly, she said, 'Let's go next door.' As she led me by the hand towards an empty bedroom, Oddie, who had been observing my progress from his chair, unsubtly gave me the thumbs up.

While Stacy and I rolled around on the bed, kissing each other hungrily as though the end of the world was coming, I decided to go for gold and whip her bra off. But without the all-important combination, I found myself struggling to decode it. After I'd decided that I'd failed miserably at the first hurdle, she sat up and punched in the code with one hand, and it was all systems go once more. Five seconds later she had my trousers off and in another ten seconds she'd stripped off her skirt and knickers. God, she wasted no time, I thought, and as I prepared to take my time exploring the mysteries of the female body, Stacy made her desires clear. 'Just stick it in me,' she demanded, and spread her legs like a budding porn star waiting for her John Holmes.

I felt my teenage erection start to fill with doubt as well as blood. I had at least hoped for some erotic preliminaries before the main event, but things were moving much too quickly and falling far short of my expectations. Stacy took out her gum and stuck it on the bedside table, 'Well?' she tutted, her eyes widening. 'What are you waiting for? We've only got half an hour.'

Did I have a time limit? I thought, wondering if she was going to charge me as well. As I stared at the girl, impatiently tapping her middle finger on the mattress and looking slightly bored as if she was waiting for a bus, I realized it was no use – I didn't fancy her in the slightest.

As soon as it had dawned on me that the situation was hopeless, my body reacted in similar fashion, when all the blood that had previously travelled south did an about-turn, reducing me to desperate virgin status once again.

'Sorry – I've drunk too much . . .' I shrugged at Stacy, who looked ready to slap me. I knew it was a lame excuse, and she certainly wasn't going to let me off the hook that easily.

'You only had three drinks,' she said accusingly. I hadn't known she'd been counting.

I didn't know what to say as I pulled my trousers up, and tried to make out I'd drunk sixteen pints, before mumbling something about 'another time, perhaps.' As she followed suit, moodily pulling up her knickers, she huffed that there wouldn't be another time. I'd had my one and only chance, and I'd blown it.

Stacy was right, I had blown it, but the whole event had been destined for failure from the start. She did nothing for me, and I couldn't pretend otherwise. Oddie was not impressed in the slightest.

'What? You went limp?!' he exclaimed far too loudly, when I'd sat back down with him and told him what had happened.

'Shut up, you bastard,' I replied, elbowing him. I looked around furtively and hoped no one had heard him advertise my dismal flop. Stacy sat at the other end of the room glaring at me and whispering to her friend, who glanced over at me with a little snigger.

'Oh, man,' laughed Oddie. 'You must be the only one to have come away from her still a virgin!'

We both started to crack up and I hoped Stacy couldn't see us as I didn't want to hurt her feelings. In contrast, though, she had opted to ride roughshod over mine. As I looked in her direction, I could see she was broadcasting the news of my abject failure to half the girls at the party, some of whom cast amused glances at me, while others gave me looks of pity. I groaned inwardly and tried to ignore Oddie, who was still cracking jokes at my expense.

In the heat of the summer, the depressing reality of failing to lose my virginity was soon forgotten amidst seemingly endless parties, during which we pushed our young livers to capacity. One evening, Oddie scored some strange-smelling stuff called 'Leb', and we did our best to get stoned while listening to Duran Duran. Either the stuff was useless or Duran Duran's songs didn't complement the drug, so rather than finding any deep meanings in 'Girls on Film', we spent the whole time asking each other whether we were high yet.

By that final year I realized that I'd never fit in with either school or the life that everyone was expected to lead as adults. Apart from making music or being a journalist in an exotic country, I couldn't imagine doing any 'normal' job. The thought of working in an office from nine to five made me feel ill and I sensed deep down that there had to be more to life than that, surely? I resolved to find it, wherever it was, and if that meant leaving school with only one qualification then that was fine by me.

O-level exams came along and I didn't even bother showing up. Instead I got high with some punks in a park – someone offered me a bag of glue and I breathed in until I was flat on my back, dreaming of other worlds. If it wasn't for the jarring spectacle of another punk dribbling, with peeling layers of glue stuck to his mouth, I may have continued to pursue this cheap high, but the unpleasant sight combined with a splitting headache put me off solvents.

I did turn up for my English examinations though, and was one of only three people in the county to get a distinction in the oral test. I decided it wasn't worth attending the presentation evening for a single O-level result, and instead received my certificate in the post. Attached to it was a Post-It note containing the words, 'For what it's worth, well done.' I took the certificate and the anonymous note into the back garden and burned them both, too disillusioned with life to appreciate my achievement.

For reasons unknown, and despite having only one O level, I was asked to stay on in the sixth form. I turned up on the first day, had a fight with another pupil and got suspended for a week. I decided not to bother going back once the suspension was over; I'd recently experienced a musical revelation that compelled me to seek out others with whom to share this new-found love – school didn't fit into the equation.

# 17 | *Another World*

---

DURING MY TIME at Altwood, I'd become great friends with Noel, who was the cool school goth. He was always trying to lure me away from my beloved Beatles with goth compilation cassettes that he'd painstakingly put together for me. I'd arrive at school the next day and he'd demand to know my views. I'd usually reply that they were 'okay', but too depressing for me. I felt disheartened enough with my life as it was without adding to it further.

But Noel wasn't about to give up. The third tape he gave me started like all the rest, starting with a song by The Cure, then a Bauhaus track – and then the third song came on. I sat there, listening through headphones, not quite believing what I was hearing. I rewound the cassette and played it again, and then again; over and over for the next two hours until my ears ached.

It was 'RIP' by Alien Sex Fiend and I'd never heard anything like it before. There was no trace here of the complaining and introverted strains of Robert Smith that somehow repulsed me; Alien Sex Fiend were savage and raw – the energy and anger of punk, coated with layers of dark melody that turned my suffocating world upside down.

I knew that something I'd been looking for – though I had no idea exactly what – lay somewhere inside that song. I also had a burning feeling that if I followed the directions where the music was pulling me, I would eventually find it. So, I went out and bought every Alien Sex Fiend record I could find, got on first-name terms with the girl at the make-up counter at Boots, and a month later there was no turning back – I was a fully-fledged goth.

Noel and I formed a band called Fetische, a name we borrowed from an Xmal Deutschland song, and started to rehearse in the bass player's basement. With the exception of our guitarist Damien, we were pretty appalling. Noel couldn't afford drums and instead banged away on his mother's Tupperware collection, hopelessly out of time, while I did my best to sound like Bauhaus's Pete Murphy, throwing in as many references to shadows, ghosts and the moon as possible, but without really knowing what I was singing about.

One afternoon we jumped on the slow train to London, wearing more make-up than any woman on the train. Shortly after disembarking at Paddington, we made our way to the Tube, bound for the King's Road, but something didn't seem right; hardly anyone had given us a second glance, despite our gender-bending goth look. But in Maidenhead, it was a different matter entirely. Wearing make-up and sporting a purple Mohawk in public places guaranteed me attention from curious passers-by. Whenever I went out with my small group of fellow weirdos, not only were we rewarded with endless hostile stares, but we also attracted the violent attentions of the casuals from the local boys' school, Desborough. Although I was a useless fighter, I soon became a fast runner. A few times, though, it was impossible to outpace so many of them, we'd get a good beating from mobs of bored, middle-class thugs.

The police weren't much better. One night I was stopped by two officers who searched me for drugs. When their quest proved fruitless, they jabbed me in the face with my eyeliner, called me a 'fucking homo' and said that if they ever saw me wearing make-up in public again, I'd be in trouble.

Consequently, I was desperate to leave Maidenhead far behind and as quickly as I could, and so when I arrived on the King's Road I realized I had found my Mecca. Punk may have just passed its zenith by 1984, but no one had told that to the multitude of punks, goths and freaks lining the whole street. My jaw hit the floor and I felt a fire inside me that wouldn't stop raging until I made myself a part of this amazing scene. Though I might have been a clueless sixteen-year-old, I felt I had found my home at last. Ordinary people wandered past the lounging groups of Mohawks and shaved heads without batting an eyelid, seemingly unaffected by the sight of men wearing make-up and sporting facial piercings.

Back in Maidenhead, with its natural sense of outrage at anything that didn't conform to 'normality', I found escape in a new sub-culture that was growing out of sight of the masses. Behind hidden doors in Maidenhead's suburban facade I went to parties where older-looking guys would sit like cool gurus in the middle of the room, rolling endless joints and snorting speed, while The Sisters of Mercy, Alien Sex Fiend or Bauhaus blasted out from the stereo. Witnessing such unreal scenes, I felt my mouth open wider and wider. I couldn't get enough of it.

Getting stoned opened up sounds in the music I hadn't heard before, and when I was on speed I felt as though my already racing thoughts were saturated to critical mass – all I sensed was the buzz in my brain and not the thoughts themselves. It was the recipe for escape I'd been searching for. My hunger to go deeper into this strange world was insatiable and before too long I'd made contact with a drugs supplier in Maidenhead.

I'd met J at a really bad party, shortly after leaving school, and I'd liked him immediately. While everyone else downed pints of vodka and danced to chart music, he drank orange juice and smoked the largest spliffs I'd ever seen. Though I had to endure his obsession with Cabaret Voltaire and Velvet Underground, it was a small price to pay as we smoked joint after joint and snorted speed in his small room piled high with records and old clothes. He was a really sweet guy and I loved spending time in his chilled-out company.

Even when he didn't have drugs, which was rare, I'd hang out with him for hours, going through his massive record collection and trying my best to appreciate the Velvets. One afternoon, he reached into a bag and gave me a small square of card.

'Is this what I think it is?' I asked, breathlessly, having asked him so many times to score me my first acid trip. He nodded with a huge grin and called it 'White Lightning'. It could not have been more aptly named, and as I climbed higher and higher, I knew my life would never be the same again.

I'd heard various stories about what to expect, but nothing could have prepared me for my first experience that afternoon. Thoughts and feelings played out in colours and in the music I was listening to. I felt as if I was being born again and that the life I would be going back to could never match the one from which I eventually started to come down.

The contrast between the acid high and my disintegrating home life couldn't have been more stark. I'd discovered my mother's Valium one day when I lifted a cigarette out of her bag. I knew that things there were bad, but I'd never paused to consider how much she must have been suffering. I couldn't – I was too absorbed in my own struggle for survival to stop and think, or even care. Instead, I helped myself to a handful of her pills as well as the cigarette.

Our breakdown in communications had begun when I was fifteen, and by the time I was nearly seventeen we hardly spoke any more. Sometimes she gazed at me sadly as if I was a stranger, and in a way I was. I'd separated myself from the part of me she knew and loved – because I hated him.

The 'sweet little' child whom my mother was still desperate

to see in me was responsible for so much pain, and all I wanted to do was blot him out and bury him. It must have destroyed her to witness my self-destruction and extreme mood swings, but I was on a downhill slope that was the only route open to me – if anyone had shown me an alternative course, I doubt I would have deviated from my chosen path. My stepfather's explosions of temper and threats seemed a permanent part of family life, Iain and I only spoke to each other to argue, and poor Anthony kept his head down to avoid the dramas unfurling around him.

To make matters worse, I picked up the phone when my father happened to call one day. I'd avoided speaking to him for over a year and hadn't seen him for nearly two, but there was no escape when he asked me in a small pitiful voice why I didn't come and visit him any more. I mumbled out excuses, desperate to slam the phone down on him. I had done my best to forget he even existed and the longer I spent talking to him, the worse I felt. At the point when he almost begged me to see him, I felt as though I'd been pierced by a huge spike. I shouted at him to leave me alone and slammed the phone down. I ran into my bedroom and repeatedly punched the wall as hard as I could until I felt something split and only then did I feel a little better – although I was in excruciating pain, it felt strangely comforting, and the upset of hearing my father sounding so hurt and desperate to see me started to subside.

I didn't realize it at the time, but I was clearly deeply depressed. Before I'd be able to hide my true feelings; I used to find it so easy to push down the anger and pain to a place where it wouldn't bother me any more – I could slap on a mask and dazzle everyone around me with my clown routine and silly jokes. Only three years before it seemed as if I was running on an endless stretch of trampoline; as fast and hard as I'd come down, the higher I'd go back up. Not any more.

The drugs I was taking were helping to keep me in denial, but instead of a grin I wore a scowl, and the only time I went up or down was through the highs of being wasted and the crushing comedowns that would leave me numb and filled with thoughts far worse than the ones from which I was trying to escape.

I knew that if I stayed in Maidenhead much longer I would crack up. The thought of suicide had briefly crossed my mind, but it scared me so much to think that I had descended such depths to be able to consider such things. Every time I imagined what it would do to my mother and brothers, the death fantasies would subside, but the thought always felt so strangely comforting and warming that it came and went when I least expected it. I decided to keep in mind the Harry Haller character from Hermann Hesse's novel *Steppenwolf*, who clings to the mental raft of suicide, knowing that he can end everything at the hour of his choosing; merely having that knowledge gives him the strength to carry on living and see what lies around the corner.

One afternoon, a couple of months after my seventeenth birthday, my mother and I had an argument about something stupid and she slapped me round the face. I was almost certainly asking for it and, I suppose, was desperate for an excuse to leave home. At the time, though, I simply stared at her in disbelief, rubbed my smarting face, and told her she'd never see me again.

I packed a battered old blue suitcase with as much stuff as it could hold, shoved my cheap electric guitar into its case, and left the house. My mother didn't try to stop me. She might have thought I was bluffing, but I think she also knew that if I meant it she couldn't have prevented me from leaving.

I jumped on a train bound for London without really knowing where I was headed, but thinking that even if I ended up in a gutter it would be infinitely better than the miserable home life from which I was fleeing. As I stepped on to the platform at Paddington, the first thing that hit me was the cold. I was dressed in ridiculous clothing that offered no protection from the approaching winter. I'd left the house in such a rush that I hadn't packed any jumpers. With only a few pounds on me, I couldn't afford a B&B and didn't know where I was going to spend the night.

The running away part had felt great an hour previously, but my confidence started to fade when I took stock of my situation and realized there would be no gothic reception committee or little kiosks for runaways on the station concourse. I jumped on the Tube and decided to play it by ear. I got off at Sloane Square, but rather than walking down the King's Road, I ended up on Chelsea Bridge. It was one of the most beautiful sights I had ever seen. The Thames slumbered below and the whole stretch of the Embankment was lit up. I gazed in wonder at the city in which I was going to try to make a home.

It was hard to believe I was really there and that only a few hours before I'd been staring at my depressing bedroom walls. I felt better and surer of myself the more I took in the view, and I stayed there for a couple of hours, absorbing my new surroundings. When it started to get too cold to stay in one spot, I left Chelsea Bridge and set off on my travels again.

I carried on walking until I ended up in a huge park, which I later discovered was Hyde Park. I recalled how once I'd slept in a Maidenhead park after far too much to drink, so if I could do it there I could surely do it here. But this wasn't Maidenhead, I wasn't drunk, and it had been summer time when I had fallen in an unconscious heap on a roundabout. It was far colder in London, but luckily there wasn't a frost that evening, so I found a tree and huddled up to it, wrapping my coat around me as tightly as possible. I soon realized it wouldn't be easy to fall asleep in the bitter cold. As the night drew on and the temperature dropped, I thought I could see shapes forming around the trees in front of me. Paranoia hit me and I clung tightly to my guitar for fear of being robbed or attacked.

As I sat there, hunched up to the tree, wishing for sleep, but knowing it would never come if I didn't stop shivering, the doubts returned with full force. I thought of everyone back at home tucked up in their beds, safe, warm and sleeping soundly. It was a tormenting image that chilled me even more. But I knew I couldn't go back – my pride couldn't accept being greeted by expressions that said, 'We knew you'd come crawling back.' I knew that if I returned home I'd have no choice but to move away again, so this was it; somehow I had to make a go of it, or at least die trying. My mind ran round and round in endless circles until dawn broke, and I took that as my cue to get up and find signs of life.

Like nearly all runaways to London, I ended up in the West End. I wandered around the backstreets of Soho, amazed to see people starting work at 5 a.m., and watching weary drivers unloading goods from their delivery trucks.

I swiped a loaf from an unattended crate and carried on walking in random directions, munching on dry bread that sapped my saliva but tasted so good. By the time London had woken up properly, I found myself in St Anne's Gardens, a little park in Soho, and wished that I'd stayed there the night before. It was like the Ritz compared to the site of my first night in the capital. There were benches, flowers and a well-tended lawn; it was also far less exposed than the other park. I gathered my belongings around myself and, trying to ignore the cold, I dozed off for a bit on an empty bench. Minutes later I was rudely awakened by someone screaming in my ear and I grabbed my guitar to try to protect myself and my belongings. A tramp had sat down next to me with a bottle of something foul-smelling and was shouting at me incomprehensibly, showering me with spittle. I moved to the end of the bench, a little shocked but determined not to be forced from my place of refuge. Another tramp prodded my shoulder, telling me, 'You're on his bench, mate.'

I decided it wasn't worth arguing with them about it – two pissed tramps against one spun-out, frozen runaway was no contest. There were plenty of places to sit on the grass, but as it was glistening with icy frost I decided to take in the sights of my new home in the company of daylight.

I wandered around the whole of the West End and on my unguided tour I sat down in Trafalgar Square while tourists took photographs of Nelson and the pigeons, bought an over-priced sandwich and some tobacco, took in Parliament buildings, crossed London Bridge, gazed across the beautiful murky depths of the Thames and tried not to think about jumping in and solving all my problems.

During my sightseeing trip I'd kept warm by dropping into a Soho cafe and spending the last of my money on a cup of tea which I'd cradled until I could feel my fingers again, then sipped it over the space of thirty minutes. I must have looked a pathetic sight in my Oxfam trench coat, ripped, skin-tight, black jeans and squashed Mohican, but no one seemed to mind. The cafe owners either took pity on me or they were too wary of me to ask me to leave.

By the end of that second evening, I'd run out of money and felt very hungry. I cursed myself for my hasty exit from home, wishing that I'd waited until after dinner before storming off into the unknown.

I'd seen a couple of people begging near the Tube stations and so I decided to give it a go. The thought of asking strangers for money filled me with shame, but if I wanted to eat I didn't have a choice. I'd considered stealing from the food store off Trafalgar Square, but I discovered they had video cameras as well as some vigilant employees, so instead I started to approach people near Green Park Tube station.

I must have been the politest beggar in the history of the profession. I'd begin by apologizing profusely for asking for money and then spend so long explaining my circumstances that most people walked off halfway through my monologue. After making only one cigarette and five pence in the space of half an hour, I opted for the more effective one-liner: 'Spare some change, please?'

During a couple of hours of begging in the freezing cold, I made just over fifty pence, one foreign coin and two cigarettes. I was ignored most of the time, physically pushed away twice, and threatened with a good kicking by one very well-dressed businessman. It was one of the most demoralizing two hours of my life. After the threat of being beaten, I gave up. I bought another cup of tea from the same cafe I'd occupied earlier. The guy who poured my tea informed me sarcastically that they closed in two hours, so I'd better drink it quickly.

I ended up in front of Hyde Park by the time it was dark, but I told myself I couldn't go through that again. It was far too creepy in those huge parks, where every sound threatened and accentuated the cold, and where the freezing air felt trapped by the trees and turned the whole place into one giant refrigerator. I walked on until my legs felt like jelly and my fingers were too numb to grip the handle on my suitcase. Eventually I found an empty bench on a side street and sat down to consider my situation. I decided that it was no use; even if the weather was warmer, what did I expect to happen? I'd come here with no plan, no money and if I was expecting help when I got here, or to rely on the kindness of strangers, then I was deluded. Since my arrival I'd received nothing but strange stares from passers-by and sometimes even disgusted glances from suited office workers. My romantic idea of London was gradually fading as reality set in.

Suddenly I was being shaken, gently. A small far-off voice kept saying, 'Wake up . . .' For a moment I thought I was back at home again, but I couldn't work out why it was so cold in my bedroom. As I opened my eyes it felt as though they had been sprayed with frozen water – it was hard to see anything and I couldn't work out where I was. I kept hearing a voice telling me to wake up and I recalled a bad dream of parks and tramps and of being homeless in London, before the crushing realization hit that it was no dream.

I jumped up and away from whatever it was that had been touching me and looked around wildly for my things. My body felt as though it had been beaten with a cricket bat, but it was the freezing temperatures that had assaulted me and not the owner of the voice intent on rousing me from my slumbers. When I was finally able to focus, I saw a man standing in front of me, holding his hands out in front of him as if I were a dangerous animal he was trying to pacify. I screamed at him to fuck off and demanded to know where my stuff was.

His voice remained calm as he pointed and said, 'Don't worry, it's there.' I followed the direction of his finger and realized my belongings had been next to me the whole time. I grabbed everything off the bench while he kept trying to reassure me, telling me I shouldn't be afraid and that he wanted to help. I looked at him properly while I clutched my possessions, and started to relax a little. He was reasonably well dressed and softly spoken. As gently as he could, he explained that he was from a Christian group who tried to help people like me. He assured me that I didn't have to sleep out in the cold like this because, if I wanted, there was a warm bed that he could arrange for me at a centre.

I'd been on my guard for weirdos ever since I arrived in London, but once I realized that he seemed okay, I decided I could trust him a little. The second he said the words 'warm' and 'bed', any doubts I had seemed to disappear.

He drove me back into the West End in a battered old van filled with piles of Jesus-praising pamphlets and flyers, but I still kept alert to the outside possibility that he might be a lunatic. He parked somewhere in Soho and took me into Piccadilly Circus underground station, leading me down one of its many passageways. Tucked into one of these tunnels was a small office and advice centre. On entering he chatted briefly to the girl at the front desk about how he'd found me and how I should be looked after. She picked up the phone and repeated over the receiver what she'd been told. After hanging up she gave me a smile, said I'd be okay and that I should trust the man who'd brought me there and go with him to get a warm meal and bed. She also told me how lucky I was, but I didn't particularly feel it – I was doing my best to stay standing, but every now and then I felt as though I might black out.

The guy patted me on the back, seemingly overjoyed, and we set off on foot into the unknown once again. While he chatted excitedly about God's wonderful ways and how Jesus had led him to me, I didn't say a word. I only put up with it because I realized he was genuinely trying to help and that, thanks to him, I wouldn't be trying to sleep on a freezing bench that night. I still wished he'd shut up about God though. His intense fervour was starting to annoy me so much that I almost felt like walking off, warm bed or not. As he went on and on about 'lost sheep', and how I was welcome to join their group meetings, and that they'd like to pray for me, I decided I'd had enough. I appreciated what he was trying to do and I could see he was a good man, but hearing him tell me that this was all part of God's plan made me feel ill. 'Look,' I told him, 'if you're taking me to a load of Jesus nuts, you can forget it. If you really want to know what I think, God doesn't exist, and if he does then he's an evil bastard.'

For one moment, as he stared back at me without saying a word, I thought he was going to leave me there, alone with my thankless attitude, and I wished I'd kept my mouth shut. I'd never felt so cold and hungry in all my life, and the thought of going back home kept getting louder, no matter how much I tried to shut it out.

Instead he gave an understanding smile and told me not to worry; the place where I was going wasn't religious at all, and we could talk about something else. I breathed a huge sigh of relief on both counts and we carried on walking down Shaftesbury Avenue in silence.

Sandwiched between two theatres was a huge black gate I hadn't noticed when walking down this street before. He rang the bell and told me that in two minutes everything would be fine. As we waited for a reply, I looked at him more closely. He reminded me so much of the decent and well-meaning people from the church where I used to sing. 'Thanks,' I said, and he beamed back at me, as happy as if I'd told him I was going to convert.

A figure approached us from behind the gates and the good man who'd brought me there told him who we were and why we had come.

The huge black gates opened and I found myself being led inside to the warmth and relative safety of Centrepoint night shelter.

# 18 | *Seeking Sanctuary*

CENTREPOINT was a charity-run centre set up to cater solely for young runaways. Situated in Shaftesbury Avenue during my visit, it has since moved to different premises; its location always kept secret to protect its vulnerable residents from being tracked down by estranged relatives or the people who had caused them to take to the streets.

When I arrived there was a mix of boys and girls, different races, diverse styles of dress and personalities, but all had one thing in common: the screw-up factor. No one was there because they felt like a break from home or they wanted to see London for a few days. Everyone was running from something or someone and had been lucky enough to end up at Centrepoint instead of in the hands of unscrupulous gangs that toured the West End, I later discovered, in search of new flesh to recruit and sell.

I sat down and thawed out while a chatty, impish kid called Wiggy, who looked no older than thirteen, welcomed me to 'The Pit' as he called it. He talked at length about how everything worked and what you had to do to make the most of your stay, but I was too busy taking in my new surroundings to pay him much attention.

The place itself was very clean, with tables and chairs filling most of the open-plan, medium-sized ground floor. From the kitchen on my left came the welcoming smell of food being cooked. The Smiths played from a stereo on a high shelf in front of the bubbling pots and pans, and a small office was tucked away in a corner on the right-hand side of the kitchen area. A few band posters served as the only decoration on the white walls. It seemed as though it was just us, the workers, some food and a safe roof over our heads.

I wolfed down a meal, and thought it was the best thing I'd ever eaten. After having seconds, one of the volunteers asked me for a chat, to tell her some basic information about myself. I told her my name and where I'd come from, and she asked me why I'd left home. I was stumped. I realized that I didn't really know the answer; or at least not one I could explain in a few words. I decided I didn't have the strength to speak at length on this difficult subject, and opted to gaze blankly around the room instead. She asked if I was being abused at home, and I said I wasn't. Wiggy made a yawning gesture in my direction and giggled.

The volunteer looked at me for a while, before explaining to me that everyone here was running from something bad that they didn't necessarily want to talk about at first. She assured me that whenever I wanted to talk, she'd be there to listen and to help. Without knowing why, I felt pangs of emotion well up inside me. I couldn't remember the last time someone had made me such an offer. The last time I'd tried to speak to my mother about my various worries and fears, she had looked at me with vague, faraway eyes and been no help at all – the wonders of Valium.

Instead of showing gratitude to my caring new acquaintance, though, I asked her to leave me alone. She didn't move and carried on sitting by me, not saying a word and looking at me with large sympathetic eyes. I kept staring at the table, wishing she would go away. She placed a warm hand on one of mine as I picked away at my chewed-up fingernails on the other, and I didn't know whether to fall into her arms or slap her away. In the end I pulled my hand from under hers, at the same time wishing that she'd take hold of my other one.

She told me she would put my belongings in the office for safety, then got up and left me sitting there, concentrating on the table and trying to hide the fact I was nearly in tears.

Wiggy came back over to join me. He was originally from Manchester and had a naturally direct manner. 'Don't worry. I blubbed like a baby the first night I was here too,' he explained, honestly. 'They get you when you're weak so they can all talk about you when we've gone to bed.'

He made me laugh instantly, even though I was pissed off and confused by a raft of mixed-up feelings. We soon got talking to each other, or rather he spoke while I tried to keep up with his incessant stream of words. Within a short time he'd revealed that he'd been sexually abused by his father for as long as he could remember and had tried killing himself two weeks before arriving at Centrepoint. Munching away on fruit, he spoke about his past as if it was no big deal, and interspersed tales of horrific abuse with descriptions of his favourite parts of Manchester and how good the music scene was up there.

At about half past ten, we were all led downstairs to the basement dorms and I got into bed with my clothes on, delighted not to be sleeping on a park bench that night. There were about fifteen beds in total and although it wasn't very warm down there, the camp bed felt like a cloud and there were enough blankets to keep out the chilly air. I couldn't wait for sleep.

I lay in that strange bed, in my temporary new home, as a pale orange light shone through a small reinforced skylight, eerily illuminating the whole room, when a sudden fearful cry came from a bed to my right. I jumped up from my horizontal position, thinking someone was being attacked, but everyone was in bed and no one was moving. Another low moan came from the far corner of the room and echoed off the high walls.

Although I recognized the sounds of nightmares, it didn't make it any easier to try to sleep through. Did I sound like that when I had a bad dream? I tried to block out the noises by covering my ears with my pillow, but it was no use. It was as though one dreamer's nightmare influenced others and a broken, pitiful chorus reverberated around the room for the next few hours.

Each time I started to feel myself drifting into the realms of sleep, another shout or short scream would assault my senses and I'd be wide awake. Once or twice I heard Wiggy – who was in the bed next to mine – shout out, 'No!' which made the night even worse, as I imagined what he must have been through in his short life.

At about five o'clock or so the sounds had stopped, and by the time I'd finally started to nod off properly, all the lights came on and a loud cheerful voice called us all to wake up and get upstairs for breakfast.

The day started horribly early at Centrepoint. It was half past six, and an hour later everyone was expected to be out of the centre until six o'clock in the evening. Bleary-eyed and shattered, I found the girl whom I'd spoken to the previous night and asked her how we were supposed to spend almost an entire day on the streets of London. She replied that there was a lot to see and do, as though we were reluctant holiday-makers who wanted to lounge around the hotel all day.

Wiggy told her that he was going to rob a bank and buy us all decent food that evening. He was forever cheerful and smiling, and when we hit the streets he followed me everywhere. I wasn't sure if I'd adopted him or he'd adopted me, but either way I liked his company. He was a lovely kid and never stopped cracking jokes, but underneath all his clowning I could see the damage; the eyes never lie. I wondered if I had looked the same when I wore my own little suit of armour. Perhaps my eyes sometimes betrayed a similar shattered look? I would never have known, though, as I couldn't bear to see my own reflection, and would only use a mirror when I was covering my face in make-up.

Outside, we wasted no time in using the luncheon vouchers we'd been given to buy a packet of tobacco to share and a communal sandwich that we split with an Irish guy called Martin. He was a bit older than Wiggy and me, but seemed all right. He didn't say too much, but then no one really had the chance when Wiggy was in full flow.

We settled for a while in St Anne's Gardens, the place where the mad tramp had screamed at me the day before. While I strummed 'Bela Lugosi's Dead' on my electric guitar, Wiggy performed a cruel but cuttingly accurate impersonation of me, walking around the park like a B-movie zombie, singing at the top of his voice, 'Bats! Coffins! Vampires!'

I fell about laughing and was reminded of how healing and restorative a bout of laughter could be. Despite the cold, things seemed much better.

That night at the centre I finally had a good night's sleep, despite the noises all around me. The second my head hit the pillow I passed out and woke up feeling better than I had done for a long time. Then it was back to the boredom of life in London and trying to stay warm, but being in Wiggy's good company seemed to make the time pass quickly. After a while we were joined by a guy called Ben whom I liked instantly. As we sat in the park and I strummed a Cure song that Wiggy groaned along to, Ben asked if he could have a go. To my amazement he was practically a virtuoso. I'd never seen the guitar played so well before and I asked him why he wasn't famous with such talent. He smiled and told me that fame would be the worst thing that could happen to him. I told him he was crazy, but he ignored me and carried on playing Spanish classical on my cheap electric guitar, while Wiggy and I sat enthralled.

Later in the afternoon, having used up all our vouchers, we went our separate ways; Wiggy needed to make a call to his sister in Manchester and I felt like a wander on my own. I strolled around for a while, looking at the seemingly well-adjusted office workers and tourists, feeling intense envy and homesickness. I wondered if I'd ever see my mother again. I missed her more than I dared admit and as I thought about the call that Wiggy would be making to his sister, I decided to swallow my juvenile pride. I went to the phone booths in front of the Windmill Theatre, dialled the operator and made a reverse-charge call back home. I wanted to hear her voice and let her know I was safe, but also, deep down, I really wanted her to ask me to come back and tell me that we could work things out. I knew that if she did I'd refuse, but the offer would have convinced me that she really cared.

Iain answered the phone and seemed pleased to hear from me, which made me so relieved. I'd been such a bastard to him over the last few months and so if he'd put the phone down on me I wouldn't have blamed him. Eventually I got to the point and asked him about our mother, and what she had said about me. Iain's reply, that she had barely mentioned me at all since leaving home, left me reeling. My legs began to shake and a feeling of complete numbness took over me. I hung up on him and stood still in the booth, in a state of shock.

I was yanked back to reality when someone rapped hard on the perspex and told me to hurry up. I opened the door to face the same kind of well-dressed suit who'd threatened me with a good beating when I'd tried begging earlier in the week. I saw red and lost control. A tirade of abuse spewed from my mouth and I threatened to kill him as he backed away from the booth, stunned at my reaction. I walked off, glaring at everyone in my path and daring anyone to give me a reason to take out my fury on them. Thankfully, the storm that raged around me must have been like a red distress beacon, because people seemed to go out of their way to avoid the six-foot-something punk storming towards them. I knew that I had to get away from people as soon as possible, otherwise I was bound to do something I'd really regret.

I went back to the little park in Soho and sat there for hours. The rage left and something much worse consumed me – the desperate feeling that I had no one but myself any more. I thought about how close my mother and I had used to be, and couldn't understand how, within such a short space of time, we had found ourselves estranged.

Dwelling on an endless stream of negative, self-pitying thoughts, it struck me that my life to that point could be summed up by two words: suffering and futility. Perhaps the sooner I left it the better . . .

Wiggy caught up with me later. I kept quiet about my troubles and let him chatter on about his wonderful younger sister. He missed her terribly, and had decided to return to Manchester that evening. I was stunned by his news, not only because I'd miss him, but also that he'd even consider returning to his father.

'But isn't your dad at home?' I asked him.

'Yep,' Wiggy replied, not looking at me.

'You're mad,' I said, adopting Wiggy's direct approach. 'Why are you going to go back to that bastard? Why can't you move somewhere close to your sister?'

He didn't say anything and stared down at the floor.

'What if your dad touches you again?' I asked. 'He will, you know. You'll end up back here.'

I'd assumed he hadn't thought things through, but I was wrong. He grinned at me and said that if his father so much as laid a finger on him again, he was going to stick a knife in him. I knew he meant it, and rather than warn him about the possible consequences of attacking one's abusive father, I advised him to make sure he did it properly.

I never saw Wiggy again. He collected his belongings from the centre and left without saying goodbye to anyone. I like to think that when he returned to his sister, his father left him alone, and that he made a great life for himself working as a mechanic, the job he wanted to do more than anything else, and now has the happy life he deserved. He didn't wallow in the kind of self-pity and self-loathing that I had wrapped around me like a shroud. Instead, this most sweet-natured of youths had succeeded in laughing at life, and made it his aim to spread happiness among everyone he met.

After Wiggy's departure, it was back to normal at the centre, fending off well-meaning questions from the workers and trying to fill the monotonous, cold daytimes with anything I could. Martin, the silent Irish guy, joined me one day as I sat on the steps outside the National Gallery. He was much chattier than before and revealed that he was in trouble with the IRA back home in Northern Ireland. He asked me if I'd like to make some good money, which seemed like a stupid question when all I had was a daily £1.20 luncheon voucher; I'd tried to claim supplementary benefit from the Westminster dole office, but was told I wasn't eligible and I would have to come back in six weeks.

Buoyed by my positive response, he started talking about a sub-post office somewhere in north-west London, which was run by two old Indian codgers whom he hinted would be a 'pushover'. He opened up his coat, looked around furtively, and nodded to his inside pocket as he reached in and pulled something partially into view. I reeled back when I realized he was showing me a gun. Never having seen a gun before, I wasn't sure if his was a replica, so I asked him if it was real.

He looked at me scornfully. "Course it's fucking real. You think I'm gonna walk into a robbery with a fucking water pistol?'

I decided I preferred the old Martin; the silent one.

We sat on the steps a while longer as I eyed a group of

magnificent punks hanging around Nelson's Column, wishing I could go over and join them.

'Well?' said Martin, as if he'd asked me a question needing a reply. 'Are you in?'

I hadn't realized what he meant until the word, 'What?' had left my lips. Now I was really starting to test his patience.

'The fucking job, numbskull. Are you up for it?'

I almost burst out laughing. The idea of taking part in an armed robbery was completely ludicrous to me, but gun-toting Martin wouldn't have seen it that way, so I decided to play it cool.

'Eh, nah . . .' I replied as casually as possible. 'Don't think so.'

He shrugged and stared straight ahead at Trafalgar Square. We sat in an uneasy silence, while I grew increasingly uncomfortable. I told him I was going to join my mates over by Nelson, and walked off, leaving him behind. As I reached the steps down to the Column, I looked back to find him still sitting there, staring in my direction, watching me approach my 'mates'.

That left me with no choice but to make a bold introduction to the gang of about a dozen hardcore punks, who were sitting by the fountain drinking from two-litre bottles of cider.

'All right?' I said, trying to sound hard, but failing miserably.

'Fuck me,' said a short fat punk with a huge Mohawk. 'It's a little goth.'

A few of them laughed, but most of them didn't seem interested.

'That's a fucking big goth, you mean,' another one replied.

'You come to beat us up?' the first one asked.

'No,' I replied, thinking they were being serious. A few of them howled with laughter and I felt I'd made a small impression on these seemingly intimidating guys who were all older than me.

A cider bottle was passed round to me a few times, and half

an hour later I was quite light-headed, not having touched alcohol for a while. I was grateful to them for making me feel like one of the group so readily. One of them, though, a small, thin skinhead who looked more like a bald Nazi weasel, didn't seem happy to have me around. He kept making comments about my shite hair and make-up, so I pretended to ignore him. Eventually, after going on and on, he stood over me and demanded, 'You a poof?'

The largest member of the group jumped up from his seat, punched him on the arm and told him to fuck off and leave me alone. The weasel skulked away and sat on the edge of the fountain, staring at me menacingly. The guy who'd sprung to my defence was a Yorkshireman called Alex. He assured me that he didn't give a shit whether I was a poof or not and that I was all right. I warmed to him immediately.

The punks made their cider money from American tourists by charging money to take their photos. Alex told me that if I wanted to get in on the act, and make some easy cash for myself and the group, I'd have to do something about my collapsed Mohican. I tried my best to spike it up using water from the fountain, but it was useless. Drastic action was needed, so Alex gave me some money to buy a bar of soap.

I sped off to a nearby store, and on my return, with soap in hand, two of the punks started work on my hair. After a while they took a step back to admire their artistry. My Mohican fully restored, I was able to start my brief career as a London punk-goth model, posing for American holidaymakers. It wasn't so bad, although every third photo would involve a disbelieving woman yanking at my hair and screaming out, 'Oh my God! It's real!'

As it grew dark, I realized it was time to return to Centrepoint. I didn't know whether they had a curfew or if I'd be locked out if it got too late. When I announced to the others that I was leaving, Alex told me to forget the hostel and to stay at their squat in Kennington. I thanked him, but explained that as all my stuff was there, I'd have to go back for at least one night. As I left the group behind, I heard the weasel call out, 'Yeah, fuck off little goth.'

When I got back to Centrepoint, I was surprised to learn from one of the workers that I'd been there for over a week and had therefore reached the end of my allotted stay. Fortunately, I wasn't about to be booted back out on to the streets, and instead was lucky enough to be offered a place in a good hostel in Kensington.

I considered my options carefully, and wondered whether to accept Alex's invitation to stay at the squat. I probably would have opted for Kennington over Kensington but for one small matter: the weasel. It was clear that he had taken an immediate dislike to me, and I didn't feel at all safe in his presence. I decided that it would only be a matter of time before he started making trouble for me and the last thing I needed was hassle or violence, so I agreed to try out the hostel.

The next day I was given an address and directions, and sent off to one of the richest-looking streets I'd ever seen. My first thought was that there had to be a mistake. Surely there couldn't be a hostel for runaways in such a wealthy area? I walked along a row of white, Georgian, three-storey houses, which looked more like mansions, and eventually found the right building. I climbed the steps tentatively and rang the bell. The door was opened by a harassed-looking girl of about twenty, who, without even asking for my name, looked at me for an instant and beckoned me indoors.

With that slightly unceremonious and hurried reception, I entered into the bizarre world of 'BG', moving ever closer towards another difficult experience that would add yet more weight to my increasingly overloaded baggage.

# 19 | *Rent*

I SOON SETTLED DOWN to life in my new home. There were about twenty residents in total and so it was relatively easy to get to know the other kids, or at least those who wanted to communicate. Some preferred silence and distance from everyone else, which scared me a little, though I wondered how much simpler life might be by avoiding all contact with people. There was an unspoken rule among the inhabitants of both Centrepoint and BG that no one asked questions about why you were there or your background unless you raised the subject yourself. This mutual understanding created a more relaxed and peaceful atmosphere.

Eight spacious bedrooms containing two or three beds filled the sprawling house. Although the boys' rooms were kept separate from those occupied by the girls, there was naturally some fraternization between the sexes, particularly after dark. Late into the night you might hear the soft click of doors opening, whispers and giggles, with the occasional low moan that definitely wasn't caused by any bad dream. The on-duty staff were undoubtedly aware of what was going on, but wisely or charitably turned a blind eye to it all.

The idea of a hostel for the homeless might conjure up grim images of peeling walls, dirty carpets, and drug-addled and unwashed troublemakers, but nothing could have been further from the truth. The whole house was kept spotlessly clean and we didn't need reminders to keep our own rooms tidy. Though we never expressed it in words to each other, we all knew how lucky we were to be there instead of trying to keep warm and stay safe from attack while sleeping in shop doorways or on cold park benches.

After a couple of days spent observing the way things worked at BG, and getting used to the fact that it was safe, well run and friendly, I had my first face-to-face contact with Graham, one of the workers, who sat me down for a chat. It was similar to my Centrepoint experience, with him asking me questions from a form and me answering, hoping desperately that it wouldn't get awkward. But of course it did.

He put down his notes and folded his arms, giving me a smile. Graham was someone who looked permanently tired, and even though his eyes were always bloodshot from lack of sleep, he was never short of wisecracks and sarcastic put-downs when dealing with the cockier residents. He asked me to tell me about home and so I explained the situation concerning my mother's emotional detachment, my stepfather's aggression and threats, and how life in Maidenhead was so utterly soul-destroying. The offhand way I described my problems made them sound comparable to a slight toothache.

I thought that would be it, or he'd tell me to bugger off to make room for someone who really needed their help, but instead he looked thoughtfully at me and said, 'Tell me about your real father. How are things with him?'

I wasn't expecting that one.

'Fine. No problems there,' I replied briefly, feeling my heart pumping much too hard. If he was going to head down that road, I would have to bring the interview to a timely close.

Instead, Graham said, 'O-o-okay. How were things between your mother and father?'

I knew he'd sensed there was a reason for my reticence and so I didn't reply. I wanted to fob him off. I wanted to be far away from these questions, but to say that my parents had anything remotely resembling an amicable relationship would be a lie too far even for me.

He leaned forward and told me that if I didn't talk about what was really going on in my life, then he wouldn't be able to help me. He reminded me that my stay at the centre could only last for so long and it was important to take the opportunity to be helped and supported for the future.

Because I liked him, I didn't want to be honest and reveal that the very last thing I wanted was his help. Furthermore, I was resolute in my belief that there was no way anyone could ever help me – I was too far gone to have strangers wave a magic wand over me and cure me of all my troubles.

He started talking about the ethos of the hostel, how we all had to work together and how everyone here was at risk – his task was simply to help. I assumed he'd misunderstood what I'd just told him, so I pointed out that I wasn't at risk: 'My stepfather's an arsehole, but he's never actually hit me, and the worst thing my mother's ever done is to pretend that nothing's wrong.'

Graham didn't say a word and continued to observe me with the same expression. I wondered whether my defensive attitude might result in my eviction from BG. If it did, I wasn't too bothered. I hadn't stopped thinking about my fun afternoon with Alex and the other punks in Trafalgar Square, and I'd even begun to imagine that there was hope for me and the weasel to work things out.

Instead, Graham told me gently, 'You don't have to be at risk from other people to need our help.' He stressed the words 'other people' and as I sat there, wondering what the hell he was talking about, I saw real concern in his eyes. His next question floored me.

'Have you ever thought about taking your own life?' he asked in a low, quiet voice.

Suddenly I felt petrified. It was as though a dark secret that I hadn't even known existed had been ripped out of me and exposed for all everyone to see. My mind seemed unable to cope with the explosion of thoughts that were released, and kept blasting out the inner fanfare, 'You're a suicide and you didn't even know it!'

Waves of nausea came over me and my suspiciously weak reply of 'No' to Graham's question must have sounded like a resounding confirmation.

He got up to bring me a glass of water, and told me not to worry. That was easier said than done. I hadn't known how strong the thoughts of killing myself had been until the question was addressed so directly. It had come as a shock because the feelings I had were so deeply buried, and yet someone else was able to see them written on me so clearly. I realized that I wasn't the master of disguise I believed myself to be, and felt stripped and exposed; the urge to crawl away and hide myself from view was overpowering.

Wisely, Graham chose to suspend this line of enquiry and changed the conversation to something less awkward, but I cannot recall exactly what. His voice grew distant as my mind became flooded with thoughts of the times I'd given serious thought to suicide. There had been many occasions, but I'd successfully crushed them all.

At the end of the chat and after Graham promised me we'd be speaking again, I went to my room for a while and gave myself a harsh talking-to: 'So what? So what if I *do* decide to finish things when I want and how I want? It's my life.' I told myself not to make such a big deal out of it, but most of all, to make sure that I never allowed anyone to read me so effortlessly again. I felt better having reconciled myself once more with the Harry Haller approach of knowing that the exit was always mine to take, if I chose to do so.

★ ★ ★

After a few days I'd made friends with a number of the BG residents and had begun to feel more at home. I got on particularly well with two guys called Karl and Sam, who seemed different from everyone else. They were curiously more sorted and sure of themselves, and each displayed a confidence that stood out from the rest of us.

Karl was dating a beautiful goth girl called Laura, who visited him every few days, while Sam insisted that all human relationships were futile and that forming attachments to anything would lead to certain doom. He was well versed in philosophy and I'd listen enthralled, often totally lost, by his world view, which mainly seemed to involve taking whatever you could from anyone who had it.

Karl and Sam always seemed to have cash while I had barely anything. I'd signed on at the local dole office and was told that I was entitled to £17.50 a week, but wouldn't receive any money for at least three weeks. I wondered how they both managed to dress so well and have money for pot and pints on such a pittance. Fortunately, they were generous people and always shared their grass and bought me sandwiches when we were out during the daytime.

One night, a few days after getting to know them, they took me to a pub in Earl's Court and introduced me to a crowd of older men with whom they appeared well acquainted. A mature gentleman, who dressed and sounded like a 1950s theatre actor, bought me drinks and fussed over me. He made no secret of the fact that he was gay and told me that if he were thirty years younger, he'd marry me. Most of the group were high camp and funny, and I realized that this was the first time in ages that I'd socialized with normal people with jobs, homes and no obvious hang-ups. I felt relaxed in their company. Everyone's gaydar was in full working order and my purple Mohican certainly wasn't floating any gay boats, so I wasn't having to turn people down constantly, but one guy standing at the bar kept staring at me oddly, and only turned away when I flashed a threatening look in his direction.

I grew bored of listening to the faded thespian and his marriage proposals the more drunk he became, so I made my excuses and moved away to look for Sam. Eventually, I found him standing by the bar with an older guy who kept touching his face and staring at him as though he wanted to devour him. Sam didn't seem to mind this intense attention and gave him a kiss on the cheek after whispering in his ear.

The penny dropped. The nice clothes, the money – now I knew how they were getting it, but I was angry they hadn't told me they were rent. I had no moral issues with the practice, but I'd thought they were my friends, and felt stupid for not realizing it much sooner. I went back to my table and sulked into my pint while the old queen carried on complimenting me on my long legs and slurring about what he'd like to do to me if I'd let him. He was starting to annoy me so I told him to shut up. Worse still, the weirdo at the bar had begun staring my way again. The old boy made some remark about my bad behaviour and, to my relief, staggered away.

I knew I had to leave the pub and shake off my blackening mood, but before I could disappear, Sam came over and plonked himself next to me, looking very pleased with himself.

'Why didn't you tell me you were gay?' I sulked.

'Because I'm not,' he laughed.

I told him I'd seen him at the bar with his older companion and that their body language looked far from platonic.

'That's business, not pleasure,' he patiently explained to me, as if I were a naïve young child with no clue about life's realities. 'I've got a girlfriend, actually, but that doesn't stop me from earning a living.'

I shrugged, still irritated, but at least I was being put in the picture finally.

'Karl's gay,' Sam continued, 'but what do you expect him to do? Say, "Hi, I'm Karl, I'm gay?" It's no big deal, you know.'

I was about to explain that I couldn't care less whether they were into bestiality or necrophilia, when a sudden thought hit me. 'Hold on, Karl's not gay. He's going out with Laura.'

Sam gave me a wry smile. 'Haven't you guessed that Laura's a boy?'

I was stunned. Laura was one of the most beautiful 'girls' I'd ever seen – and the fact she was a goth made her even more attractive. One thing was certain: if she hadn't been going out with Karl, I would have gone after her myself – the fact that she was a he definitely wasn't an issue for me.

Over the next few days I spent more time with the guys and every evening we'd end up at the same pub, they'd buy me drinks and I'd usually end up going home by myself or with Karl. Sam was exceptionally good-looking and had no difficulty attracting punters. Naturally, the thought had crossed my mind that I could try it too. Spending time in that environment regularly made it seem quite normal, and the fact I still didn't have a penny to my name made it all the more tempting. The idea of buying some new clothes and shedding the ones I'd been wearing for the last month was very appealing, but each time I'd survey all those old men and their lustful eyes, my mindset would change and I wouldn't make the leap. On one of these nights, though, temptation called, and greed and curiosity found me out.

On this particular night, Sam and Karl were doing the rounds as usual while I was waiting patiently at our table. The chair next to me pulled back and a guy leaned over and asked me if I wanted a drink. I was about to accept the offer, as regulars often bought me drinks, until I realized it was the weirdo who'd been staring at me on my first night in the pub. I turned him down and told him I was waiting for my friends. He asked if he could join me and though I wanted to say no, I opted for a non-committal shrug of the shoulder. He sat down at the table. I tried to look in any direction except his, but despite my obvious disinterest he started chatting. I pretended to ignore him until he offered me an unusual apology: 'Sorry if I was staring at you the other night, but you're beautiful.'

I was taken aback and, ridiculously, I felt flattered by his comment. No one had ever said anything like that to me before and, despite myself, I ended up talking to him. I discovered he was an antiques dealer, and was in London for a big auction. Every now and then he cracked a lame joke that made me laugh more out of sympathy than genuine amusement. He seemed harmless enough and I blamed my initial gut reaction about him on a bout of misplaced paranoia.

After the third or fourth drink, he nudged me under the table and gestured for me to take something. I did as he asked, wondering whether it was something to smoke or, better still, some coke. He slipped a small roll of notes into my hand. I looked down and saw a bundle of fivers.

My heart began to race. I looked at him, he nodded back at me and I understood the proposition on offer. I'd been in similar situations when I was at Centrepoint; it was quite common for middle-aged men to walk straight up to us on the street and flash money about, but the only reactions I gave them were angry screams and verbal abuse. When I discovered that one of the younger kids at Centrepoint was involved in such transactions I felt sickened at the thought of filthy, predatory hands placed on someone so desperate for a little money.

But here I was, in another time and place, and wiser to the realities of life and my own predicament. I thought about all the things I could do with that money. My boots were falling apart and they stank no matter how much I washed or sprayed them; my trousers were barely holding together; I'd been wearing the same T-shirt for nearly a month . . . The list went on and on, and the logical arguments grew louder and louder, but when I thought about what I would have to do to earn the money, it didn't seem like such a great idea. I wasn't against the idea of going with a guy – especially after finding out about Laura's true identity – but looking at this older man anxiously staring back at me wasn't remotely enticing. He must have sensed my hesitation and told me that I didn't have to do anything more than let him touch me for a while.

The proposal seemed more practical. Surely it wouldn't be such a big deal to let him grope me a bit? I could always close my eyes and imagine it was someone else, and I couldn't ignore the fact that I was curious about being with another man.

'Okay,' I told him, 'but you can only touch me. If you try anything else, I'm off.'

We finished our drinks and went to his hotel, which was a ten-minute walk from the pub. The whole way there a voice was shouting in my head: 'Keep the money and run.' Ignoring my inner warning system, my legs kept going as if they were beyond my control.

A part of me wanted to see what kind of world existed outside the one I already knew. Hungry for experience, I was like a moth to a flickering light that was going to reveal a side of life I had not yet seen. I had the money in my pocket, I knew he was only in London for two more days and I could easily outrun him, but despite my racing heart and bad feeling, I was drawn to the situation, whether it was with him or someone else. The intense curiosity that I felt overruled my intuition and gave me the sense that I might even enjoy it.

His hotel seemed cheap and depressing, even though it had a porter who barely glanced at us when we entered the lobby. The frontage was shabbier than BG and inside there was the aroma of damp carpets and stale food. His room was tiny and messy. It looked as if he had been living there for quite some time rather than renting it for a week, as he had told me. I tried to appear confident in these unfamiliar surroundings, but had no clue what would happen next nor what I was meant to do.

He asked me whether I wanted a drink, and I replied that I definitely did.

'Have a shower first, eh?' he suggested, as he reached out for a bottle of vodka on a table piled with papers.

'I had a shower this morning, thanks,' I told him, and sat down on a small chair next to the bed.

He suddenly looked unsure about something. 'Oh, no . . . you have to be very clean. I can't do anything unless you've had a wash.'

Warning bells. Ringing and ringing – and I didn't listen. I assumed he was a hygiene nut and perhaps he could smell my stinking boots. I left him alone and walked into the en suite bathroom, undressed and quickly showered. I didn't want to return to the bedroom naked, so I got dressed again, leaving my offensive footwear by the basin.

When I opened the door to rejoin him, I could smell something strange that I hadn't noticed before. It was like a mix of aniseed and petrol, but I was too nervous to give it much thought, and forgot about it as soon as he handed me a drink.

I knocked back the large shot and, after a few moments, things didn't seem quite so freaky or intimidating. I relaxed even more when he began chatting about his business and how it was a lonely profession, travelling so much and being away from his wife and kids. My worries started to fade and I felt surprisingly good. It occurred to me that perhaps he'd changed his mind about being intimate and only wanted to talk. This made me feel even better; all I wanted to do was have another drink and chill out.

The odd smell persisted though and I decided to ask him what it was. He explained that he'd spilled some cleaning liquid earlier and couldn't get rid of the fumes. I didn't think to ask him to open a window because my thoughts seemed to be grinding to a halt, so slowly were they entering my mind. Then my head started to spin. My body felt as heavy as lead and I could sense him touching my chest as he told me to undress. I thought I was going to pass out; I was suddenly so tired and unaware of what was happening or where I was.

I leaned back against the wall, trying to shake off the debilitating effects of the large vodka, and felt him undoing my trousers. I wanted to explain that I'd changed my mind, but it was impossible to get the words out. Through the disgusting smell and my spinning head I heard him tell me how beautiful I was. I felt hands over me and I could feel his rough chin as it scraped my stomach. Confusion and repulsion hit me – I couldn't even remember taking my trousers off, let alone my T-shirt, and all I could hear was him breathing heavily over me, and saying, 'Beautiful.'

That was the last thing I remembered before I passed out.

I came to in a darkened room, but I couldn't move. It felt as though I was strapped to the bed and for a frightening moment, I thought I really was tied up. Eventually, muscle by muscle, my body came back to life and I managed to swing myself off the bed before crashing on to the floor. It was soaking wet with some unknown substance and smelled awful. Instinctively, I pulled my head back from the stench, and the memory of the previous night's events slowly started to reveal itself to me.

I stumbled around the room in the dark, looking for my clothes, but I kept falling back down. Each time I moved, my legs gave way, but I was desperate to get away from that overpowering odour. I needed some fresh air to avoid passing out again.

I managed to stumble over to the door, and then tried to turn the handle. At first I thought I'd been locked in. The more I wrestled and fumbled with the door catch, the more it seemed that I'd been imprisoned. Fortunately, after several minutes of frantic twisting and turning, the door swung wide open, and I sunk to my knees in the sunlit corridor, gasping deep breaths of relatively clean air away from the poisonous fumes in the room behind me. The smell of that corridor and the memory of that patterned red-and-blue carpet and the dirty yellow walls will never leave me.

I stayed there for a while, breathing in the hotel's stale air, waiting for my body to start to feel normal again. After my head had cleared a little, it occurred to me that I was stark naked and kneeling on a hotel carpet – I had to get dressed and leave this place as quickly as possible. As I slowly got to my feet, the strange feeling I'd had before in my legs returned, but this time it seemed to be higher up. I reached around to pinpoint a small but definite ache, and as my fingers touched my backside I could feel bits of dried matter clinging to my buttocks and around my anus.

It took a few seconds for me to work out what had happened, but at the time I was more concerned with getting out of there, and the fight or flee instinct took over. I grabbed my clothes and got dressed, holding my breath as best I could. As I looked around for my missing boots, I noticed there were several small brown bottles with the lids off scattered all around the hotel room, and at that moment I realized where the smell was coming from, and what it was. I'd seen clubbers pass these little bottles back and forth to each other, but had never tried amyl nitrate myself; to me it was too much like glue-sniffing on the dance floor. Ironically, I probably had enough of the stuff in my nervous system to keep a whole club high all night.

I continued searching for my boots, smashing anything that got in the way, and then I remembered the bathroom: they were still there.

As I left the room my thoughts returned to my attacker, and I worried about what might happen if I met him on the landing or stairs; I was too weak and uncoordinated to do much more than struggle. I stumbled down winding staircases, taking wrong turns in search of the main entrance. I was so afraid of colliding with him as he returned to his captive guest, and of being grabbed, hauled back up there and finished off properly.

Eventually I found the main lobby and, ignoring the porter who shouted something in my direction, I fell outside into daylight and the safety of the street. The air was sweet and restorative, but I didn't have a clue about how to get back to BG. I asked so many people for directions but kept getting lost, even though I knew I was close to home. It was only when I finally found the right road that I sat down on the pavement and felt safe again.

It didn't take too long for my head to clear enough for me to piece together the evening's events, even though it was the last thing I wanted to bring to mind.

I remembered the odd request the man had made about my having a shower and how he'd looked at me when I said I didn't need one: he was nervous about something and wanted me out of the room. At first I wondered whether it was to fill the room with poppers, but I couldn't understand why he hadn't collapsed as well. I recalled the strong vodka and the effect it had had on me, like acid laced with morphine, and then I realized that he'd dosed me; the amyl nitrate was for him, the spiked drink for me.

Although I wasn't in severe physical pain, I could feel the dull and aching reminder of his attack, and I pathetically gave thanks for the fact that I'd been unconscious. Nonetheless, little jolts in my arse accompanied the pounding of my pulse and the more I remembered every detail, the more numb I became – until I didn't feel anything at all.

I slipped into BG quietly, hoping that no one would spot me or ask any awkward questions. Fortunately, no one did. I went into the room I shared with a guy called Clive, grabbed my washbag and went to the bathroom to scrub myself free of the filth that clung to my body. As soon as it dawned on me that perhaps I'd never be clean again, I returned to my room, picked up a disposable razor and broke it open to expose a thin strip of razor blade.

I was completely without thought or feeling; all I had was

the urge to punish myself for what I'd let happen to me. If I bled to death then fine, but what I needed more than anything was to hurt myself. I needed to feel something and as far as I was concerned, this tiny strip of dull metal was the only thing that could arouse from the waking coma into which I was slipping.

How could I have been so stupid and blind to the dangers of the situation? All for a few pieces of clothing, and because I was a selfish, greedy bastard who wasn't satisfied with what he had. I knew I had deserved everything I'd got.

I climbed into bed and cut my wrist once – just enough to hurt, not enough to finish myself off for good – and I watched as a wide gash opened up and blood start to pour from my wrist. The relief was exquisite. I felt everything wash out of me as if I was being cleansed of his stinking touch and voice. The dull throb of pain soothed me and the stream of blood turned into a nursery rhyme calling me to row my boat. I settled down under the sheets and pressed my wrist into the mattress to hide the flow of blood, hoping that when I slept my arm wouldn't fall out of bed and let me be found out. It crossed my mind that I might have cut too deeply, and could bleed to death, but that thought gave me even greater comfort as I closed my eyes and went to sleep.

I slept for a long time and awoke late at night with a burning and dull pain in my wrist. I remembered what I'd done and went to the bathroom to inspect the damage. In the bright light I could see that it wasn't pretty. The blood had congealed and clotted, but every time I moved my hand I could see I'd gone in too deep. The gash opened up wide to reveal bone and a bloody substance resembling Rice Krispies; it made me feel sick to look at it. I knew it needed stitches, and that would mean awkward questions.

In desperation, I tried to think of a genuine household accident involving a razor cut to the wrist, but my mind was a blank. Even if I had to tell the truth about my self-inflicted wound, one thing was certain: I'd never tell anyone why I'd done it. It was yet another secret for the vast collection that by now felt like an overpacked suitcase that I could barely close.

I left BG a few days later, after getting myself stitched up at the local hospital. I had tried to explain away my injuries to the examining doctor by saying I'd fallen down heavily on some broken glass. He quickly surveyed the damage and with a sardonic grin introduced himself as Dr Spock. I'd tried to slip the bloodied bedsheets into the washing machine the next day, but had been discovered by the staff who fussed and clucked around me with endless concerned questions, while I stayed mute.

I decided to phone home, and spoke to my mother. She seemed so happy to hear from me and begged me to come back. It was the best thing I'd heard in weeks. When I said I was surprised she wanted to see me, having learned from Iain that she hadn't even mentioned me after I'd left home, she sounded shocked, and told me that she'd cried for days after I'd left home that day. At first I was furious and felt betrayed by Iain for the lies he had told me, but then I remembered how badly I'd treated him for well over a year before I ran away – threatening him, deriding everything he said and did. I couldn't blame him because I'd probably have done the same in his shoes.

As I contemplated my next move, I was bothered by the fact that I'd failed to make it by myself in London. I'd gone there with no clue about anything – neither life nor people – and I'd been shocked into waking up to a world that demanded more respect and care about where you trod. I had to admit to failure and learn from my experiences.

But one thing I had discovered while I did my best to survive in the midst of that huge uncompromising city was that I loved it. I loved the way you could be anything you wanted and no one said 'No'; the way that the people you met accepted you, faults and all, and didn't judge you; the way that anything seemed possible if you knew how to go about achieving it. I hadn't learned that knowledge yet, but I knew I would.

Most of all, I missed the Thames at night; that beautiful, glistening witness to everything happening overhead as it rolled on past illuminated bridges, breathtaking buildings and through a city that wouldn't be the same without it. I knew I'd return to London and that I'd do things differently next time. All I had to do was to restore my strength at home, plan properly and avoid making the same mistakes again.

If I'd known back then that the biggest mistake I was ever going to make was lying in wait for me back in Maidenhead, I'd have stayed in London, homeless or not.

## 20 | *The Drowning Man*

O N MY RETURN to Maidenhead, my mother greeted me with open arms and did her best to welcome me back to the family, but I felt I was among strangers. Although my brothers and I were happy enough to see each other again, a brooding unease seemed to fill the whole house whenever I was there and I knew I was the reason for it. Everything suffocated and depressed me one day, then scared and angered me the next. It was clear that all the happy-family days of old had gone for ever, and so I quickly made my next exit plans.

True to form, I pushed the rape incident deep down inside me to join my collection of suppressed bad memories. It wasn't too difficult. Perhaps if I'd known exactly what he'd done to me after I passed out, then dealing with the knowledge would have been much harder, but instead I counted myself lucky to have been drugged and to have survived the horrific experience.

I teamed up with my old schoolfriend Noel when I returned home. He was my one rock of sanity in that narrow-minded world of Saturday night mob fights, where broken beer glasses were jabbed in your face and the threat of violence loomed as punishment for standing out from the masses.

We often stayed over with a good friend of ours, Jim, who lived on the borders of Maidenhead. He was one of the most happy-go-lucky people I'd met, and despite his fearsome reputation as a crazy fighter – it was known that three guys twice his size failed to send him to the floor when he was attacked one night – he had never started a fight in his life. He wasn't a fellow goth, but he enjoyed our company as much as we loved his. Whenever I turned up at his place, he'd answer the door dressed like the ultra-casuals who normally chased us at night, in his Pringle top and trendy jeans, welcome me joyfully and sincerely point out that my eyeliner was smudged. Even when I was at my most depressed, Jim had a knack of reducing me to fits of laughter with his off-the-wall sense of humour. After my spell of homelessness in London, I spent some fantastic nights in the company of Jim and Noel.

Despite having some great times at Jim's house, listening to Noel's endless collection of goth C90s, having parties and drinking till the early hours, it still wasn't enough for me. Being stuck in the confines of Maidenhead gave me the sense of extreme claustrophobia, and the urge to escape was unbearable. I started to jump the train to London, hiding in the toilets to escape paying my fare, and spent long afternoons and evenings trawling my old haunts. I revisited BG to see if Karl and Sam were still there, or any of the others I'd known, but everyone had since moved on. I left a message for Karl with one of the workers, but never heard from him. I even went in search of Alex and the other punks in Trafalgar Square. There were a few there, loitering in the same spot where I'd first met the old crowd, but I didn't recognize any of them. One of them said he remembered Alex, but didn't know where he was and thought he'd returned to Yorkshire after being arrested.

Although these irresistible weekday escapes proved somewhat futile, a new club had opened in Bayswater that gave me an important reason to be in the city every Friday and Saturday night.

The Kit Kat was a subterranean paradise of narrow passages and black and red walls, and home to a mythical world of spiked coloured hair, Mohawks, fantasy-inspired characters, drug dealers, vampires and vermin. But everything seemed beautiful to me and made all the other goth clubs I'd visited look like school discos in comparison.

My first thought, as I paid my £3 entrance money and walked towards the cloakroom, was that I had never seen so many goths and freaks gathered under one roof before; they were breathtaking. As the music pounded all around, you had to push your way past tripping punks and heavily-painted, staring eyes to reach a single red door that was a gateway to even greater sights and sounds.

On my first visit, the door swung open and a turbine engine of music almost took me off my feet. 'Body Electric' by The Sisters of Mercy had the small dance floor heaving with dark, twisting, writhing creatures – making it look like a pagan rite. Although it was one of my favourite songs, and the speed I'd taken earlier was screaming at me to dive in and join the worshippers, I couldn't dance. It was too much like walking into the best dream I'd ever had. I sat down in a daze with my mate Foggy and we looked at each other in amazement, as if to say things could never be the same after this.

I spent my weekdays in the company of Noel or Jim, with occasional trips to Kensington Market or the King's Road, all the while counting down the minutes and the hours until the weekend and the freedom of the Kit Kat. Following my discovery of the Bayswater club, it felt as if a fuse had been lit deep inside me. Though it was slow burning, I knew there was sure to be an end result; an explosion that would take me with it. I can only describe it as a beautiful feeling of fate and finality.

Since going to the Kit Kat, I'd become friendly with a smackhead called Jem, and before too long I was smoking heroin with him, either in the club toilets or sometimes at his squat in Chelsea. I was always careful, though, as my favoured highs came from being wired by speed or banged out on acid; I was less keen on being zonked out and unable to move. Also, despite having an addiction to speed, I felt disgust at the thought of being dependent on heroin. When I asked Jem whether he was hooked, he looked at me with an amazed expression, scratched his arms wildly and told me he could take it or leave it, and at first I believed him.

He hated the way that I chose to smoke it instead of injecting. He'd point his syringe at me as if he were a university lecturer, and rant about how stupid I was: 'It's a fucking waste, man. You're missing out on the real thing.' But there was no way I was going down that route. I'd seen what a waste it was when he'd mainline and then lean back with his eyes rolling backwards, the syringe still dangling from his arm. My fear of needles and a laughably snobbish attitude to becoming a smackhead like Jem no doubt spared me from an early death.

I knew I was already deeply hooked on speed, but having convinced myself that it was nothing more than a psychological addiction, I felt justified in comparing my situation to that of a smoker craving a fix of nicotine. Heroin was different, though, and seemed to exercise a different set of barbed hooks; the urge to do it again so soon after the last fix remained in the pit of my stomach rather than in my head, and so I could limit my usage to weekends only.

The waves of bliss I experienced while lost in opiate dreams, followed by the huge line of speed that made the experience complete, soon made me wish that the mindlessly boring weekdays in Maidenhead could compress into one tiny moment, so that the weekend headfuck could start all the quicker.

Shortly after moving back to Maidenhead, I'd had something of a windfall: for some reason, the bank had sent me a cash card for my overdrawn account, and, inexplicably, I'd been able to use the card to take out money and withdraw almost £2,000. With enough cash to live recklessly, I'd bought drugs and spent days in amusement arcades, losing myself in the fruit machines, the bleeping noises and the hypnotizing reels. Occasionally I'd end up in a bookmaker's, placing £20 or £30 bets on horses despite knowing nothing about racing. I'd pick a cool-sounding horse – the weirder the better – and watch as it invariably staggered home last. Sometimes, though, I managed to pick a winner, and the feeling in my stomach at having cheated the odds was incredible and not unlike the sensation of an amphetamine rush.

But the party didn't last for ever, and one day my card was swallowed up in the ATM. The dreadful words on screen – 'Insufficient Funds. Card Retained' – announced the end of the ride. It was as though someone had pulled out the plug that powered the only thing in life that meant anything to me – getting wasted and gambling.

I panicked and tried desperately to think of a plan to get some more money. I went to my bank and attempted to convince them I was working and was due to get paid, but my pleas fell on deaf ears, and I was strongly advised to start paying back the money I owed. I sold everything I had to raise a little cash, but it wasn't even enough to fund a single weekend in London, and ran out halfway through Saturday night.

Then, one evening, a golden opportunity presented itself. I'd gone to Jim's house to see if he fancied a night out. I often entered his place by the back door, and when I saw the lights were on in the kitchen I knocked, but there was no reply. Instead of jumping back on my bike and going home, I peered through the window. My heart started pounding as a small vicious voice told me to go in. A handbag belonging to Jim's mother was on the kitchen table, lying wide open, and next to it a cash card and some loose change. I didn't think about the consequences of my actions, that by stealing the card I would be shattering the trust of people who loved and had faith in me; the only things on my mind were the chemicals I could buy if I had only had some money.

Without a PIN, the card was less useful to me, but fate continued to smile down on me as I fumbled around in the bag and eventually found what I was looking for – a slip of paper containing the card's four-digit number.

It was inevitable that one day my thoughtless actions would cause the whole house to come tumbling down around me, while I remained blind to the damage done to those caught in the falling rubble. I had no thoughts at that time for anyone but me – I was my world. I loved my friends, but only because they were playmates in my drug-dominated recreations. I was trapped in a glass cage, staring out at distorted faces and surroundings. I didn't understand anything, but didn't care enough to ask the questions that might have prevented the child philosopher from turning into an adolescent bulldozer.

I spent the next month or so on a binge of speed, heroin and LSD, courtesy of the money stolen from Jim's mother. Any feelings of guilt or remorse were easily suppressed by the drugs flooding my mind and body. Only the dreaded comedowns allowed the voice of my conscience to speak out, and so I did my level best to keep it muffled by ensuring I was never without a supply of speed – or indeed heroin, which I'd started to buy from Jem, whose old hospitality had dried up when he realized I had money to spend.

Half the time I didn't have a clue where I was and I'd often wake up in houses or squats in different parts of London, with people I didn't know, and frantically hurry to cut another line or use the stolen card to get more money if I was running low. An addict's life is dominated by forward planning and the worry of finding that next fix.

I had started renting a cheap bedsit on Blackstock Road in Finsbury Park, which I used as a bolthole when my head couldn't handle any more and a place to hide my drugs. I didn't care about getting caught and though I knew I would, sooner or later, I simply couldn't stop myself. It was yet another example of life getting beyond my control, which resulted in my trampling and hurting anyone or anything that got in my way.

One Sunday morning, after a weekend of chemicals and clubbing, I came back to crash at Foggy's brother's flat in Maidenhead, where we'd often go either before or after the Kit Kat to collapse on the floor with other burnouts, hoping that unconsciousness would reach us quickly.

I tried to get some sleep, but couldn't. Although I hadn't slept for a few days, the speed and acid from the night before refused to let me wind down, and so I was sitting on the floor, staring at the moving walls and faces, when the doorbell rang. Someone was alert enough to open the front door and in walked two CID officers from the local police station, flashing warrant cards and staring at the shocked and confused faces that filled the room. At first everyone thought it was a drugs raid, but instead the men had asked for me. Despite being so wasted and barely able to stand up, I knew they'd come to arrest me. I felt a huge wave of shame and relief that it was finally all over.

They searched me and found the stolen bank card in my pocket. While I did my best to stay upright and avoid the freaked-out and disbelieving expressions of the others in the flat, I was read my rights and led to the waiting police car, before being driven to the station to be charged formally with theft and obtaining money dishonestly. I was still heavily tripping, particularly after the unique experience of being handcuffed and bundled into a police car. Unfortunately, the whole morning turned into the longest bad trip I'd ever had.

On arrival at the station I was taken to an interrogation room where the same two detectives fired endless questions at me. In my drug-addled state I made little sense and so was moved to a cell until I could speak more coherently.

The walls of the white cell closed in on me from every direction, squeezing out all the air from my lungs and I knew I was finally in hell. I felt I'd been hurtling towards this moment all my life, and now here it was – I'd reached the nadir of my existence and the end of the cursed race was in sight. The secret dark life that I had so zealously embraced was open and exposed. I was naked at last, and the poison that coursed through the veins of the seemingly sweet kid whom mothers trusted and friends loved was revealed for all to see.

Eventually, I was taken away for questioning, but I remember few details of the occasion – apart from one thing. As one of the officers told me to sign my statement, the other leaned forward and said that I'd broken the trust of a good woman who would never be able to put faith in anyone else. If anything could have brought me crashing back down to earth, it was the thought of Jim's mother, weeping – crushed by the fact that someone whom she had invited into her home on numerous occasions could take advantage of her so heartlessly.

I waited to be returned to my cell and tried to work out how I could finish the story the way it was meant to end. Everything of any use to me – my belt, my studded wristband and necklace – had all been bagged up and put away, but I knew I'd work something out; if not in a police cell, then somewhere else.

As it turned out, I didn't go back to my cell and was released on police bail. I was discharged from custody and my belongings were returned, but just as I was about to leave the station, a strong hand grabbed my arm and a voice told me to stay put. I looked up to see the face of the policeman who'd once jabbed an eyeliner pencil at my cheek and threatened to punish me if he ever saw me again. Good, I thought, hoping he'd be true to his word and take me to a quiet corner to beat the living daylights out of me. 'Wait there,' he said.

So I did. I waited for him to return with three or four other queer-hating coppers to take me to a small cell for instant justice. I looked over and saw him talking to one of the detectives who'd questioned me. After a couple of minutes, he came back alone and asked me, 'Where are you headed now?'

I lied that I was going home to my parents and he stared at me intently for a few uncomfortable seconds. Then, in a voice far removed from the sneering homophobe who'd once intimidated me, he said, 'You're not going to do anything stupid, are you?'

I must have looked in a terrible state. I was still coming down from the night before and hadn't been able to stop crying since the arresting detective had told me about Jim's mother. In an attempt to reassure him, I said, 'No, I'm fine. I won't do anything stupid.' He seemed to believe me and nodded, before opening the door for me to leave. For a worrying moment I thought he might have kept me back at the station. I couldn't understand why the bastard from a year before had appeared so concerned about a freak like me.

The relief at being given my temporary freedom was enormous. I had told the truth when I said I wasn't going to do anything stupid, and had been able to look him straight in the eye and convince him. The fact was I wasn't going to do anything remotely stupid: all I was going to do was to kill myself, which in my view was far from stupid; it was the only logical and right thing for me to do.

I jumped on a train bound for the capital, thinking only of the task in hand, and headed back to my north London bedsit. As I walked down the Blackstock Road towards that depressing little room, I realized that the stash of substances hidden in my suitcase wouldn't be enough to carry out my plan successfully. I couldn't remember exactly how many tranquilizers I had, but I knew there weren't many, and I only had half a gram of heroin left, which was useless – especially as it was nowhere near pure – unless I could find a syringe. My deep fear of needles still prevented me from injecting, despite the obvious temptation, and I didn't even know where to get hold of one at such short notice. Instead I toured the local late-night shops for the missing ingredient for my recipe.

The first couple of stores I tried didn't stock the item in

question, but the third shop yielded a result. I decided not to bother with subtlety. I launched myself over the counter, grabbed the display box of Anadin Extras from the shelf behind the frozen shopkeeper and strolled out of the shop. There were no shouts or scurrying footsteps behind me as I hurried back to my bedsit – perhaps he was too stunned at the speed and oddity of the theft to raise the alarm. Nonetheless, I quickened my pace, as the last thing I needed was to be arrested again for shoplifting. Fortunately, my room was less than five minutes' walk away, and it wasn't long before I was turning the key in the lock to be greeted by the sad, bare walls that I intended would be the last thing I ever saw.

There was a bottle of vodka on the small dressing table – the only piece of furniture in the whole drab room – which I drank while I wrote my final letters. As far as I recall, they weren't the usual suicide farewells – such as life isn't worth living, there's nothing left for me, etc. etc. – because those weren't my reasons. I had to impose the ultimate punishment on myself for what I'd done to everyone around me and to end the torment I was suffering as a consequence of my actions. In common with other suicides, I was motivated by two things: selfishness and cowardice.

I clearly remember the letter I addressed to Jim: I tried to explain that I was beyond sorry for what I'd done to him and his mother, and that I believed I was sick with an unknown disease I couldn't cure, but that I hoped one day they'd both be able to forgive me. The others, to my mother, Noel and Foggy, were apologies for taking the easy way out. I was under no illusions that I was a coward and accepting this fact gave me a sense of peace that no drug had so far managed. I sealed my brief shrugs of defeat in small envelopes and left them propped up by the bed.

I had a small tape recorder in my room and knew that I wanted to go out listening to *Faith* by The Cure, which is possibly the most beautiful and depressing album ever recorded.

I started the tape rolling and as the music began playing I had the strongest feeling that I had been here many times before.

I checked my suitcase and fished out my collection of drugs. I had to be as organized as possible regarding the procedure and order of consumption to avoid the risk of passing out halfway through, which was a prospect that filled me with dread.

I emptied out every Anadin from all the packs I'd swiped earlier until there was a pile of about 200 pills on the bed. I knocked back the twenty tranquilizers from my suitcase with the vodka, then laid out the heroin on foil and smoked it in one hit. The effect was instant and before I knew it I'd fallen back on to the headboard of the bed, struggling to stay awake. I know I lost a few minutes, because 'Other Voices', the third track, was hauntingly wafting out of the tape player. I wanted to stay where I was and not bother moving, but I snapped at myself to finish off the task in hand.

One by one, I forced the tablets down, counting them all to keep myself together and to focus on hitting my target of 200 pills. By the time I'd reached 100, it was almost impossible to manage any more. I'd finished all the vodka halfway through the count and had to fill the bottle with water from the sink in my room, and it felt as though my whole body was bursting with the foul taste and smell of the tablets. My throat was on fire and as I reached 120, I knew I'd reached my limit. I simply couldn't bear to swallow another one, and in any case the danger of vomiting was something I knew I had to avoid.

I felt sure I'd taken enough to do the job properly, so I crashed back on to the bed and waited for tomorrow never to come.

# 21 | *Near Death and Life*

A HUGE BLACK HOLE stretched out in front of me as I slowly slipped down the waiting slide. Way off in the distance I could hear 'The Drowning Man' call me to final sinking sleep. It felt so perfect, so complete and joyful to have finally made it to this point – almost as if this moment had been waiting for me all my life, and that each and every failure that stretched behind me could now be forgiven – perhaps even understood.

I felt arms around me, strong consoling wings that seemed to wrap me up and lift me into space. The black hole wasn't down after all, it was up and I could see something there, waiting. No bright light, no celestial sounds, or white-winged angels, just an opening that grew wider the higher I rose. And then I was awake. Wide awake.

Sunlight poured into my room and I sat up with a start. I could hear birds singing outside, which was strange because I'd never heard them before in this most urban part of north London, unless I'd never paid them any attention till now. A second later, I found myself in the garden outside my room. It was the most magical place I'd ever seen. Children were playing hide and seek, running after each other and falling, laughing with delight as they played their weird and wonderful games. They looked familiar, but before I could get near to them I was back in my bed. The curtains were drawn and I couldn't understand how I'd been able to see the children through the window, or how there could be bright daylight in my room when the curtains were closed. I sat up and tried to work out what was going on, unaware that I'd overdosed. I had a burning feeling there was something I'd forgotten, something important, and it would be helpful if I could remember it.

Suddenly my room was full of people, which struck me as bizarre. One minute the room had been empty and the next they were in front of me as if they'd always been there. I saw faces I recognized immediately and then I realized: the night-time visitors from my childhood were back. There were others too, whom I didn't recall from those silent visits years ago, but even they looked familiar and had the same inscrutable expressions that set them apart from people made of flesh and blood.

I was so happy to see them, and I felt like crying tears of delight. I wanted to run to them, but for some reason I couldn't move. It didn't matter though; just to have them so close to me was wonderful and I felt such exhilaration that even though I knew I couldn't move, I felt certain I was dancing.

I saw the old woman standing to my right, smiling down at me. I hoped she could see that although I couldn't reach out my arms to hold her, I had missed her so much.

A figure approached my bed. A tall, good-looking man dressed in a well-tailored suit and waistcoat looked down at me as if I was a child trying to wriggle out of going to bed. Confusion hit me, though I had no idea why. Bending down slowly and giving me an all-knowing grin that admonished the naughty child he was about to tuck up in bed, he said, 'You're going nowhere.' His smile broadened. 'It's not your time yet. Sleep. Wake up.'

I realized he was right, and at that moment his bemused expression slowly started to fade, along with everything and everyone else in the room. The confusion I'd felt at his presence among my crowd of ghosts faded as I understood what was out of place here: this man wasn't a ghost, angel, dream or hallucination; I felt I knew him from the real world from which I'd tried to escape.

Darkness was the last thing I remember before I awoke to find myself sitting up in bed, the curtains shut and the muted light of the day revealing an empty bedsit once more. I couldn't move a muscle for what seemed like many long hours. It took me even longer to start processing what I'd witnessed. In fact I might have lain in that position for days. If the near-death experience was etched in my mind like a tattoo, the re-emergence into life was as cloudy as a thick mist. Before checking my bed and basin for any vomit – and finding nothing – which would have provided a more logical explanation for my survival, my last act was to go to the window, open the curtains and look for the garden I'd seen as I lay dying in vain. A concrete patio provided the only hint of a back garden, while rows of faceless windows from the block of flats in front of me was my uninspiring view as I struggled to make sense of what had happened. I stood there for a long time, remembering the bizarre events of the last few hours, and having no idea of what to make of any of it.

Dead zones, black holes or times in your life that have become detached from reality are common to all heavy drug users, but the one that followed my failed suicide attempt was the daddy of all voids. I don't remember leaving the bedsit, or how I ended up in a derelict house in Wood Green, or for how long I was there. All I can recall is the searing pain in my head and ears as a policeman dragged me by the hair across splintered floorboards and threw me out on to the street, while a black guy shouted at him to leave me alone and bent down to check that I was okay. I staggered off, not knowing whether I was asleep or if it was all a dream. It was only when I managed to make it to Jem's squat in Chelsea that I knew I was definitely awake. He answered the door, with black eyes that spun around wildly. 'Got any gear?' he gasped.

But I think I passed out before I could offer him a reply.

## 22 | *Back to Reality*

IT WOULD be reasonable to assume that having such a close encounter with death would have changed my life and my perceptions of the world for the better. I had, after all, taken enough drugs to do the job a few times over, but I hadn't vomited, been resuscitated or revived, I wasn't doubled up in pain with internal organs collapsing, and I had had an experience that seemed to indicate I still had a part to play in the world – although the afterlife was waiting for me, admission was not yet available.

Instead, I felt cheated and filled with a sense of abject failure. I had given death my best shot and been thwarted in my attempt, which was damning. Despite the mystical nature of my experience, and the fact that I'd survived with no bad after-effects, I reached the conclusion it had been a massive hallucination. The figures I saw in my room were clearly just memories dug up from my subconscious, and my temporary relocation to the garden outside could easily be explained by the hallucinatory results of such a large and varied drug intake. An inner voice boomed loud and large that I was overlooking the obvious fact I should be dead, given all that I'd taken, but I opted to ignore this point.

Although I thought I had seen the ghosts of my childhood, and had apparently flown out of the window into a garden that wasn't actually there, the figure who'd approached me with that whimsical, chastising smile was very much alive. I hardly knew Ian, the DJ at the Kit Kat, and had only seen him a few times from my low vantage point on the dance floor, while he was elevated in his little box, spinning the tunes to which we all danced.

I'd approached his booth a couple of times, and asked him to play the odd song. He always listened politely to every request, even when he was juggling three or four records in one hand and balancing refreshments in the other, but I'd never said much more to him than, 'Hi, can you play . . .' It baffled me as to why he had featured in my near-death hallucination, but of course the mind can play strange tricks, particularly when certain drugs are in our system.

So, as much as I would have loved to have believed in angels or destiny and a life that was somehow 'meant to be', I couldn't. In truth I was pissed off at Ian's random inclusion in my incredible visions because so much of it felt much more than just a delusion and I truly wanted to believe that something special had happened. But there it was; I had to accept that I was a failed suicide and cope with the life I was stuck with.

The way I dealt with my existence was firstly to stop dabbling in heroin and settle for a steady life of drugs that I could take or leave. My brush with death wasn't going to make me join the born-again brigade, but I did know that I had to clean myself up, for a while at least.

If I didn't believe in angels standing round my bed, then I definitely believed in Barry. I'd met him at the Kit Kat a few times and had taken to him instantly, but had never had a chance to get to know him properly. He was old-school post-punk, never short of witty comments and stories, and a likeable guy.

I was quietly honoured by the fact that not only did he seem to like me, but he also invited me to various places and introduced me to his friends. Despite being able to smoke whole hash-producing regions dry in one sitting, Barry was always completely together. No matter how stoned he was, he could always be relied upon to deal effortlessly with life, day-to-day affairs or even out-of-the-blue emergencies. I was in total awe of him; he was like an older brother who looked out for me, making sure I was on the right track and yanking me by the collar at the first sign of any trouble.

We spent quite a while hanging around a huge squat in Chelsea called Cheylesmore House, which overlooked an army barracks. Each and every one of the hundred or so flats was illegally occupied by an assortment of punks, anarchists and goths. I'd visited a few times before to score smack and had briefly gone out with a girl who lived there.

One memorable night of tripping started to wind down when someone turned the television on at six or seven in the morning. There was a newsflash about an IRA bomb that had been discovered in an army base and was about to be detonated in a controlled explosion. It was all very dramatic, and we sat there like little kids watching a cartoon as the camera showed a familiar block of flats and the army barracks, while a caption appeared on screen carrying the message, 'Bomb discovered in Chelsea Barracks.' It took us a few more seconds to realize just how close we were to the action when someone piped up, 'Er . . . isn't Chelsea Barracks, like, outside?'

At that we ran to the window with a chorus of 'Cool!' The whole of the street below was filled with police vans and army trucks. No sooner had we stopped giggling at being in the centre of something really quite serious than the front door burst open and three soldiers piled into the flat, no doubt searching for IRA suspects or bomb-making equipment. Instead they found something much more confusing – a bunch of spaced-out trippers. I heard one of us shout out, 'Bang bang!' and then saw Barry groan as one of our number passed a soldier a spliff. Much to our surprise he took a deep hit on it, thanked her and then shot off with his colleagues to continue their door-to-door search.

Any time I felt like escaping to a different realm I'd drop downstairs and spend time with a guy called Sean. He was an artist and musician who'd strum the most exquisite chords and riffs from a semi-acoustic as he wandered through psychedelic Elysian fields of various hallucinogens. Visiting his squat was like entering another dimension; the walls were practically bare, except for the odd beautiful sketch stuck up haphazardly with drawing pins, but his mind had a way of taking you with him as he pondered the existence of other worlds and dimensions out loud.

Sometimes he'd wander off, tripping up to his eyeballs, and leave me alone in his flat. Once he advised me in a meaningful way that I had to listen to The Chameleons. 'It's quite important that you do,' he told me as he floated out of the flat. I rifled through his vast collection of acid-inspired and trip-accompanying records and found the LP he'd mentioned and stuck it on his turntable. I liked it. It was good, but it didn't blow me away. I had trouble understanding what the singer was saying and some songs sounded similar to me, but it was all right. I felt a little let down by Sean's earnest entreaty to listen to this band, as I'd expected to hear something magical within their music.

One night, when everyone else was out clubbing and I didn't have the money or the inclination to join them, I was alone at Sean's place and looked for some good music. Most of it was from the Sixties or too weird and wacky for my liking, so I put on The Chameleons LP, *Script of the Bridge*, which I'd heard before. This time, I stretched back on his mattress to see if I could pick out any more of the lyrics.

The fourth track, 'Second Skin', had been playing for less

than ten seconds when the hairs on the back of my neck suddenly stood on end. My ears opened wider and my mind seemed to follow suit. By the end of the record I was stunned. I had never believed that guitars could produce such exquisite sound or that impossible drum lines could hold their own unique melody, and above all, that a single voice and those lyrics could so magically encapsulate the pleasures and pain of living.

I played the album over and over again, and it was still on the turntable when Sean floated home six hours later. With eyes as wide as saucers from the acid he'd picked out that night, Sean looked down at me with a satisfied grin saying, 'I knew you'd get there eventually.'

After a week or so spent hanging out in Chelsea, Barry and I were invited to stay with some friends at a squat in Borough, south London. I jumped at the chance to get away from Cheylesmore because although it was a wonderful and crazy place, there were too many temptations of the opiate variety. I'd already succumbed a few times, despite my vow to steer clear, and I knew it wouldn't be long before I did it again.

The squat 'owners' were due to move elsewhere and so gradually transferred the place over to us in the space of a week or so. What I couldn't tell anyone – especially Barry – was that I'd started to get withdrawal symptoms now that I'd moved away from my drugs supply at Cheylesmore. I knew I'd get no sympathy from Barry. If he'd known I'd used to slip off to smoke heroin at the junkie's squat downstairs, I'd be in for a hard time. I'd heard the way he spoke about 'smackheads' once or twice before, and couldn't face his particular brand of scathing derision or, even worse, him disowning me.

The cramps came on after two days at the new place and the nausea quickly followed. I hadn't expected any withdrawal symptoms at all because, compared to the junkies I knew, I hardly touched the stuff. In fact, I didn't even know I was withdrawing at the time, only that I felt as though I was dying both mentally and physically. I told Barry I was just sick and stayed in bed, trying my best to keep warm despite the regular blasts of cold air that breezed through a large hole in the window. I was also having nightmares and driving Barry crazy with my nightly shouts and screams. Perhaps a little unnerved by my unexpected behaviour, Barry left the squat for a few days, leaving me to recuperate alone.

I don't know how long I survived in that squat, my muscles squeezing shut, ripping apart and continually drenched in cold sweat, but it felt like months. Rats, real and imagined, occasionally shot around the freezing mattress that was lying on the floor. I was constantly frozen, even when I hunched over the single-bar electric heater and pressed my chest to the safety grill. I wondered if I was going to die like this; alone in a filthy squat, with puke stuck to my neck and chest. As I crouched over the fire, on or around the third day, I saw Barry's small tape recorder and wondered why I hadn't thought of it before. I grabbed the cassette I'd made of Sean's Chameleons album and pressed the 'play' button. It never left the tape deck; as soon as it finished, I'd rewind it and play it again. It wasn't long before my physical suffering was soothed by the calming melodies on the tape.

About two or three days later, I woke up one evening feeling ravenous, so I dragged myself off the mattress, went out and shoplifted a few cans of baked beans for dinner. In fact, I lived on baked beans for the next week or so until Barry finally showed up, clearly relieved that I had lost the insane glint in my eye. He bought me breakfasts and dinners every day until I left the squat for a few days to return to Maidenhead and to sleep in a real bed where rodents were absent, thankfully.

Even though they were some of the most frightening moments of my life, I had only experienced minor withdrawals because I had only dipped my toe into opiate waters; thus the hooks hadn't fully sunk in. I can barely imagine what real addicts with a daily need for heroin have to go through to rid themselves of their habit. I had a brief insight when a friend tried to clean up and he asked to be locked in a room to let the cold turkey do its work; his screams were horrendous, and driven mad by his cravings, he managed to squeeze through a tiny window, only inches wide, and jump from the first floor, hitting the concrete below before limping off. It made my experience seem like a touch of the flu.

My court case loomed for the theft charges and I prepared myself for the worst. My solicitor was based in Maidenhead and so it made sense to spend a few days there and avoid London for a while. When I walked in through the front door, my mother grew pale when she saw the state I was in. I'd lost a lot of weight. When she weighed me I was just over eight stone, which was not good for a six-foot-three man. During my brief stay with her, she made it her mission to feed me up and would find any excuse to go to the kitchen and return with various snacks. So convinced was she that I was going to vanish into thin air, I forced myself to eat to make her happy.

As my mother and I attempted to reconnect, I discovered that things were not going well with her and Dick, and hadn't been for quite some time. She mentioned the possibility of divorce and I started to realize how hard everything had been for her. Both she and I had one shared flaw: the refusal to face up to the past, the present, ourselves and each other. We spoke properly for the first time in months, and began to repair the damage we'd both caused.

Meanwhile, my solicitor didn't seem optimistic about my chances in court. I'd stolen over £1,500, illegally entered a property and was being charged with burglary as well as theft. I asked him if I could end up in prison. He looked at me, shrugged, and told me it all depended on which magistrate was sitting that day. Before I left, he offered me one piece of advice: I had to make sure I turned up.

It hadn't even crossed my mind not to appear for sentencing. I knew that I had to face up to the consequences of my actions and a small part of me even hoped I'd be jailed because I knew I deserved it.

I told my mother not to worry because I was only likely to be fined, but I asked Barry to look after my few possessions if the worst happened.

On the day of the hearing at Beaconsfield Magistrates' Court, I tried my best to flatten my Mohican and give the impression of being an upstanding member of society. Instead I ended up looking more like an escapee from an asylum in my white Oxfam shirt and the only decent pair of black jeans I owned that weren't shredded or decorated with splashed bleach.

As I travelled to court the only person on my mind was Jim's mother and how she must have felt to discover that someone to whom she had always shown such kindness had thrown it all back in her face. All I could hope was that she would one day come to understand that I was an aberration, and that all Jim's other friends were exactly how they appeared – decent, honest and not prone to fucking people over.

At the magistrates' court, I was met by my solicitor who told me I was extremely lucky – the burglary charge had been dropped, and now I only had a fifty-fifty chance of being sent to prison. I didn't say anything in response as I was only concerned with getting into court and accepting my punishment.

Once inside, and faced with a grim-looking magistrate who looked at me as though I was wearing a Sex Pistols T-shirt and spitting on the courtroom floor, I began to doubt the fifty-fifty odds that had been mentioned earlier. The charges were read aloud and, naturally, I pleaded guilty.

When the formalities between my solicitor and the court were completed, the magistrate looked at his notes and peered imperiously at me through his reading glasses. Informing me that the offence was a serious one and that he was duty-bound to reflect that in the sentencing, he told me, 'I therefore sentence you to a period of two years' imprisonment.'

I froze in disbelief. I had prepared myself for six to nine months – but two years? My legs shook and I thought I was going to drop to the floor. I clutched the rail of the stand and tried to steady myself, as the magistrate continued, after a well-timed pause, '. . . suspended for two years with two years' probation.' But all I could still hear was 'two years' imprisonment' and hardly understood what he had said after that. One of the clerks led me off the stand, telling me, 'It's okay, you're free to go.'

I couldn't take anything in as my head was spinning too much, but once my solicitor had led me outside, he explained the sentencing to me and how I would only serve the two-year prison sentence if I appeared in court again for any other offence within the two-year period that had been imposed. I had also been heavily fined and ordered to repay the stolen money, but I'd missed that part of the sentencing when my mind shut down over the prison issue. He patted my shoulder and told me that the magistrate was a crafty old sod and had intended to give me a helpful shock. He seemed quite amused at the court theatrics, but I wouldn't appreciate the magistrate's cunning verbal twist until years later.

When I returned to London, to my few belongings and the freezing squat in Borough, I certainly didn't feel like celebrating my freedom. The bare floors and broken windows of the flat made me feel as though I'd returned to an open prison that I'd chosen to live in of my own free will. I had to get out fast.

I grabbed my possessions, told Barry I'd find him at the Kit Kat and broke into a small, abandoned flat in Clapham. After a week of shoplifted baked beans and death threats from the next-door neighbours, I woke up one morning to find a huge rat asleep on my feet, so I fled, like any self-respecting loser, back to Maidenhead and my long-suffering mother.

23 | *First Love*

---

D EBBIE WAS SOMEONE I'd met at the Kit Kat who had
become a good friend. Some time ago she had discussed
the possibility of getting our own place with some mates
whom we knew and trusted, but as my court case was looming,
I hadn't paid much attention at the time.

Now that my day in court had been and gone, I mentioned
it to her again when we next met at the club. She was still keen,
so we decided to work out who else might be interested in
leaving the unstable rodent-filled world of squatting behind.
Barry was my first and only choice, and I knew I'd get on well
with Debbie; she had been going to the club as long as I had
and was what we affectionately called a 'hippygoth' – a
mutation of flowers in the hair and a barbed-wire corset.

In the summer of 1986, finding a landlord tolerant of people
signing on wasn't easy, especially when they looked as bizarre as
we did. Fortunately, Debbie's then landlord was happy enough
to entertain the idea of five government-supported, signing-on
goths moving into one of his many properties in north
London, as long as we came up with a month's rent and deposit
in advance. In my poverty-stricken circumstances there was no

way I could rustle up that kind of money, and when I asked a depressed-looking worker at my local dole office whether there was any chance of my receiving an extra £1,200 next week for a flat, she laughed hysterically and told me she loved me.

Fortunately, though, we had heard of a little-known dole-office secret that meant it was possible to receive this sort of money as long as you had legitimate contracts and a written letter from the landlord confirming the cost of a month's rent and deposit. So, the five of us piled into a Tottenham dole office, explained our situation and listened to them telling us over and over that we would not be receiving any more than our usual £30 a week. We sat down by the plexi-glassed counters and told them we wouldn't leave until we got what we were entitled to. Eventually, more than eight hours later, and with doubts raised over whether we'd been misled on the subject, a harassed supervisor emerged from a back office and barked at us to come and collect our cheques.

We could hardly believe it. Somehow we had walked out of there with £6,000. It had taken determination and a sit-down protest, but at least we were now on the way to a more legal and stable way of life – no more police kicking in the door and turfing us out on the street, no more excuses for carpet-less rooms, over-friendly rats and permanent colds.

Our chosen destination was a house on Mount Pleasant Road, one of the longest streets in Tottenham. It ran parallel to the Broadwater Farm estate, the scene of the grisly murder of a policeman during the worst riots London had experienced in recent times.

Number 133 was about halfway down the street and looked like a small paradise to us. There were six good-sized rooms, a living room, a tiny washroom and a garden. My upstairs room faced the street outside and was next to Barry's slightly smaller one; a womanizer called Gordon had the next room down the hallway and a girl I'd known from Maidenhead called Sam, who was obsessed with rabbits, took the room at the far end.

The front bedroom downstairs was occupied by Debbie, who, in just a few hours, had transformed it from a landlord-white box to a hippy love nest of candles, wall hangings and incense. Helen, formerly of the Cheylesmore squat, moved into the room next door. We threw a huge party as soon as we'd settled in; a party that lasted over a year.

Nights and days in Mount Pleasant Road were lit up by joints reflected in mirrors on the carpet, which we crouched over in worship while snorting massive lines of speed and coke. There was a never-ending supply of everything.

With my appetite for all things chemical increasing once again, I realized how easy it could be to finance my habit if I started dealing. Giving absolutely no thought to the two-year suspended sentence hanging over me, I began selling drugs at the Kit Kat. At first it was just small amounts of speed and acid, enough to fund my own intake. After a while, though, as word got round I was supplying, I'd be clearing ounces within a few short hours.

Barry's small room was the main focus of the whole house. He'd sit like a grinning king, skinning up endless joints for his subjects, and we'd observe him reverently, enthralled by his many stories. They were magical evenings and mornings spent in his company and they seemed to go on for ever. Indeed there were many times, cramped though we were in that room, when I really wished the experience would never end.

The summer of 1986 melted into autumn and then winter, but there were no seasons in that house; you partied until you dropped and when you woke up, you'd do it all over again. The Sisters of Mercy ran on a permanent loop from mine and Barry's bedrooms, so when one of us called time, there was always another small club to go to and endless chemicals to keep you wired. Downstairs an old video of Pink Floyd's *The Wall* played endlessly on the television like moving wallpaper, as people tripped and skated through the house. Half the time I had no idea who was who, as the house had quickly established a reputation among the Kit Kat faithful and beyond as being the place to go and also the place from which it was difficult to escape.

Whenever it was announced that there was to be a party that night, for the next three or four days there would be an endless procession of people filling the rooms, five different stereos blasting out a variety of goth tunes, and enough drugs to put us all in prison for a long time. In the aftermath of the Broadwater Farm riots and the resulting lack of police presence in the local area, our small world had the feeling of being untouchable and we exploited it mercilessly.

The blur of parties saw us explore and grade every possible source of manufactured high. On the rare occasions that the speed supply had run dry or we were waiting for a delivery of acid, we'd even sit sucking on gas canisters or munching on magic mushrooms like fly agaric. On one memorable evening, Micky, a gentle giant of a punk, proudly wheeled in a huge cylinder of nitrous oxide that he'd swiped from a local hospital; the carnage from that particular party was impressive even by our standards. Goths lay collapsed and giggling on the pavement outside, while indoors bodies lay crumpled like hysterical soldiers dying in a twitching mess on a battlefield.

There was an almost desperate quality behind the hedonism and decadence of those celebrations. We shoved and strained at our mental and physical limits, determined to do as much as we could as quickly as possible, for fear that it could all be over at any moment. As the endless nights rolled on, it became obvious to me that my own endgame wasn't too far away. The more drugs that filled the house, the greater my desire to absorb even more.

On another matter entirely, it seemed that I was going to be stuck with my virginity indefinitely. Although I'd laid the foundations on a few separate occasions, every time it came to the moment of penetration I'd feel a wrench inside my stomach as I lost all physical ability to do the deed. After a while, I'd stopped trying. Fortunately, it didn't feel like such a big deal to me any more. When I was wrecked, all I wanted to do was to get even more blasted; the mystery of copulation and erections didn't seem worth solving.

Around the time that I'd all but given up on the holy grail of sex, things changed unexpectedly one night when I was tripping with a friend, Heather, at a party. In the heat of the moment, we started to writhe around on the bed in a state of horny, ecstatic bliss for an hour or so, when suddenly – and much to her disbelieving cries of 'You're freaking me out!' – I shouted out to her that I'd just lost my virginity. It no doubt came as quite a shock when she realized she'd been hanging out with a nineteen-year-old virgin.

I had managed to convince myself that losing my virginity would change my world in some way, that I would perhaps stand taller and prouder, with a deeper masculine voice. In reality, though, it felt no different to passing my driving test; I had my licence at last, but I still preferred to take the drug bus, albeit without the use of needles.

Suddenly, at Mount Pleasant Road, there were syringes everywhere. Even people who used to sneer at friends who regularly jacked up had got in on the act, sitting on the sofa and casually tying up their arms and hitting their veins. I was the only one that couldn't. I wanted to. God, did I want to. I knew that I wasn't getting my fair share of body electric and it drove me crazy, but somewhere deep inside, someone or something had implanted a failsafe device that couldn't be bypassed, no matter how much I tried. I realized how effective it was when I was at a speed dealer's one night; as he fixed himself up, I told him to hit me quickly as well. He never even got to press the trigger, or so he told me afterwards, because I passed out cold the second the needle slipped into my arm. I gave up even thinking about it after that.

Whatever sensation I was being denied because of my needle phobia, it was more than compensated for by the discovery of two sources of powerful amphetamines – a mix of pure speed and crystal meths. There was nothing else like it. Even if you took it close to 5 a.m., it felt as if the party had just started. I lost no time in showering the club with it, then snorted up and gambled away my considerable profits. Though I was usually on the go for long enough to make the most of my partying, this new stuff could easily keep its users awake for many days. There was so much of it that my own intake was now running to several ounces a week. The more speed I sold, the more I took; the more I took, the more I wanted.

When I wasn't throwing £100 on a horse or into a fruit machine, I'd be snorting half-gram lines like they were cups of tea. I'd get so wired that I'd start to hallucinate and I didn't know when to stop. While my highs were getting higher, the resulting comedowns saw me plummeting to earth without a parachute to break my fall when I hit the ground. Nothing could spare me from the burning in my brain, the shakes and the paranoia that wrapped itself like giant tentacles around me. I'd close my bedroom door and curl up into a little ball, hallucinating demons and insects crawling all over my body, knowing that I was dying and wishing it could all be over.

I knew my party was coming to an end, and Barry could see it too. My skin was a permanent shade of yellow, which I masked with layers of make-up and foundation, but I couldn't hide from Barry's scrutiny. On one occasion he warned me to slow down, but resentfully I thought he was interfering in my life – I couldn't see that he was being practical and offering help. The last thing I wanted was anyone trying to throw me a lifeline. I knew I was burning out and couldn't wait to go up in flames.

Every two or three days, when I decided to sleep, I'd wake up in agony, with the strange sensation that something had invaded my being. I wouldn't know where I was and would throw myself into the corner of my room, shaking and hallucinating, believing I was slowly going crazy. I was terrified, but not because I cherished my life; I had expected my body to give up on me before my sanity, and it was obvious that I was heading down the road of losing my mind before that of losing my life. I was disintegrating, I knew perfectly well why, and yet I still continued to fill my system with substances that would pull me even faster to complete meltdown.

Even being rushed to hospital one night, and having a doctor tell me that I'd be dead in a few months if I didn't stop what I was doing, failed to make an impression on me. In fact, the first thing I did when the taxi dropped me back home was to drop acid.

What I hadn't anticipated was the arrival of something even more powerful than the helter-skelter ride toward my own self-destruction; someone who would bring me to my senses and make me focus on my last remnant of sanity.

Nicky was part of what I regarded as 'the beautiful set' at the Kit Kat. Her long, red hair and physical beauty combined with her all-black goth regalia made her look every inch the dark princess. I had silently admired her from the sidelines and often wondered what it would feel like to be with someone so lovely. I'd never imagined that anyone like her would even bother talking to me, but as I would discover, Nicky was much more than just a beautiful face; there was genuine warmth and an amazing personality behind her outward beauty.

To my delight she had started to offer me lifts home from the Kit Kat, which gave me the perfect opportunity to get to know her better, and the more I learned about her, the more I started to fall in love with her. Aside from my crushing lack of self-esteem, there was a bigger problem to overcome. At that time she was going out with my housemate Gordon. Their relationship was far from perfect, though, as he'd regularly finish with her so he could parade a new girl around. Unfortunately for me, he would always pick Nicky back up like a trusty old leather jacket once he got bored of his new toy, and she would let him.

So, as it had been with Maria many years ago, I had little choice but to keep quiet, enjoy Nicky's friendship and forget all thoughts of anything more. It wasn't easy as we were spending more time together and I was falling ever deeper.

Meanwhile, a curious thing had started to happen. Since I'd started to tie myself up in knots over Nicky, I'd noticed that the drugs weren't having the same effect on me any more. After snorting a few lines, I'd feel as if something was wrong. Then one day, I counted the number of wraps in front of me and realized that I'd practically halved my intake. Spending time with Nicky was better than any drug I'd ever taken and I found I couldn't get enough of her.

The situation was far from straightforward, though, and what was even more frustrating was that she still believed Gordon was being faithful to her, despite the endless flow of girls I'd see coming and going from his room.

I bit my lip and said nothing. All I could hope was that one day she'd realize the sort of person he was, and allow me to open up and tell her how I really felt. I'd be ready to be let down gently, of course, but at least I'd have proven myself able to feel love again and not felt forced to bury my feelings as I had with Maria.

Not surprisingly, it was becoming increasingly hard to look Gordon in the eye. I felt guilty for having feelings for his girlfriend, even if he was a liar and cheat. There were some lines you couldn't cross, no matter what, and it didn't feel right to be thinking about someone else's partner in that way. My guilt was eventually alleviated, though, when one evening Gordon said something that proved he wasn't worthy of Nicky's affections.

A group of us was getting stoned in his room when he brought up the subject of his latest list of conquests. Then, without even looking up from the line of speed he was chopping up, he remarked suddenly, 'Actually, Nicky's the worst lay I've ever had – she's so shit she sends me to sleep.'

I sat there in disbelief, stunned at how he could be so

disrespectful of his beautiful girlfriend in front of so many people. My fist curled up into a ball as I waited for him to say one more bad word about her. Then I left the room quickly, without saying a word, unable to trust myself to keep a lid on my emotions, but realizing it might be time to act on my feelings, otherwise I might regret it for the rest of my life.

I sat in my room knowing that what I was about to do would cause a great deal of friction in the house and possibly end up with me losing many friends, but I knew I couldn't keep my feelings quiet any longer. Although I stood little chance of getting together with Nicky, I had to be honest with her. All my life I'd trained myself to keep my feelings and secrets buried and out of reach of others, and now, the one time I felt like shouting them aloud from the rooftops, the consequences I faced would be heavy.

The days passed by and I stayed holed up in my room, avoiding everyone in the house apart from Debbie, with whom I'd shared my dilemma, and wondering whether I dared tell Nicky how I felt, knowing that the inevitable rejection would be hard to accept. And then it dawned on me that during my contemplative malaise I had neither smoked a joint, nor taken any speed or acid. The mist was finally clearing from my eyes and it was time to end to my increasingly self-destructive behaviour.

I had long days and nights to go over what had happened during the past year or so, and think about what I'd been doing to my mind and body. What had started off as a wonderful long party was now nothing more than a mindless routine of getting blasted, crippling comedowns, selling chemicals and wondering when I'd get busted. I felt like a sleepwalker being shown the film of his night-time travels and it took a long time for me to understand how far off course I'd staggered. Then one evening, as I sat listening to The Chameleons' 'Second Skin', the realization dawned on me like a bolt of lightning: I hadn't been using drugs at all; they had been using me.

I knew then that it was all over: the house, the drugs and the dealing, perhaps even Nicky, because even if I couldn't have her, I certainly didn't want this life any more.

I called my mother and asked her if I could come home to clean my life up once and for all. She almost cried down the phone and told me that there was nothing she wanted more. At that moment I knew that whatever happened with Nicky, or during my return home, my time at Mount Pleasant Road had ended.

Saturday evening came and as I sat with Nicky in my room, I told her I had something important to tell her, and that it would change everything and possibly mean the end of our friendship. A solitary candle flickered, and in the half-light I noticed that Nicky had turned to face the carpet, as if she was afraid she was going to hear something unpleasant. I carried on regardless, and told her that I was in love with her. I explained that I realized there was no chance of us being together, but that if I didn't tell her how strongly I felt about her I would be making one of the biggest mistakes of my life, and I was tired of making mistakes. I finished up by telling her not to worry too much about the situation because I was planning to leave Mount Pleasant Road soon as life had become intolerable and it was time to start afresh elsewhere.

I prepared myself for her shocked reaction; for her to touch my face sympathetically and tell me that she was happily in love with Gordon and could only ever see me as a friend. But Nicky didn't tell me that there was no chance of our being together or that Gordon was her one true love. Instead, she remained motionless, kneeling on my floor, still gazing downwards at the carpet with her head bowed for a worryingly long time. Then she looked at me and said simply, 'Oh, God.'

I didn't know how to react to that. Oh, God, what? Oh, God, you idiot – how could you? Oh, God, why have you ruined our friendship? I couldn't work out what she meant because her face told me nothing. So I asked her a question that I knew would give me some indication as to where we both stood: 'Just tell me if you feel anything for me beyond friendship?'

She looked at me, with tears forming in her eyes. 'Of course, I do . . . Oh, God, what a mess . . .'

At that moment, hearing those words, my life got back on track. I had dreamed of this moment so many times without ever believing it could come true. We held each other tightly for an age, and with that embrace the pleasures and pains of Mount Pleasant Road became consigned to my past. My future lay with Nicky.

## 24 | *A Dark Light Goes Out*

A FEW DAYS AFTER my confession to Nicky, I returned to Maidenhead to get away from Mount Pleasant Road for a while and work out what I was going to do next. Once Gordon discovered he had a rival, he was determined not to lose Nicky; not because he loved her, but more on a matter of principle. I wasn't prepared to witness his pathetic attempts to keep her as his property, and decided to leave him to it.

Nicky had told me that she needed time to think about everything and I felt the same way. I wanted her to reach her own decision based on her feelings for me and so I didn't reveal what I knew about Gordon and his philandering ways. If she chose me, then I wanted it to be for no other reason than because she loved me.

I arrived back in Maidenhead somewhat changed from my last visit. My mother was astonished and told me she couldn't remember the last time I'd looked so happy. She paled a little at my weight though, but as I'd only been living on Tracker bars and Dr Pepper for a few months, it was no wonder. So I let her try to build me up, knowing it made her feel better. Bridges had been rebuilt between us and our relationship was back on track. For the first time in many years, I spilled my heart out to her and we ended up talking late into the night, as we had done regularly in my youth.

Even my brothers could see the real change that had taken place in me and, to my surprise, I found myself telling them all about the past year, how my drug habit had almost destroyed me and how falling in love had made me realize how close I'd come to losing myself. Iain and I seemed to click again, and I knew that whatever happened back in London, I still had fences to mend with my family, but that we would get there eventually.

When I returned to London, Nicky told me that she had ended her relationship with Gordon, and we celebrated in the best way imaginable – with a kiss.

It would be impossible to describe the sheer intensity of that first kiss. All I know is that I had never really felt anything before that moment, and every second of that kiss and what followed is burned into my memory as if it happened only yesterday.

A week later, Nicky asked me to move in with her. To me it was like a dream that had once seemed remote, but was now becoming a reality. In one of my last nights in Mount Pleasant Road, I lay on my bed, planning how we would make things work. I knew it wouldn't be easy and had already told her so. I was screwed up inside, and kicking my drug habit was just the first in a long line of difficult obstacles to be overcome. Despite this, I really believed I could make it, knowing she was at my side, a pillar of wisdom and strength.

Suddenly, I was yanked back into the present when my bedroom door flew open. I leapt out of bed, thinking that the drugs bust I'd always feared was finally happening. Someone switched on my bedroom light, but instead of rampaging police and sniffer dogs, the figure entering my room turned out to be Trevor, my supplier's runner. He sat on my bed and looked around my room, sneering at the black bin liners and the posters on my wall.

'Get dressed,' he ordered. 'Rob wants a meeting.'

I was still reeling from the shock of having my door kicked open and an uninvited guest in my room, but the second he mentioned Rob's name, I knew there was a problem.

'But it's three in the morning,' I told him. 'Can't it wait until tomorrow?'

'Now,' he snapped back, and it dawned on me what this was all about: I owed Rob money.

I dressed quickly, as Trevor stood in the doorway, and then he beckoned for me to follow him. A car was outside and we were driven the short distance to the house I'd visited on so many occasions. As I emerged from the car I decided that Rob was overreacting. With all the drama of the last few weeks I had forgotten to pay him back, but the amount wasn't a fortune, and Rob always got the money I'd owed in the past; he knew I would settle eventually. We both got on and I liked him – I thought the feeling was mutual, but perhaps I'd miscalculated.

I did some mental arithmetic to work out how long I'd need to pay him back the £500 that I still owed, and told myself he'd be happy with two months. But when I entered his front room, I could see that it was more serious than I'd anticipated. Two huge guys sat on one sofa, glaring at me as I came in with Trevor, while Rob sat on a chair looking nervous. I'd never seen him so subdued before and I began to fear for my safety.

Rob gave me a small nod and tried to put me at my ease with a strained smile, and invited me to sit down. I felt as though I was at the dentist, about to get my teeth pulled out. Rob apologized for dragging me over to see him at such a late hour, but he was calling in all his debts and had no choice. I lived closest to him, so I was the first, but he'd be busy for the rest of the day collecting what was owed to him. It was clear he didn't like the situation any more than I did.

'I know I'm behind, Rob,' I reasoned, 'but I'll get you the money as soon as possible. I've stopped dealing and I'm trying to clean up. I'll have a job as soon as I can. You'll get it within eight weeks, I promise.'

Rob shook his head slowly and a voice boomed out from the sofa: 'You'll get it *now*, fucker. You're telling us that you've stopped dealing? So how are you going to pay the money back?'

The voice belonged to a huge, scary-looking guy. His mouth didn't seem to be moving behind the thick, dark beard that covered his face, but the contempt in his eyes was plain to see, and told me he wasn't a man to be messed with. When I tried to explain I'd have some paid work soon, the bearded guy told me to shut up. I did as he said. Rob repeated that he needed the money now.

I understood his situation and why he seemed so uneasy. He owed money to his suppliers and they were calling in what was due. The men on the sofa were doing what Trevor had done to me, because their employer wanted his money – now.

When I explained that they'd have to wait because I didn't have a penny, I saw the bearded guy nod slowly and braced myself for a baseball-bat beating.

'Okay, fuckhead. Then we'll get our money another way, right?'

I looked back at him the way I felt – stupid.

'You're going to have to do a little delivery work for us. You got a passport?'

I nodded mutely. Even though I didn't have one, I knew what was coming.

'Good. If you don't pay your man what you owe him by this weekend, then you're going to have a little trip somewhere, with a little suitcase and you're going to bring it back to us. Then we'll call it quits. And don't even think about trying to do a runner – we know your friends, we know where you club, we know Maidenhead and we know you're a fuckhead.'

The true seriousness of the situation became acutely apparent the moment they mentioned my hometown. How they knew where I was from, I didn't have a clue, but one thing was certain: I was in deep, deep trouble.

I sat there in silence as Rob stared at the floor.

'Well?' the beard asked me, as if I'd missed something. 'Fuck off then.'

On the walk home I wondered how quickly I could get a passport and what I needed to get one. There was no way I could find the money. No one I knew had that kind of cash and there was nowhere to run, that was clear. I had no choice. I couldn't believe the bitter irony that just as my life was about to begin again, I had to dive even deeper into the world of drugs to settle a debt I should never have allowed to build up in the first place.

For the next couple of days I lived in my room, feeling the full weight of my suspended prison sentence, plus the long term I would face for smuggling. It would be a miracle if I kept myself together going through customs; the odds were stacked heavily against me. Then, as if things couldn't get any worse, a friend of someone else to whom I owed money came round to warn me that Jimmy would be paying me a visit to pick up his cash. Although it wasn't much, that wasn't the point.

Jimmy was part of a small East End firm that I'd ill-advisedly got to know. He'd given me a few ounces and when I'd asked him how much and when he wanted paying, he waved his hand and said, 'Don't worry, pal. Whenever. Give me what you want.'

It seemed an odd way of doing business to me, but at the time I was just happy to get my hands on such good stuff. A week later, I discovered that Jimmy thought it was hilarious to slash faces with a cut-throat blade he always carried. I also learned he was meant to be on medication for schizophrenia, but he never took his tablets. So a visit from Jimmy was the last thing I needed.

Swab was a regular caller to our house in Mount Pleasant Road, and after Barry he was probably the person I got on with best. I'd known him for a couple of years and during my drug-taking days I'd loved nothing more than dropping acid while he did his best to freak me out and entertain me.

On this occasion, when he banged on my door, walked in, and stood there grinning in his trademark top hat, even seeing Swab wasn't going to help me forget my ever worsening problems. Usually, during my frequent depressions, he always had the knack of dragging me out of them – mainly by lampooning my gothness – but this time it wasn't working. He asked me what was wrong, so I told him about the debt and who was involved.

I'd never seen Swab look so serious before, and seeing his grim reaction made me even more depressed. As he mulled things over, though, he gave me a grin and told me not to worry; he was certain something would crop up. I wished I could share his confidence, but I was glad I'd shared my fears with him.

Later that evening Nicky turned up unexpectedly at the house. We hadn't been due to meet until the weekend, for the move, but it was great to see her and for a moment, at least, I could forget the mess I was in. She sat down on my bed and said we had to talk. So worried was her expression that for a moment I thought she was going to call everything off. Instead, she revealed that Swab had told her everything – the money I owed, the threats and the job I had to do for Rob – and she said to me, 'I can't let you do it.'

I could see how concerned she was, but she clearly didn't understand what or who was involved. 'I've got no choice, Nicky. You don't know who these people are and they're not going to go away.'

'No – and neither am I,' she replied, firmly. 'I've got some money saved up and I need you to tell me exactly how much you owe, so we can get you out of this mess.'

It was the last thing I wanted and I told her that I couldn't take her money, but we both knew that pride wouldn't keep me either out of prison or hospital. So, the next day she turned up with £700 from her savings that had taken her months to build up. She beamed a smile at me, knowing that it finally marked the end of my old life.

After clearing up my debts with both Rob and Jimmy, and clearing out of my room in Mount Pleasant Road, I rushed excitedly towards my new life with Nicky. She had a room in a house in Edmonton where there were no all-night parties and no dealers nor wasted strangers wandering in and out. She'd go to work during the day and leave me to get used to a world without chemicals and comedowns. The sun would shine through the two large windows in her room and hurt my eyes – I wasn't used to daylight nor the rhythm of the daytime that, over time, I had forgotten how to move to.

Before settling down with Nicky, I'd been a chain smoker; my chest heaved and spluttered with the heavy deposits on my lungs. With her support and encouragement, though, I began to ration the number of cigarettes I was smoking, and suddenly went from a hundred fags a day to only ten. Gradually, the gunk cleared from my chest and a feeling of good health slowly started to manifest itself. As my energy levels started to pick up, I channelled my feelings of vitality into my new favourite hobby of jumping her the second she got in from work and not stopping until she groaned that she had to get some sleep.

Other former users have spoken about how empty they feel after cleaning out and trying to join the real world; the boredom and the gaping hole that stare you in the face every morning. But I didn't experience any of that. The physical symptoms I endured included minor cramps, colds, headaches and sickness, but compared to the two or three days in that freezing squat in Borough, it was a breeze. There was no doubt in my mind that Nicky was the reason for my survival – to me she was the best medicine on earth.

With this in mind, I felt that the time had come to be completely honest with Nicky about the details of my past. It took me a week to build up the courage, but I finally had the chance to do something I should have done with both Noel and Barry, but simply hadn't been able to when it came to the crunch.

We sat down one evening and I told her as much about my father as I could, but as I prepared to reveal all about the night I attacked him, my mouth froze. I couldn't move it. She sat in front of me, not saying a word, and the more I tried, the more my lips refused to open. I had to close my eyes and try to imagine I was telling myself. I heard my voice recounting what had happened and when I'd finished, I waited for her to move away from me in horror, in the way I'd always feared anyone would if they found out I'd tried to murder my own father. She put her arms around me and held me for a long time saying nothing. Then she whispered in my ear, 'You saved them. You saved your family.'

In all honesty, I hadn't looked at it like that for a very long time. Maybe I never had – only during the night itself did I know exactly why I had to do what I did. The years following that night saw me heap so many layers of guilt upon myself that, eventually, all I was left with was the unmitigated feeling that I was some kind of monster who'd committed an act of pure evil. I had simply forgotten why I had been driven to such an act.

Read as a sequential order of events, it seems hard to believe that I could ever forget why, but guilt carries a shovel, conscience is the hole and once you're down in it, you're trapped.

In my mind I knew what Nicky had said was true, but the problem was I didn't feel it to be true. It was that crucial difference that couldn't justify me climbing out of my hole just yet, but I knew I'd made an important first step on the road towards leaving the pit and the graveyard far behind me.

Barry had started to go out with Nicky's best friend and suddenly we were back on track again. With my head clear at last, I appreciated him more than I ever had and the four of us would go to Trent Park in north London for long afternoons that made the past year seem so unreal.

They were perfect days that made me smile for the first time in a long time. But just as we were finally getting used to sharing some good times together again and renewing our all-important friendship, Barry was arrested. He'd been caught in a car with a tiny amount of speed while driving, and been charged with possession. At first it seemed there was nothing to worry about. He wasn't dealing and only had enough for himself and the night ahead. So he was facing a fine and a slap on the wrist, nothing more. Then a letter came from his solicitor with a shock attached. One of Barry's friends, a guy called Paul who'd been arrested with him, made a signed statement that Barry was a major drug dealer and had supplied various clubs in London for the past two years. Most of the sworn statement was false, but now Barry was being charged with conspiracy to supply on the basis of Paul's attempt to wriggle out of a minor charge of possession.

When his case came to court, Barry was sentenced to eighteen months in prison. We couldn't believe it. It didn't seem possible that he could have been sent to jail for a crime he hadn't committed. I spent the next three days in shock and wondered how it could have happened to him.

With Barry's exit, everything collapsed. The house in Mount Pleasant Road couldn't carry on without him; he had been at its centre, and one by one everyone who meant anything moved out. Not long after, the Kit Kat was spectacularly raided by police – the front page of *The Sun* featured a surreal photograph of a cop dressed as a punk arresting a clubber – and then forced to close, probably as a result of Paul's statement.

And so a door swung shut on the mythical world of the Kit

Kat, that dazzling dark underworld of the eighties where you could be anything you wanted to be, and which would one day become the stuff of post-punk legend and nostalgic longing. At the time, though, the significance of its demise was lost on me; I could only feel relief that I'd quit dealing in time to avoid an inevitable prison term.

With its passing, people vanished into the real world of jobs and responsibilities, old familiar faces wiped off make-up and put on shirts and ties, some jumped on to the house-music train that was building up steam, while others floated in limbo, unsure of their place in the new world of the nineties.

## 25 | *'Real' Life*

NICKY AND I soon found our own place. Her house had been enough to make a start in, but there was little real privacy. Things had got worse when a crazy guy moved in with an Italian girl downstairs and they seemed to spend all their time arguing. It reminded me too much of another couple from my past.

To escape the madhouse we decided to get our own place. As luck would have it the small one-bedroom house next door became available for rent and so we could make the move with ease. Although the place was tiny, full of damp patches and had walls that wobbled like scenery from *Crossroads* every time we trod too heavily, it was all ours.

As we hauled our belongings in, Nicky stood in the middle of the front room, looked above her at the ceiling and said, 'I've got a bad feeling about this place.'

'What do you mean?' I asked her, worriedly. 'You mean for us?'

She stood there in silence, assessing the situation. 'No,' she said slowly. 'Not for us – I think. The house . . . like something bad is going to happen to it.' She sniffed and carried on unpacking as if nothing had happened, but I didn't like the way the hairs had stood up on the back of my neck and hoped she was misreading something.

Ignoring Nicky's ominous feeling, we got down to the crucial task of painting the walls and making it look more like a home. She had an eye for what looked good where and which colours worked best, and so between us we created a small sanctuary for ourselves.

The first year or so was bliss. Most weeknights would find us cuddled up on the sofa watching B-movies and *Blackadder*; our weekends were spent in parks and drives to the country. Neither of us were interested in clubbing any more, and whenever we felt like dancing we could turn up the volume on Nicky's stereo and dance away indoors.

We were also able to host a visit from my mother, who, after finally divorcing Dick, had come over to London to see our new home and wish us well. I was delighted to see her looking so radiant. As far as I was concerned, the divorce had been long overdue and it seemed her newfound freedom was proving to be a tonic.

Once we were properly moved in, my first priority was to get a job. Ideally I wanted to do something that involved music, but I couldn't afford to be choosy and had to start earning money quickly; I didn't want to be relying on Nicky after she'd helped me to clear up my debts.

The first year saw me selling bin liners; computer parts; stationery; photocopiers; telephones; dating-agency services and Savile Row suits. I found a few fun jobs as well, and for a while I worked as a chat-line operator and also took calls for a horoscope line. When I found out that I'd have to read out random horoscopes to my gullible callers, and tell them that terrible things might lie ahead (so they'd continue to call back for more information), I decided to start making things up. I'd pretend to tap their details into the computer and then sit back and tell them how wonderful the week was going to be as long as they smiled at least ten times a day. While spreading a little bit of happiness, I learned that calls to the horoscope line quadrupled during my time there. As I worked alone from midnight to six in the morning, I had carte blanche to do and say what I wanted. I loved that job, but was sacked when the company realized that I was spending hours dialling random numbers in the US and comparing cultural notes with complete strangers.

My other jobs were far less rewarding. With all of them I'd wait until I was on the verge of swallowing my own tongue, collect my pay packet and not bother to show up the next day. Nicky would come home from her own steady job in an advertising agency and look at me as I sat guiltily on the sofa, and groan, 'Oh, God. Not again?'

I just couldn't do it. I tried so hard to conform to the nine-to-five ideal and even attempted some night work, all for Nicky's sake. I felt I needed to prove to her that I was on the road to normality, but despite all my efforts nothing was working out. Every time I had to lie through my teeth about the product I was hawking or obey commands from ravenous managers about never taking 'no' for an answer, I knew I was selling a piece of myself for a miserable few pounds an hour.

I could feel depression setting in with each new job. My creative urges remained unfulfilled and although I had started singing in a band called The Host, Nicky had unthinkingly referred to it as a 'hobby' too many times for my liking, which made me realize we had very different ideas about what made my life tick.

Meanwhile, Barry had finally served his sentence and was due to be released. I'd never managed to visit him in prison. Although I'd written him long letters, I couldn't cope with seeing him deprived of his freedom. More importantly, I could hardly bear the guilty feeling I had that he'd served a sentence when I'd escaped all punishment for my own dealing crimes. The injustice was difficult for me to accept.

While filled with nervous energy over his impending visit, I prepared the house as best I could. When he walked through the door, I did my best not to cry, knowing that he would simply tell me to shut up, and gave him a quick hug. I was amazed to see how well he looked after almost a year in prison. We sat down and I asked him how it had been. 'It was shit, of course,' he said, not giving much away. I toasted his health and couldn't believe how grounded he was. Even if he'd been forced to endure some terrible times inside, he would never tell.

Barry stayed with us for a few days and while we were together we acted like children or rather I did, just to see his expression as he laughed at my foolishness. I hadn't realized how much I'd missed him and was grateful that he never asked me why I hadn't visited him. I felt I'd failed him in this regard, but I think he knew exactly why.

To take the edge off the drudgery and the desperation I was feeling over my precarious employment situation, I'd started to smoke hash again. What I didn't want to face up to was that love couldn't wave a magic wand over the inner disaster that was mySelf. If you don't know yourself, you'll never know anyone else properly, and if you can't love yourself, you'll never know how much someone else loves you.

Sometimes, without reason, I'd blow up in a terrible uncontrollable rage. I'd see Nicky's scared reaction to my irrational frenzies and hate myself for what I was doing, but in these such moments I couldn't shake off the grip of anger that seized me and tossed me effortlessly around. Of course, I didn't lay a finger on Nicky, nor come remotely close to threatening her, because all my rages were directed at me and me alone.

One day, I picked up a dinner plate in a blind fury, threw it across the room and stood there, frozen, looking at the pieces of broken crockery while listening to Nicky's sobbing, and I remembered how I'd seen my father do exactly the same thing. It shocked me deeply.

And then I began to gamble again. Although I thought I'd left that part of my life behind me, I hadn't realized that the monster was merely sleeping and waiting for the right time to re-emerge. The more my anger intensified, the more it stirred, and it didn't take long before it had found an escape hatch.

At first I kept it a secret from Nicky because I thought I could deal with it. As far as I was concerned it was only a phase, but the phase turned into months of spending all my savings and then eating into my overdraft. It was obvious that if I didn't stop soon I'd be making the same old mistakes from my past. I had no choice but to tell Nicky about my gambling habit, past and present. She was stunned, of course, but far too level-headed to overreact or cause a scene. Her sole concern was to help me, and the next day, she gave me the address for Gamblers Anonymous, telling me that she knew I could overcome this problem, but only with proper help.

The following Sunday, Nicky drove me to a huge church hall to attend my first meeting. My initial reaction was to turn away. If the meeting had anything to do with organized religion, I simply didn't want to know. But when I turned back to look at her sitting in the car, I knew that even if they were Bible-bashers I had to give it a go – if not for me, then the woman I loved who had never let me down and who believed in me.

Fortunately, there were no Bibles or any bashing – just a group of about twenty men, no women, sat in a circle. I was surprised to see so many attendees. I wandered over and asked if I was in the right place for the GA meeting and was warmly greeted by them all. The chair of the group suggested that I sat down and listened for my first meeting and told me not to worry about making a contribution. 'The first meeting is always the one that leaves you speechless,' he grinned.

A ripple of laughter went round the group and I noticed how ordinary everyone seemed. I'd half-imagined I'd be faced with the kind of shabby old men that I used to avoid looking at in betting shops, but most were reasonably well dressed and spoke eloquently about their lives and how gambling had affected them. The more they revealed about themselves, the more I felt part of a frightening compendium of individual horror stories all linked by the common theme of gambling.

Most of them had lost everything. They had sacrificed their homes, jobs and families, and all they had left was the hope that they could start again. It was tragic to witness them break down in tears as they told the group how they'd stolen from their friends, employers, and even their own children.

Such bitter truths got me thinking about Jim and his mother's money, and how much of it I'd spent on gambling as well as drugs. It seemed I wasn't alone, for at that precise moment, a fellow addict began talking about his own drug problem that compounded his gambling habit, while another spoke about how his alcoholism and gambling relied on and fed off each other. I decided I didn't want to keep quiet after all, so I stood up and told them exactly what had led me here and how my compulsive personality had seized on gambling first, then drugs, and then both. I was applauded for my contribution, but the inner applause I felt was even louder.

I attended three meetings in total. Some people have to go their whole lives, as though taking regular shots of medicine for an incurable illness; others attend for a year or so, some 'break out' and come crawling back wracked with remorse. The lucky few are fortunate enough to have a moment of clarity, understand the workings of their compulsive personality, and put a stop to it before it destroys them. I was one of the lucky ones. Unlike most of the men at the meeting, I hadn't been gambling all my life and so catching a glimpse of what my future might be if I didn't put a stop to it now was more than effective for me, and I never gambled again.

I cannot claim to be 'cured' of my compulsive or addictive urges, because I don't think you ever really can be. Nevertheless, it is possible to learn or discover ways of channelling your compulsions into activities and projects that are positive and creative, not negative and destructive.

When a surgeon is faced with a bullet-riddled patient, the first thing he has to do is remove the bullets and shrapnel; only then can he ascertain the extent of the damage and continue treatment. I may have extracted a few bullets, but if I imagined the surgery was over I was deluded. In the beginning, I thought that losing my damaging addictions would change my life for the better, but all it did was trigger a new set of problems. Depression and rage still frequently consumed me, and no one felt it more than Nicky.

I couldn't understand what was causing me so much anger and unhappiness. I loved Nicky with all my heart, but sometimes she felt like a stranger. I hid myself from her far too often, preferring to escape to the back room to compose depressing songs that I couldn't bear to listen to again.

To an impartial observer or a therapist, it may have seemed obvious what the real problem was, but I had no interest in going down the therapy route. I tried it briefly once, purely out of curiosity, but I left the session more confused than before I went in. The therapist was far more interested in how often my parents shagged, than how regularly I heard them screaming.

I instinctively felt that therapy would complicate matters and create a reliance on strangers that I wanted to avoid. Instead I preferred to examine the problems that I faced in the present rather than the past, and discuss my worries with friends and lovers who cared about me rather than professionals who were simply doing their job.

The dissatisfaction I felt with my working life was definitely still part of the problem. I'd managed to hold down a job in the sales room of a courier company for two years. Admittedly, for a nine-to-five position it wasn't a bad set-up. I had my own office, was my own boss more or less and got stoned whenever I wanted with the bikers and drivers. I'd stuck at it for so long mainly because I was tired of listening to Nicky's complaints every time I walked out of a dead-end job. But it was still a job that involved selling, which I despised. I was earning money from the business of persuasion and that clashed violently with my own ethos of a peaceful life. I was nothing more than a nuisance to the people I had to call and would regularly be subjected to verbal abuse and phones being slammed down on me. Hardly the most rewarding way to earn a living.

The only time my anger abated was when Nicky and I went away together. Being out of the city brought me a peace that enabled us to rediscover how close we could be and how much we loved each other. On a trip to Wales one summer, we drove through a rainbow, visited the fairy glen of Betws-y-Coed and had a wonderful time taking in the breathtaking scenery. One night we got lost while driving around in search of a bed and breakfast. We took a turn up an old dirt road towards a distant farmhouse in the hope that they might have a room. It was pitch black, except for a couple of dim lights from the farmhouse ahead. Luckily enough we were offered a room for the night, and so, tired from our endeavours, we sank into a huge comfortable bed and fell asleep instantly.

The next morning I woke uncharacteristically early. Normally I slept like the dead until Nicky either jumped on me or splashed cold water over me, but as I opened my eyes, feeling Nicky still asleep next to me, a sudden and violent inner earthquake tore through my body. It was like having a huge electrical current ripple through my body. I wasn't scared because I instantly knew what was happening. The vibrations increased and suddenly I was floating above my body, looking down at my sleeping self and Nicky lying next to me, curled up with her pillow. I knew that I had left my physical body. I had the fully-conscious knowledge that I wasn't dreaming and the feeling of freedom was extraordinary. I shouted in delight and flew upwards, through the bedroom upstairs, through rafters and the roof, until I was hovering above the farmhouse itself. To my right, I could see three huge trees, a broken fence and some sheep grazing. The second I thought about being there, I was there. The branches of one of the trees surrounded me and I gazed at the droplets of dew on the leaves, sparkling like precious gems, each one filled with a myriad of beautiful colours.

The feeling was indescribable. I had experienced fleeting moments of connectivity on LSD, but this was total and purely natural. I'd come down off a trip and be left with only the fragments of things I'd seen, but every finite moment of this experience was crystal clear and I wouldn't forget a single second for the rest of my life. I'd read about such experiences and had always kept an open mind on the subject. All I could think, as I floated through those jewelled droplets and branches, was that nothing would ever be the same again for me.

Then, I felt movement next to me somewhere – Nicky was stirring.

'Oh, please, no,' I thought as I hovered among the trees. 'Not now! Stay asleep, Nicky!' But her arm fell over my body and she moaned that we had to get up. She hadn't even finished her sentence before I shot back into my physical body and instantly jumped out of bed.

She screamed – she'd never seen me move so quickly out of bed and it scared her.

I breathlessly paced the room, crying out, 'It's true! It exists! Oh, my God!'

She looked at me, seriously unnerved by my odd behaviour, and demanded to know what was wrong and so I explained what had just happened. As I told her, I threw my clothes on as fast as possible; there was something I had to confirm.

While Nicky remained behind in the room, no doubt wondering whether I'd finally flipped, I ran out of the farmhouse, hoping and praying that my suspicions would be proved right.

There it was. I could hardly believe it, but ahead of me everything was just as I'd seen it during my unscheduled morning flight: three trees to my right, about three hundred yards in the distance a broken fence vanished into the field like a slide, and several sheep were contentedly grazing. Because we had arrived at the farm the previous night in utter darkness, with no lights to show us the way, we had seen nothing of the surrounding area until the morning, so how on earth could I have known what was there before seeing it with both feet on the ground? I let out an ecstatic, 'Yes!' and spent the rest of our trip on a natural high and full of boundless energy.

The incident made me realize how blind I'd become to the world I lived in and also to myself. I started to recall things I'd either forgotten, blocked out or dismissed as imagination, including my near-death experience, which stayed in my mind for a long time afterwards. I had told Nicky a little about my failed suicide attempt, but hadn't mentioned that I'd seen Ian, the Kit Kat DJ. It didn't make sense to have seen him during the event and so I simply gave her the bare bones of my experience. Now I couldn't stop thinking about it, despite an inner voice of logic trying and failing every time to dismiss it as a mere hallucination. I felt as though I was lying to myself and accepting a convenient answer rather than giving proper consideration to an unorthodox possibility.

I was sure there was a reason for it, because it was clear that there was something much greater I had yet to understand. Fortunately, it didn't take long before a trusted hand began guiding me in the right direction, leading Nicky and me to embark on an important journey of discovery.

Noel, my old mate from Maidenhead, had been on an enlightening trip to India. He told me all about it when he came to visit one day, and the more I listened to his adventures, the more fascinated I became. I was compelled to learn more, and read a book on Rajasthan; with each new page and photograph, I felt my heart pump faster and a distant bell ringing inside me. I knew that I had to go, with or without Nicky, but to my delight she agreed to come along.

Deep down we both knew that the trip would be the greatest test of our relationship. If we were still holding hands at the end of the planned six-month journey, we'd make it through anything, but if it exposed even more cracks, we would have to face the fact that perhaps a fresh start for each of us was the best way forward.

It was during this period, as we were slowly winding things down in London, that I received a knock at the door. I opened it to find my father standing in front of me. His unexpected appearance caught me off balance. I hadn't seen him since 1987, when I turned up to our meeting wearing make-up, and he'd spluttered, 'Oh, for fuck's sake. What's that on your face, son?'

When I told him it was eyeliner, he'd replied, 'Oh, Christ. You're not a poof are you?'

'Sometimes, yeah,' I'd said, savouring the moment I'd been waiting for all my life. Strictly speaking, though, that wasn't true. My curiosity in the subject had ceased following the incident in that popper-filled hotel room some time before, but it felt great finally having the guts to say it and watch his reaction.

Surprisingly, instead of responding with fists and fury, he rolled his eyes heavenward and, with the faintest glimmer of a smile, he muttered, 'Christ. I always knew you were.'

Taking advantage of the rare moment of good humour, I spent the rest of the day teasing him by camping it up and making him crack up and choke on his pint. It was undoubtedly the best day I'd ever spent with my father. When we parted company, he hugged me goodbye and told me he loved me. Though it meant a lot to me, it also added considerable weight to the guilt I'd been carrying around inside me for years.

Even though he had looked ill the last time, and his hands trembled as well as his jaw, he still seemed healthier than he'd been during his earlier visits. On this occasion, though, the man who stood before me didn't look anything like my father. He had lost so much weight that the worn-out suit he was wearing hung off him shapelessly, further emphasizing his bony physique. His appearance shocked me into a long silence.

The main reason for his visit to London was to see his brother Tony. He had been accused of shooting a man in a Holloway pub, and was in prison awaiting trial. I was shocked to hear the news and couldn't imagine my softly spoken giant of an uncle being capable of such a crime.

Initially I was happy to see my father, although it was hard to take in how unwell he looked. The more he chatted away, the more I thought to myself, '*I* did this to him.' Eventually it became unbearable to hear him telling me how much he missed his three sons. All I wanted was for him to go away.

After he'd finally left, I rushed to the bathroom and threw up.

Within six months Nicky and I had saved enough money for the trip. In October 1990, we said all our goodbyes, placed our possessions in the safekeeping of our parents, until finally we were standing in the middle of an empty front room. It had seen many more good times than bad, but I felt happy to be leaving it behind and embarking on a new adventure. Nicky smiled at me as we stared at our former home and reminded me of the bad feeling she'd had about the place when we were moving in.

'Well,' I told her, 'you can't be right all the time.' And off we went, into the waiting taxi and on to a land with more magic than even I had dreamed possible.

Two weeks later, while the place was still unoccupied, the boiler exploded in the bathroom and destroyed half the house.

## 26 | *Under Indian Skies*

TAKE ONE addictive personality, place it in a country where the hash costs less than chocolate back home, and leave to simmer for three months. Together, Nicky and I learned that India is a recipe for anything you desire: we both wanted to find out whether we had a future; Nicky needed to know where her happiness truly lay; I was desperate to uncover the real source of my deep discontent and rages – we each discovered much more.

India is an impossible place to explain. Osho, the revered and reviled guru, perhaps came closest when he said that the country is situated over an energy field within our planet that is unlike anything else on earth. For me, it is a place beautiful beyond words and ugly beyond comprehension. It can both chew you up and spit you out or hold you to itself in a loving embrace and help guide you to your true Self. Disrespect India at your peril.

The first twelve weeks of our trip were filled with fear and excitement: we stayed in the war zone of Kashmir, while rockets launched by the mujahideen exploded next to our houseboat; we faced the prospect of being kidnapped; stared in disbelief at the Taj Mahal; drank bhang lassi – a government-approved cocktail of hashish and curd – and prayed for death; caught dysentery; saw stars explode like fireworks; and watched people either burn out or dazzle in the midst of India's unflinching intensity.

After the third month, we ended up on the small island of Diu in the state of Gujarat. Its colonial past was clearly evident in the Portuguese-inspired houses and architecture we discovered in the centre of the town. We headed off to the small coastal region about five miles to the west and found the site that we had been told was the most incredible place in India.

Back then Diu was a well-kept secret among visitors to its shores, and became known as the alternative Goa for it lacked raves, hard drugs or heavy commercialization. The fear was that the more people who knew about it, the more likely it would become overrun with hotels, hawkers, motorcycles and techno, and lose its untouched beauty.

The sight that greeted us on our arrival was an unblemished vista of jagged rocks, pure sands, a scattering of beach huts and the emerald waters of the Indian Ocean, which reminded me of an ever-moving front lawn. Eventually, after a protracted bargaining period with a screaming villager, we settled in our own small hut. We soon learned that the bartering process was almost always punctuated with screams and shouts from the locals, so didn't take it personally.

Our back garden consisted of a jungle of palm trees that flashed and sang with swooping parrots and exotic birds. Water had to be collected from a well a mile away, candles provided all the light we needed and amazing food was cooked on open fires. I took to this simple way of life instantly and started to feel at one with the world around me.

We soon discovered that we had a lot in common with everyone in Diu, as we were all intent on connecting with the natural world around us. Nights were spent around small fires on the beach, gazing at stars, smoking joints, sharing chillums, but never saying too much to each other for fear of breaking the spell.

One night, as we sat in relative silence, the sound of the waves was broken by a noise that made the hairs on my body prickle. I had never heard anything like it. It was haunting, like a choir of babies singing the strangest of hymns. No one said a word as it continued until a low voice asked what it was.

'Jackals,' someone replied. 'Isn't it the most beautiful sound you ever heard?' I silently agreed. Though it lasted for less than five minutes, the supernatural quality behind those mournful voices stayed with me all night. I hoped to hear them again often during my stay, but their arresting performance proved rare.

Until our arrival in Diu, our journey had consisted of non-stop sightseeing and endless travelling, so when we settled down to enjoy the peace on the island, we had ample opportunity to start looking at the state of our relationship. At first glimpse, to me the signs weren't good. I'd watch as Nicky gazed sadly at the ocean and ask her what was going through her mind. All she could do was shrug, telling me she didn't know. It frustrated both of us and communication between us started to falter. Then, to make matters worse, I caught a bout of amoebic dysentery and could do little more than stay in the hut while spears dug into my stomach.

While in Diu, Nicky and I had met a guy from Manchester called Dominic. Prior to my illness, when I discovered that he knew the drummer from The Chameleons, I badgered him incessantly with questions about the band. Now, though, as I lay crippled with severe stomach pains, I was forced to listen to him laughing and joking with Nicky outside, making my agony mental as well as physical. It was obvious that Dominic had latched on to her, but Nicky didn't choose to see it at the time. I couldn't blame her, though, as I was a whining mess and whenever I tried to make her smile, she'd turn away.

After about a week of trying to starve the infection out of my system, I felt well enough to leave the hut and meet the new residents of the hut round the corner. There were about six Greeks crammed into that small shelter, all seemingly insane. Somehow they had managed to get hold of more than twenty kilos of the most powerful hash I'd ever smoked. The leader of the group spoke no English, but grinned communication through his two remaining teeth, while the others smiled in agreement. None of them said more than 'Namaste,' but the rest of us didn't care when an ounce was on sale for less than six quid.

There was also an unwritten rule that you had to smoke with them with every purchase, and so once we began smoking it in earnest, our small community became consumed by thick clouds of hashish that clung to the air all day and night like incense. It didn't take long to realize that these guys were hardcore smokers. Somehow, they had constructed an underground chillum – a huge tunnel ran underneath their hut and connected a huge bowl and pipe out of the ground. Although I had seen joints the size of didgeridoos before, when Barry had been in a sadistic frame of mind, the sights I witnessed in Diu were frightening.

Naturally, I had to give it a try. As the leader smiled his slightly manic grin, and motioned for me to pick up the end of the pipe, I saw him reach into his holdall and produce a lump of hash that at home would have lasted me a week. As he walked into the hut to get the ritual going, I laughed to myself as I considered how crazy it would be if he used the whole block of hash.

Crazy or not, that's exactly what he did, and crumbled the whole chunk into small asteroids on to the tobacco that coated the large metal bowl. Three of his party had gathered around me like eager scientists watching an experiment and the leader's girlfriend whispered to me excitedly, 'Breathe hard – strong!'

That would be the easy bit, I thought, as my lungs were like bellows from all my vocal training and singing – it was the likely aftermath that concerned me. A match was struck inside the hut and four enthusiastic heads nodded up and down like head-bangers while I sucked on the pipe with everything I had . . .

I came to lying on my back and opened my eyes to see the Greeks sitting around me on the floor, smoking their equivalent of little joints – huge chillums that wafted thick clouds over my blinking eyes. I must have been out of it for a while, because the light had shifted, but smiles and chuckles greeted my resurrection and they seemed delighted with me. As I knew I'd have to go through this every time I scored, I made sure I walked away with enough hash to last me at least a week because I knew that doing more than one of those a week would surely kill me.

So, while Nicky escaped with Dominic for walks around the cliff tops, I disappeared into impenetrable clouds of marijuana. Days melted into night without me knowing. As soon as I awoke I lit a chillum and slipped off to a place where I didn't have to think about my ever-worsening relationship with Nicky. I didn't want to face up to it, because we'd always come through the difficult times before, but this time seemed very different.

It had been three weeks since Nicky had started drifting away from me towards Dominic and I'd begun floating high on clouds. The date was 23 November 1990 – I was compelled to make a record of the following events knowing that what I'd experienced would change my life for ever – and a small gathering had come together on the beach. It had been an evening like so many before, and began winding down at about 1 a.m. Most people had shuffled off to their huts and hammocks, but I had opted to stay where I was, alone, for a little while longer. I leaned back on the sand and strummed out the chords to 'Soul in Isolation' by The Chameleons as the stars sparkled brightly above me and something indescribable started to fill my consciousness. I felt an extraordinarily lucid peace come over me as I lay there and sang lyrics that I'd always loved and related to so deeply. But as I sang the chorus, which proclaims that we are all separate and isolated, it struck me that something about those lyrics didn't hold true any more.

Before long I had the feeling that I wasn't alone — it was faint, but unmistakable. I rolled a joint and stared at it dispassionately. Once again I had lost sight of how to use drugs and instead I was abusing myself. Would I ever learn? I lit it anyway and leaned my head back on my guitar, taking in the beautiful night sky and all the lights above me, watching me.

I pulled on the joint and thought about how I had once believed in God, or a higher intelligence, but yet the only things I seemed able to relate to now were songs that emphasized how isolated we all were. Could that really be true? I knew it didn't feel true, so why did I persist in trying to find comfort there?

'Because it's easier that way,' a far-off voice answered.

Although it should have unnerved me, hearing the voice from within didn't even make me blink, because everything I was feeling and thinking seemed as natural as the waves splashing ahead of me and the stars smiling above me.

I fixed my eyes on one star that looked like it was dancing in the sky and I had the strange sensation of being pulled towards it. I remembered how I used to spend hours gazing up at the stars when I was a child, talking to God, to the night and the stars. It struck me that it was all lost and I would never have it again.

Again, a voice in my mind whispered, 'Is it lost?'

I certainly felt lost. I had lost my love and was losing myself — and no, I didn't believe in miracles and magic any more, because the only peace I could find lay in the joint in my hand.

Still the star above me pulled my gaze and my thoughts upwards. I had the sense it was somehow mocking me and yet I was drawn to that star more than any other in the whole sky.

Right, I announced to the universe, if you send that star shooting out of the sky by the time I smoke this joint, I'll never do this to myself again. Deal? I felt ridiculous for sending out such a challenge to the sky above, but at the same time the feeling persisted that I wasn't alone.

The joint burned down, the last flickering flames of the fire beside me made their last desperate jump towards the sky . . . and there was nothing, of course. I looked at the last half-inch of the spliff, looked up at my star and raised a toast to it as I pulled in the final ball of smoke and breathed out slowly. And then it happened.

At that moment, my star burst into a streaming blaze of sparks across the night sky and time stopped. I saw my whole life rush at me in images, feelings and actions; dispassionate and without judgement, every moment made clear for me to see and understand.

And then I realized what it was that had led me here to this place, to this point in time, and what had been the source of all my suffering. The intense feelings of guilt that tore through me were suffocating, and with each came a reminder of every moment I'd ever punished myself.

So much of my life had been dominated by guilt and punishment: for what our father did to us; the things he did to my mother; when I attacked him; everything I ever stole; my rape; suicide attempt; taking drugs; Barry's imprisonment; the list seemed endless. And then came the worst but most incredible revelation of all – I had charged myself with the crime of simply being alive.

My realization brought with it a sensation of extreme bliss. It was as though the universe or God or Buddha or a fallen star had shown me what a fool I'd been, but without casting judgement. If I'd been able to laugh out loud, I doubt I'd have ever stopped, but I was still caught in the moment, unable to move. Something retained its hold over me and I wasn't even sure if I was still breathing, but the white-hot glow of joy shone into all the hiding places I'd created within and rose up inside me, like a deep intake of breath.

And then I knew it was all over at last.

I had finally served my lifelong punishment, and the guilt was lifted from my conscience. I exhaled what felt like the longest breath of my life and as I did so the entire horizon, behind a strangely silent ocean, along with the whole night, breathed a sigh of relief in unison. It was audible and it was there; a sigh so loud it went right through me.

Then the inner voice said, 'Now you will go on a long walk.'

And on the cliffs, far off to my right, the jackals started to sing.

Nicky and I separated a few weeks later. We knew that there was no more perfect place to part than the small pilgrim town of Pushkar in Rajasthan.

The change that had taken place in me during that eternal night in Diu was one that Nicky had found hard to understand. I'd stopped smoking overnight, saw the path that lay ahead for me and we both accepted that it wasn't for her. The inner peace that was slowly dawning gave me the sensation of learning how to walk again after being crippled for most of my life. I knew it would take a long time, because the change was real and nothing like that of a born-again convert. I certainly didn't emerge from the experience with the urge to join an ashram. However amazing my revelation may have appeared, it was nothing more than an old useless skin being shed.

As if to add to the magic of that extraordinary evening, in January, while I was in the mystical city of Varanasi I received a letter from my mother, written in December. She revealed that she had been suffering terribly with IBS and it had got so bad she had started having problems sleeping. Her stomach had distended and she was in constant pain. Then, she continued, she went to bed one night, fell asleep and woke up in agony. Standing at the side of her bed she saw a figure, and as she looked more carefully, she realized it was me. I placed two hands over her swollen stomach and both the pain and the swelling disappeared. To this day, it's never returned. Though my mother could not recall the exact date on which this strange visitation took place, I couldn't help wondering if it had been around the time of my life-changing experience, on 23 November. In any event, her news certainly gave me plenty more food for thought.

On our last night in Pushkar, Nicky and I sat in the grounds of a former palace, now a hotel for backpackers, and spoke about what we both wanted from life. I told her that I knew London still had a part to play in my future and that the most important thing for me was to know myself truly. I didn't think there could be anything better. Nicky replied that all she wanted was to be surrounded by nature, but beyond that she didn't know; she'd wait and see. That made me happy. I felt certain she would find whatever she was searching for. India may not have turned her world upside down, but it had given her an idea of where she should be headed.

We made love for the last time later that evening. In the distance I heard a soft voice singing a Hindu prayer and we held each other just as tightly as we'd done all those years ago, when, sitting in my room she bowed her head and I first told her I loved her.

# 27 | *Quiet Wisdom Revealed*

A FTER SETTLING BACK into life in London, I had started to go to a new club called The Slimelight, which had risen from the flames of the Kit Kat. After a month or so of going, I started to find myself looking forward to the weekend ahead, meeting up with an old schoolfriend called Vicky, and reliving the best parts of the past. This time, though, I always returned home remembering every detail about my night out, without the crushing comedowns, and just the occasional hangover.

But the long walk I'd been promised back in India hadn't been an offer of a free holiday. I still had a lot of work to do and if I thought that one life-changing experience was going to solve all my problems, I was mistaken. The crippling anger may have dissipated, but a gnawing unease replaced it and the more I became aware of it, the more it chewed at me until I started to feel as though I was moving back to square one. Of course, I knew I wasn't. I had had a revelation that had turned me inside out, but India was far away from the urban jungle of London and the curse of humanity is that we forget so quickly.

After six months in Green Lanes, I moved on to a little flat in Holloway, and it was here that my brothers came to visit me, to start remembering how important we all were to each other. One night, as I sat with Iain, I took the plunge and told him about what had really happened to our father. He sat quietly for a while, in what I feared to be shocked silence, and I wondered if I'd made a mistake. Ever the considered thinker, Iain was merely taking the time to engage his brain before opening his mouth, and to my relief he replied, 'I always knew something had gone on that night. I felt it. I'm not all that surprised, actually.'

It turned out to be a long night of earnest discussion. Though it seemed that neither of us had changed much from the two peas in a pod we'd once been, who would read each other's minds and point out each other's absurdities, the little boys from our past had gone for ever and it was time to start acknowledging our grown-up selves.

One night at The Slimelight, I'd met an American girl called Lauren who was going to live in San Francisco. When she invited me out there to stay for as long as I wanted, I jumped at the chance.

I had been feeling a gnawing hunger inside me that I couldn't explain. Though I was happy enough with my life in London, my little flat, a crazy job with crazier people in a small courier company and my family, I knew that my legs were restless and more importantly that I'd yet to embark on my long walk. It was only when I travelled that I ever seemed to find the answers I was seeking, and so a journey to the States seemed like a timely opportunity.

A month before my visit I was back at The Slimelight, walking past one of the dance floors, when I stopped dead in my tracks. Sitting in front of me, with the hint of an enigmatic smile on her lovely face, was Maria, the girl I had once loved who had died on her way to school.

Of course the ghost from my childhood was long gone, and I soon found out she was a German artist called Bobbie who merely bore an uncanny resemblance to the girl from my youth. And once I got to know her it was clear she was nothing like Maria. I liked her instinctively, and her positive attitude had an immediate effect on me. There were times when I found myself battling with a lot of negativity that came bubbling to the surface, which frequently made me wonder if I'd really changed at all, but in Bobbie's presence it didn't seem to matter. I was able to stop berating myself for all the moments I'd taken a backwards step, because she'd point out to me that I'd also taken two steps forward. 'Life isn't a race,' she once said, and I knew she was right.

A part of me still believed that my connection with the universe that night in India should have transformed me into someone with total understanding of myself, at least, if not the world. Instead, I still got angry over stupid things and felt frustrated that I seemed to know hardly anything at all. In other words, I still remained a mystery to myself. But Bobbie showed me that I had to be patient and stay on the path I was treading with those small tentative steps. We grew closer daily.

I was naturally excited about my impending trip to the States, but was sad that I would have to leave Bobbie behind. There was no way I could cancel it, though, and I knew it was part of the journey to which I had committed myself. The open road was calling and I had no choice but to follow it and find whatever was waiting for me there.

One afternoon, a couple of weeks before I was due to leave the UK, I had a phone call from Nicky. I hadn't spoken to her for a while and it was great to hear her voice again. She sounded breathless with excitement and told me she had some incredible news: 'Andy, I've fallen in love! Oh, God! It's the real thing.'

Knowing that Nicky never let her emotions get the better of her, I realized that this was something big, and was delighted for her.

'But, Andy,' she continued, 'you'll never guess in a million years who it is!'

Just as I was about to ask the obvious question, everything in the room shifted as though it had been lifted up at one end, and I slid towards the vision and memory of a familiar figure: a tall man in a black suit, smiling down at a desperate young man trying to kill himself in a depressing bedsit, and telling him that it wasn't his time yet.

Nicky didn't have to say his name, but I heard her gasp, 'Ian! You remember – the DJ from the Kit Kat . . .' Her distant voice explained how he'd moved out to Glastonbury a few years ago, married, got divorced, and they'd bumped into each other. On she chattered as I stood there immobile, unable to say anything for a while, and somewhere a wall fell down with a hard thud.

At the end of our chat, I sat down in disbelief, now believing beyond all doubt that everything I'd experienced during my overdose had really happened. And if that had been real, how many other things had I dismissed as imagination, hallucination or mere coincidence? The list was lengthy.

The long road to finding all the answers began the moment I put the phone down and realized that Nicky had found the love of her life. I knew that they'd marry and spend the rest of their lives together, and time has since proved me right.

Though the mystery of how and why I saw Ian, of all people, as I lay dying all those years ago may never be solved fully, I came to accept absolutely something I'd read not long before: not only is the universe stranger than we imagine, it's stranger than we *can* imagine.

Before I left, Bobbie and I partied like it was the end of the world as we made the most of every second left to us. When I came to say goodbye to her on the day of my flight, I had the sudden feeling I was making a huge mistake. How could I walk away from someone I'd waited so long for? Was this part of an old mission of self-destruction? As I embraced her, telling her that I didn't know anything any more, she looked at me with tears in her eyes and said to me, 'You know you have to go. If you don't, you'll regret it for ever. I'll be waiting.'

So I left her with those final words shining like a beacon behind me; she'd be waiting and that was all that mattered. I also knew that whatever it was I might discover in America, it wouldn't keep me from returning to her.

As it turned out, my trip to the States was more of an amazing holiday than a voyage of self-discovery. I toured the south-western states in the company of a human dynamo called Jane, whom I'd met in San Francisco. It was definitely more than worthwhile, even if I didn't experience any enlightening moments. But that was until I wandered the streets of Berkeley, California, and was asked a question. It was a short question that didn't require an on-the-spot answer, and yet planted a seed that was to grow into my life's mission.

I'd been idly taking in the sights and sounds on the street, and appreciating the warm colourful people who passed me by, when I saw the hippy from a distance. He was sitting on a small stool, reading tarot, and a girl was kneeling in front of him on a cushion. I paused for a moment and watched as he gazed at one of the cards, his thin beard and sparkling eyes reminding me a little of Barry. Just as I was about to resume my aimless wandering, he looked up and smiled at me, and with his head slightly tilted and his eyes squinting at the sun's bright rays, asked me, 'Have you ever wondered what would happen if you broke the chain?'

He looked at me for another second and then turned back to his cards, leaving me to contemplate this seemingly random question.

Of course it could have been the case that he enquired this of everyone who walked past; perhaps it was his life's mission to make people think, or it was the one question he'd asked himself so many times that he'd worn it out and kept it alive by releasing it into the world.

All I know is that when I wandered off down that long white street, the question now belonged to me, as though he'd entrusted something precious to me and I had to work out what to do with it.

What was the chain? What did he mean? The answers to those particular questions were fairly obvious as far as I was concerned, but it would take some time before I asked myself the all-important question: *how* do I break the chain?

# A Door Closes

AFTER MY SOJOURN in the States, I returned to London briefly, to collect a few belongings, and was then on my way to join Bobbie in Frankfurt, where she'd moved just after I left for America. I had planned to stay for a few weeks, but things changed and before either of us knew it we'd been there for two years.

I got a job as a stage manager at the English Theatre in Frankfurt, and it was there that I reignited my passion for the theatre. I'd watch from the wings as the actors took to the stage and feel a burning desire to be out there, performing, rather than handing out props and pulling the curtain. When I asked one of the directors if there was any chance of taking a tiny part in a play, she looked at me in astonishment and exclaimed, 'Good grief, no! It takes years of training, darling!' As I watched some of the actors standing around on stage doing very little, I wondered how much training that took.

Living in Frankfurt turned out to be less than inspiring for both of us and after a while I was itching to get moving again. The people in Frankfurt were, on the whole, uptight and miserable, the city grey and featureless, and it was clearly not suited for anyone with creative urges. Bobbie wasn't prepared to stay there without me and so we moved back to England's capital, to our own little flat in north London.

I got a job almost immediately at a small production company in the West End, while Bobbie went off to college to fulfil an ambition to learn photography. For a while it was a situation that suited us both; in Germany, Bobbie had supported me for almost a year while I struggled to find work, and so it was my way of returning the favour.

The work itself wasn't too bad, but it still involved marketing, which I hated. Despite the good money I was taking home, I dreaded the mornings and often found myself staring blankly at the computer screen when I should have been working. After a while, my health took a nosedive. Sickness in the mornings later developed into severe pains in my ear, and just as I was wondering how much more of it I could take, Bobbie made the decision for me. I'd been putting off going to the hospital for a check-up for a while, but, afraid that something was seriously wrong, Bobbie marched me to the hospital and insisted to the doctors that I be treated there and then. Normal NHS procedure was cast aside in the face of her Germanic insistence.

The young doctor who eventually examined me spent less than five seconds looking in my ear, muttered 'Oh, God,' and disappeared with a worried look on his face. He returned a few minutes later with an older doctor, who also peered through the steel funnel rammed into my ear canal. While listening to their intense mutterings in incomprehensible medical jargon, it dawned on me that my earache was the result of something much worse than an infection or blockage. It turned out I had a massive non-malignant tumour, which had eaten into almost all of the inner ear, dissolved the bone covering my facial nerve and was steadily heading towards my brain.

The operation took six hours and required two surgeons to remove both the tumour and my entire inner ear. I was something of a minor celebrity for the next three days in hospital as swarms of doctors came to my bedside to congratulate me on having had one of the best surgeons in the country, Mr East, to whom I am indebted. There had been a real risk of my losing the facial nerve on my left side and it was due only to his skill that this was avoided.

Meanwhile, The Slimelight was still giving out its weekly call to dance and meet people. My eight-week, post-op convalescence mainly involved spending long hours doing nothing other than sitting at home watching mindless TV and studying Stanislavski, which had nearly driven me insane with boredom. As soon as I got my balance back and stopped crashing into furniture, I dived joyfully on to the dance floor. With my entire inner ear now replaced by plastic, some might have thought it strange that I was exposing myself to high-density noise, but the therapeutic effect was enormous. My favourite DJ, Pete, became an extension of my healing without ever knowing it. The depressive lethargy of the weeks before vanished completely after one night out, and after another few weeks it felt as though I'd just had my ears syringed.

Bobbie and I had become close friends with a girl called Julia who was the undisputed Empress of the club; she slapped strangers with fish, kicked persistently annoying men in the face, and generally ruled her little kingdom with an iron fist, thus proving what you can get away with when you're beautiful and an expert at kick-boxing.

Julia's former boyfriend was a guy called Bernie, whom I'd seen at the club once or twice. At six foot four, rippling with toned muscles, with a short angry-looking Mohican and facial piercings that spiked out of his cheek and lip, he looked an intimidating character. But appearances can sometimes be deceptive, and in Bernie's case it couldn't have been more true. He was wise, funny, gentle and, without quite knowing why, he absolutely fascinated me.

I had always been wary of men in general. Ever since I'd

suffered at the hands of my father, I'd erected an invisible fence around myself to protect me from any man who even remotely resembled him. It also took me a long time to build up trust in any male. But once I got to know Bernie, it seemed stupid to keep the barrier up.

He soon became one of the most important figures in my life. Not just because he told me how amusing he found all my emotional barricades and reclusive tendencies, or because he'd have me in stitches with his stories and exploits, or because I could sit in his company for hours and not need to say a word; it was because I couldn't escape the fact that he reminded me of my father. Or, more correctly, he reminded me of how my father could have been if he had been offered or made different choices.

It forced me to think about my father in ways I'd never considered before and the more I did, the more the question of the 'chain' burned into my mind.

Bernie could get angry, bitter and obnoxious, but he could control himself; all he ever did was breathe it in, breathe out and the next moment it was gone. He knew instinctively not to repress or hide anything that might seem negative or destructive – he simply swished it round his mouth and spat it out. Then he'd grin from ear to ear and burst out laughing. To me he remains the most spectacular shining example of how a strong male can attain greatness by rejecting the old, outdated ideals of what makes a man a man.

In terms of my career, I had yet to find a job that really inspired me, but a chance meeting at The Slimelight would point me in a new direction. As I chatted to a friendly Scots actress called Louise, I revealed how I envied her choice of profession. I was taken aback when she told me to stop dreaming, get off my arse and audition for the director with whom she was working;

an actor had dropped out of a play he had just started work on, and they were looking for a replacement.

Two days later, I found myself standing in front of the artistic director of a small fringe theatre company, above a north London pub, from where he ran his productions. Before my arrival I hadn't known what to expect and was dreading meeting an overblown luvvie who'd look down his nose at me and my lack of formal training. Fortunately, Enrique was anything but. He was a short but stocky, hirsute Mediterranean actor-director, who instantly put me at my ease.

'Ah, hi,' he said, shaking my hand vigorously before leading me into his little office with props and costumes stacked high to the ceiling. 'So, my friend, why do you want to be an actor?'

I told him about all the school plays I'd loved performing in, my brief time in Frankfurt's English Theatre and how much I'd yearned to be on stage, rather than handing out props from behind one.

He nodded thoughtfully and asked me if I was a poof. At first I thought I'd misheard him, the hearing in my left ear now somewhat unreliable, so I asked him to repeat the question and leaned forward to make sure I heard him properly.

'Are you a poof?' he demanded.

I was so stunned by the question that I couldn't think up a reply fast enough. I knew that the world of theatre was heavily populated by gay men, but I hadn't realized it was compulsory. The macho man in front of me didn't seem that way inclined, but you never can tell. As it turned out I was simply experiencing my first taste of Enrique's unique brand of humour, which revolved around poofs, penises and prostitutes.

'Don't worry if you are, my friend,' he explained, 'They're all bloody poofs, so you'll be in good company.'

'Oh,' I replied, still adjusting to his sense of humour. 'That's good.'

'I am not a poof,' Enrique emphatically informed me, 'but sometimes when I masturbate I think about cock.'

And that was my unique welcome to the world of professional theatre. Enrique gave me the part after a brief audition and then told me that although I'd be wearing a 'poof's costume' for the show, I'd also have a sword and so I shouldn't feel too ashamed about it.

I was on a cloud. Whether it was because Enrique just liked me, or he thought I simply looked the part didn't alter the fact that I'd auditioned against three professional actors that afternoon and still somehow managed to get the job. Even though I was by far the weakest and most nervous actor in the whole cast, I knew that I'd been waiting for an opportunity like this ever since my old school days on stage, and my lack of experience and ability was offset by my determination to stick it out and somehow learn the craft.

Despite my enthusiasm, though, in each performance onstage terrors defined my every scene. I'd look around me as other actors sailed through their lines with apparent ease, while my legs shook so much I couldn't help but wonder what the hell I was doing. Who did I think I was kidding? I was terrible and knew it. I'd made the classic mistake of watching actors who make it look so easy and then convinced myself that I could do it too.

Nevertheless, the acting bug had got under my skin and there was nothing I could do. I enrolled on workshops and gradually started to understand what it really meant to be an actor.

One evening in November 1997, my father telephoned me to see if I wanted to visit him. For the first time in my whole life, I was genuinely eager to see him. I wondered whether he'd sensed the hint of enthusiasm in my voice because he exclaimed, 'I can't wait to see you, son. I've missed you.'

Although not strictly true, I told him I missed him too. For some reason, I'd wanted to make him feel good; it felt important to me.

After I'd spoken to him, I couldn't help dwelling on the strange sensation of warmth that had penetrated all my old feelings of fear, resentment and guilt. I thought about the chain and how, without even realizing it, I'd been tracing the links back to my father and could see how strangled he'd become.

I remembered the fact that in his youth he'd chosen to go into a monastery and train to be a priest. How could this 'evil monster' who'd inspired such revulsion in me have even considered such a career? I imagined him, confronted by his personal waking nightmare of abusive brothers and his own father, and though his situation began to make more sense to me, I needed to know why he'd left such a sanctuary. What had happened?

The inevitable conclusion I reached was that he'd been sexually abused by a priest during his time in the monastery. Not only would that account for his drunken rants about 'fucking priests', but it also went some way to explaining his homophobia. I'd never find out the whole story as I never had the opportunity to ask my father about his early life, but my thoughts on this subject were later clarified by a conversation I was to have with someone who would become a highly influential figure in my life.

Robert Wilson was a director who looked like he'd stepped off the set of an old Ealing movie. Always immaculately dressed in tweeds and waistcoat, his voice was so clipped and precise that a single word from him commanded instant and full attention. He stood straighter than a soldier on guard and his eyes had a piercing quality that could unsettle even the cockiest of actors. But he also concealed an intriguingly wild personality.

He was casting for the Julian Mitchell play *Another Country*, for which Rick had generously put me up for a part, but after my brief audition I didn't feel confident standing in front of the great man. He had worked with Gielgud and other luminaries of the stage and here I was slouched in front of him like an unruly pupil about to be caned.

Robert, or Bob as I came to know him, gave me a penetrating stare through eyes as sharp as a hawk's. 'You're very tall, and your posture is terrible,' he remarked ominously, 'but beneath your coalface lurks a diamond.'

And so, over the next four weeks, he set about wielding his miner's tools in an effort to uncover the actor potential hidden within me. It wasn't an easy or enjoyable experience for me, as Bob had impossibly high standards. If a finger moved out of place – even if I was standing in the background – he'd stop rehearsals and shout, 'No, no, no, darling! Good God, this isn't a bloody ballet!' I soon discovered that even just 'standing there, doing nothing' required much more effort and concentration than I'd ever imagined.

However, thanks to Bob's intensive training, my confidence grew in leaps and bounds. He'd spend hours with me after rehearsals picking through Shakespearean monologues, word by word, line by line; he'd force me to stand for long periods in various postures, not allowing me to move a muscle; he'd take me through voice exercises that left my face hurting and my throat on fire. Most of the time I couldn't see the point in any of it and were it not for his genuine zeal, I'd have thrown in the towel after the first week.

I often wondered why he bothered with me. It was obvious I was a lot of work and sometimes, after I'd murdered simple monologues, he'd roll his eyes heavenwards and ask Shakespeare for his forgiveness. A few of the other actors in the cast had joked that he just wanted to get my trousers off, but I knew that wasn't true. Although Bob was gay, his sole motivation was to turn me into a good actor and nothing more.

Over time he became something of a father figure to me. I could confide in him on any subject, for nothing fazed him. So one afternoon, when I happened to mention to him my father's hatred of gay men and my suspicions about his time in the monastery, a part of a puzzle with which I'd been wrestling fell into place when he told me a fascinating story in reply.

It concerned one of Bob's old friends (who, coincidentally, had lived in Glasgow for many years) who had a penchant for picking up outwardly straight men and having sex with them. When Bob first heard about this rather dangerous practice, he wondered how his companion had managed to avoid being attacked, but his tried and tested technique was covert, clever and quite simple. He would sit in a pub until he spotted a group of guys drinking, then he'd join them and engage them in small talk, before steering the conversation towards the subject of gay footballers. 'The one that shouts loudest about how they're all "dirty poofs" is the one I'll take home,' he revealed.

By chance, as I chatted to my mother on the phone a few weeks later, I referred to Bob's tale in passing. Her revelatory response left me reeling.

A year into her marriage with my father, she'd been with him in a pub when he suddenly pointed to a man sitting at the bar. 'See that guy there?' my father growled. 'He's a fucking poof.' He became so angry at this gay man's presence in his local that my mother was afraid that he might launch a vicious attack on him. Fortunately, the man left shortly afterwards, and my mother was spared any potential embarrassment.

A few months passed by and my mother had all but forgotten the incident, until one night when she came home from work to find my father at home having a drink with a male visitor. She recognized him as the man from the bar, and couldn't understand why her husband was socializing with someone whom he'd previously regarded with such hatred.

At about ten o'clock, my mother was ordered to go to bed and leave them alone to talk, which she did without question. Half an hour later, she came downstairs to fetch a glass of water from the kitchen. As she paused by the sitting-room door, which was closed, she clearly heard my father say, 'Don't worry about her – she's dead to the world. Get your clothes off.'

And with this shocking news – combined with the knowledge of Bob's 'straight-loving' friend – part of the mystery surrounding my father's complex persona was solved. Not only did it reveal much about my father's violent hatred of gays, but also taught me a lot about my own fears and hatreds, of which there were many. I analysed everything that angered, frightened, or even irritated me, and I emerged with a clearer picture of myself. Often, when I caught myself criticizing or becoming angry with other people, if I took a step back I'd realize that I was using other people's shortcomings to distract myself from my own failings.

The more I delved into my father's character – as well as my own – the more my bitter feelings for him began to recede. I hadn't seen him since my return from India, and so the lengthy absence would give me the chance to gauge what effect he now had on me. As far as I was concerned, though, I felt nothing negative towards him any more; just a deep feeling of pity.

When I saw him, one Saturday evening in December 1997, I knew his life was almost at an end. He was virtually skin and bone with a terrible cough and he could hardly hold his hand still. I knew that I had to cheer him up and try to tell him something I'd never been able to admit before, because it was something I'd never felt until that moment.

In spite of everything he'd done to us, the threats, the violence, the emotional abuse, and the fact he nearly killed our mother and may well have intended to kill us all, I still loved him. I couldn't explain why or how, but it felt so good and liberating to know that I could forgive him and even feel love.

We only had time for a brief meeting because I was performing at the theatre later in the evening, but I intended to see him again a few days later. It was a cold winter and by the look of him he had clearly fallen on hard times. His worn-out suit was the one I remembered from our last meeting and the little money he did have was obviously being spent on drink. I had jumpers and a jacket I wanted to give him, and so told him I'd see him the following week. He seemed so delighted that I'd promised to return so soon, and smiled at me with great joy in his eyes.

As we got up to say goodbye, he took me by the shoulders, looked me straight in the eye and burst into tears. I was shocked – I'd never believed my father was capable of such an open display emotion, least of all in the middle of a pub and in front of me.

He stood in front of me, shaking and sobbing like a child, repeating over and over, 'Son, I'm so sorry. I'm so sorry . . .'

I pulled him towards me, and for the first time we embraced like a real father and son. And then I let him know the truth.

'Dad, I forgive you. I love you and I forgive you. Do you know what I really believe? I believe that I chose this life. I chose you as my father and I'll choose you again – and next time you'll get it right.'

I meant every word. He cried even harder. We stood hugging each other for about five minutes in the middle of that pub full of hard men and alcoholics, and none of them said a word or even looked at us.

Then, once he'd pulled himself together a little, he looked at me, almost unrecognizable, and said, 'Thank you, son, thank you. I love you so much.'

I never let a single tear fall inside the pub. I couldn't. But the moment I stepped outside, the full force of it hit me and I didn't stop crying until I got home.

My father died three days later. I never had the chance to give him those warm clothes to protect him from the cold, and so when I found out that he'd died from pneumonia, it hurt even more. But, within my grief, unmistakeable and clear, was relief. He had endured terrible hardship in his final years and no one deserved to suffer that much, no matter what their crimes. He could finally move on to a better place, knowing that he'd made his peace with at least one person whom he'd made to suffer, and had been forgiven.

I called my mother to tell her the news of his death, and she said what I knew she would: 'Thank God. At last.'

Rather than sitting at home to brood, I went out with Bernie that night. He never left my side and was the rock I needed right there and then while I danced all night.

After his funeral, I found myself in possession of even more conflicting emotions. The relief I'd felt at his passing – the fact he was now at peace – was partly motivated by selfish reasons. I began hating myself for allowing myself to think that his death meant I was free to move on with my life. I spent many months trying to accept the finality of his absence, never knowing whether to laugh or cry. Sometimes it felt as if I had no heart at all, and other times it overflowed with emotion.

Eventually, once I'd stopped beating myself up over my ever-changing reactions, a childhood memory came rushing back to me. One year, when I was six or seven, our grandparents took us away on a rare holiday for a week in Felixstowe. I asked our mother if our father would be coming too, but she laughed and said, 'Don't be silly!' as if I could even think such a thing. Then, on the day we were due to leave, he called us all into the front room, opened a giant glass jar, and tipped out its contents: a mass of coins and notes fell to the floor in a huge heap. He looked at us and pointed to the pile, saying he'd been saving it up for us to take as spending money and I remember the look on his face so clearly because it was the same one he'd given me just before we'd said our final goodbye; it was awkward and he couldn't look us in the eyes, but it was there all the same, however trapped and muffled it was – a father's love.

The strange sense of peace that had started to come over me seemed connected to developments in my acting career. Courtesy of Robert Wilson's dedicated tutelage, I had grown in confidence on the stage and my acting skills had improved immeasurably. I was always at my happiest when performing in a play or simply being in a theatre environment, and my professional and personal life was set to receive a massive boost thanks to a Russian director with plans to set up a theatre company.

In the winter of 2001, I'd just returned from a two-week tour of the stage version of *Reservoir Dogs* and needed a good dose of classical theatre, preferably in a warmer location than my recent on-the-road experiences. Enrique's proposed tour of various venues across south-east England had seemed like a great opportunity on paper, but the reality, though rewarding, was less than glamorous.

I had turned up at six o'clock on a freezing cold morning to meet Enrique and my fellow cast members for our Tarantino-inspired theatrical mayhem. The rest of the guys were already there, trying to keep warm while they waited for the tour bus to show up, and cracking jokes about the broken-down transit van that someone had dumped outside the theatre. Sal, the cast comedian, informed us it was Enrique's new office, where he hid his casting couch. Someone else suggested it was probably our official transportation and we'd end up getting towed to all our venues by the AA; with Enrique, anything was possible.

When the boss arrived, he greeted us cheerfully with his inimitable broad grin. 'Morning, bastards! Why are you waiting outside in the freezing cold? It's open!' he exclaimed, yanking open the rusting back doors of the heap of metal we'd spent the last fifteen minutes ridiculing ...

Driving from venue to venue in a rusty, smelly old former meat wagon with holes in the floor should have been a nightmare, but it turned out to be one of the best experiences

I've ever had. Although the travelling was hellish, by the end of the fortnight every cast member felt like they'd known each other a lifetime.

The acting experience was invaluable, too, and set me up perfectly for my first encounter with Russian dissident, Victor Sobchak. Imprisoned by the KGB on his wedding day and locked up in a 'correctional centre' in Siberia for performing plays deemed to be anti-social, he was then subjected to six months of medical experimentation and brainwashing by the Siberian authorities, who tried – and failed – to make him renounce his ideas about society. Were it not for an influential friend in Moscow who pulled strings to secure his early release, he would have doubtless died there like many others before.

In spite of his shocking treatment, Victor did not feel 'wronged' by the Soviet authorities, and nor did he harbour any bitterness over his unpleasant experiences. Instead he was just glad to be free of the regime that controlled all forms of expression so ruthlessly. An amazing director, Victor taught me more in one production than I had learned in the previous three years. In the same way that Robert Wilson had given me endless encouragement, so Victor assured me that if I paid attention to every detail and let go of myself, not only would I become a good actor, but I could also be great. It may take years, he once told me, but nothing comes without a price.

Together we set up Act Provocateur International, a theatre company admired and reviled in equal measure; never afraid to tackle the most taboo of subjects, from paedophilia to insanity. Sometimes the choices we made proved successful, and other times they failed spectacularly, but no matter what the outcome, our ongoing commitment to producing these 'unfashionably intense' pieces of theatre never wavered, because when they worked nothing on earth felt better or more rewarding.

## 29 | *Breaking the Chain*

Although more than a year had passed since my father's death, my life still contained a mysterious void, like a gaping wound that refused to heal. Despite my final forgiveness of him, and having gradually come to terms with the events from my past, I still believed that there was something stopping me from moving forward.

I started to feel like a pendulum on an old clock whose springs were shot. One minute I'd be elated, and the next I'd be crippled with old doubts and fears that left me questioning everything. Then, from out of leftfield, I became plagued with thoughts of suicide again. I couldn't understand what had triggered these destructive notions, but whenever I tried to suppress them they sprang back ever harder. I'd even started to plan how I would do it – as simply and as cleanly as possible – but it was always the thought of the damage I'd cause to my loved ones that dragged me back from the edge. The fact that I was worrying about others was proof that my suicidal feelings weren't as real as I'd imagined, but more likely a mere echo from the distant past. If I'd really wanted to kill myself I wouldn't have had cared about anyone but me.

In those days I was fond of picking up old pieces of discarded furniture from off the street, taking them home and restoring them. Walking back from the theatre one day, I found a small folding table with built-in drawers. The wood was all but buried by thick layers of white emulsion and it weighed a tonne, but that made it even more of a challenge. As I started work on it, using paint stripper and a scraper, the layers of paint slowly peeled off to reveal the first hint of the wood beneath, which seemed to be of excellent quality. The more I stripped it down it over the days and nights, the more the good wood revealed itself. I moved on determinedly to the next stage of restoration, and sanded, straightened, chiselled, and then fine-sanded that old table, knowing I was helping to salvage something beautiful. When I reached the final stage of staining, I stood back marvelling at the fine piece of workmanship before me – the flow and depth of the grain was breathtaking, almost a work of art.

And then I realized that there were numerous parallels between my life and the stripped-down table before me. After removing many layers of useless, stifling paint, I had simply discovered that even more work was needed before I could get right down to the grain and uncover a treasure that had lain hidden for so long.

With a sense of renewed self-awareness, I put all my efforts into focusing on the next stage of inner restoration: to keep the past firmly in the past. Even though I knew it wasn't giving me any peace, I couldn't stop basing my present life on previous personal experiences; something still dragged at my feet and no matter how hard I tried, I couldn't shake it off.

I had traced the chain that bound me to my father back to the one he had inherited from his Glaswegian forefathers. It was a chain that had passed to me as a child, and which, in adulthood, I knew I had to break in order to take control of my life once and for all. The more I remembered the little boy I once was, the more I saw flashes of childhood thoughts and feelings; intense memories like razor cuts of fear, anger, death and suicide.

It was as if two Siamese twins had ripped free of each other and were climbing a treacherous mountain with only a safety rope linking them. One was trying to climb as high as possible, while the other, too scared of what lay ahead, kept tugging at his end of the rope to keep his twin from reaching the summit.

I started having the strangest dreams that left me crushed for whole days. In my nightly visions, I would see myself as a child, watching my smiling father enter my bedroom, laden with presents and trying to make me laugh – I would end up screaming at him in terror and he'd walk away in sadness. Catching a glimpse of the sort of man my father could have been left me with a raw and empty feeling.

One night, as I danced at The Slimelight, I closed my eyes and let my body and mind be gripped by the pulsating rhythms and melodies. For many years, dance had been the highpoint of my week. I'd discovered that if you dance long enough and let your mind relax totally, it's possible to reach a trance-like state without the need for drugs. So, as I danced harder and harder, keeping focused on the music alone, I felt everyone around me start to slip away. Slowly, in front of me, I could see a swirling vortex, spinning and pulsating in time to the beat of the music. Entranced by the intriguing sight, I could have dismissed it and left it alone while enjoying my solo moment of frenzy, but as I danced, an idea entered my mind: don't just stand there – enter it.

With this thought, I instantly felt myself being pulled into that twisting tunnel of strands and spirals, softly glowing and pulling me deeper and deeper, until the lights started to fade . . .

*I'm in my childhood bedroom in Woodley. I can still hear the music coming from a long way away and the bass drum somehow seems to be my heartbeat, but I am there. And I know exactly what is happening.*

*The child lying in the bed in front of me has been crying and is trying to sleep, but is still awake. I call his name and his head turns in my direction, but I want to appear slowly, to let him see me bit by bit until he's not sure whether he's awake or dreaming. He slowly sees me and his eyes widen, but my smile is one he recognizes and trusts. He doesn't understand what's going on or whether I'm a ghost, but he's not frightened. I sit on the bed and tell him who I am, but even though he doesn't say a word in reply, I know that he doesn't believe me. He nods slowly, with a little grin, when I ask him if he would like to go somewhere magical.*

*I tell him to close his eyes and take my hand.*

*All I have to do is let the music grow louder and feel the spinning spirals that carry us both into the future-present and then we're there.*

*I open my eyes and let him see what's around me and let his ears open very gently to the music. I can feel astonishment and wonder like I've never felt before as I look out through his eyes. I carry on dancing and Bernie is in front of me, pulling a face and grinning ear to ear; you can't not smile back at that.*

*'That man,' I tell myself, 'will be the best friend you ever had.'*

*I say to the wide-eyed child that this will be a part of his world, and I explain to him about the life outside and the amazing people waiting for him. I finish by assuring him that whatever happens in the future, everything will be okay and eventually life will become beautiful and magical.*

*I can feel it's time. I close my eyes and fly back into the spirals and there I am, with myself lying in bed, eyes drooping and ready for sleep.*

*He asks me if I will come again, and just as he falls into the best dream he's had for a long time, I promise him I will.*

And I did, twice more, and with that a circle had been closed; the chain had finally been broken.

Some time after these unique dance experiences, I began to have new dreams about my childhood. I would see myself in the front room, with my father crouched on the floor in front of me, crashing my toy cars together and making noises as they collided. We'd both roll about laughing and he'd pick me up with the biggest smile and throw me high up in the air. I knew he'd catch me, but I always woke up before I started to fall.

I felt so strange when I awoke from those dreams. Tears of happiness would stream down my face as I recalled them, and I'd carry the vision of my father's delighted smile throughout the day. I couldn't ask for more when I think back to how it all started and how it all could have ended.

It would be wonderful to end this story on a high, to reveal that I am now a fully self-realized being, who never wakes up in a cold sweat or gets angry, who never thinks negatively and who has reached his prized destination, but the real world doesn't quite work like that.

As I started writing this book, a chance email came my way. It was from my old schoolfriend, Alice, with whom I used to walk to school. As our correspondence progressed, we began to share memories from our early years, and I was reminded of Alice as a happy-go-lucky girl with a grin that made me forget my troubles, and who had cheered me up and kept me giggling in dark days.

But during our reminiscences, Alice dropped a bombshell: over a period of several years, she had been repeatedly raped by her father and brothers, while her mother watched.

My devastation on hearing her news was absolute. I gazed at the computer screen for an hour in a state of shock and grief. Recalling her parents, her father especially, I would like to say that there was 'something about him', but there wasn't. He seemed so ordinary and 'normal', and there was no indication in his manner of the evil practices to which he subjected his innocent daughter.

Sadly, Alice's nightmare didn't end when she was taken into a place of so-called safety – her abuse continued at the foster home in which she was placed. She has since picked up the pieces of her wrecked childhood and has begun the long road towards finding some small measure of peace, but her story illustrated to me how false my sense of isolation had been. It was apparent, with the benefit of hindsight, that various friends and acquaintances from my youth had faced a difficult start in life, in their own personal hell, unable to break away from the charade of a happy home life.

In many ways, the burden of silence was the hardest thing for me to bear during those years. The belief that our father's violence was unique, and reserved only for us, made me feel like a freak inside. As I grew older, though, I realized that wasn't the case, but conditioned thoughts and feelings are always the hardest things to erase – the first step is to be aware of them and accept how irrelevant they are now. Alice understands this, I know, and that makes her a true survivor.

The past is not unlike a hallway of mirrors. The more you gaze on those reflections, the more real they become and the temptation to dwell there becomes irresistible. Whether you decide to smash them up, pull faces or simply close your eyes and trust your senses to help you find the way out is a matter of choice, but I do know that when I decided to reach out two arms and feel my way past those ghostly reflections, my whole life started again.

It's been ten years since my trip down my own time tunnel and since then I've moved onwards and upwards, step by step, with a few wobbles and the occasional flat-on-my-face comedy moment, but my focus is unshakable and I've a clarity now that

I've never before possessed. I couldn't wish for a happier situation than that. And at last, after seven years of hard work, with Victor Sobchak's merciless but laughter-filled instruction, coupled with my own steely determination, I believe I can finally call myself an actor.

The long walk continues for me, and though I might never reach the end, that's not the point. I've learned that it's never a good idea to stop too long and get trapped by the scenery. Our lives don't just grind to a halt because we think we've made it and know all there is to know. The journey for us all goes on and on until you can go no further, at which point you just might have found yourself.

It may take a lifetime to get there, but as a wise woman once told me, life isn't a race.

# *Author's Acknowledgements*

MY THANKS, first and foremost, go to William Whitehurst, author of *Pigeon Man Apocalypse*, which is the play that set me off on what has been the most amazing voyage of world and self-discovery; Carol Midgley, of *The Times*, for writing up my interview with such respect and sensitivity; Lesley O'Mara for wondering whether there was a book in my story; Lindsay Davies, Editorial Director at Michael O'Mara Books, for saying 'yes'; Helen Cumberbatch for her infinite patience and guidance, and to all at O'Mara Books for their amazing support.

On a more personal note, I'd like to thank Nicky for her love of hopeless causes; Barry for just being himself; Bobbie for more than words can express and for showing me that many roads lead to Tanera Mor; Victor Sobchak for his years of tireless direction and friendship – and for bringing Arthur Cork to life on the stage; Carl Kirshner, Scott Christie, Sal Ahmet and Patrick Doherty for being the best Dogs on earth; Julia K for so many jaw-dropping moments; Noel for all those precious C90s, being a rock of sanity in a sea of Pringles, and all his stories about a magical land called India . . . ; Julia W for her inner-child and Green Lanes; Bill and Genie in Tanera Mor, for being the keepers of Paradise; Joe for being the hairiest angel I've ever met and for that first copy of *Conversations With God*; and Bernie for his unconditional friendship and wisdom, and for all the stories we've yet to write.

A special thanks to my brother Iain for his endless support and love – and for never letting me give up. And to my mother for . . . well, everything.

And lastly for my partner Nika – the brightest light in my life, who has shown me that I can be whoever and whatever I want to be and that the long walk is there for anyone who wants it.